The Communicator's Commentary

Deuteronomy

THE COMMUNICATOR'S COMMENTARY SERIES
OLD TESTAMENT

Lloyd J. Ogilvie

General Editor

The Communicator's Commentary

Deuteronomy

John C. Maxwell

WORD BOOKS, PUBLISHER • WACO, TEXAS

THE COMMUNICATOR'S COMMENTARY SERIES, OLD TESTAMENT, Volume 5: *Deuteronomy*. Copyright © 1987 by Word, Inc. All rights reserved. No portion of this book may be reproduced in any form whatsoever, except for brief quotations in reviews, without written permission from the publisher.

Library of Congress Cataloging in Publication Data
Main entry under title:

The Communicator's commentary.
  Bibliography: p.
  Contents: OT5. Deuteronomy/by John C. Maxwell
  1. Bible. O.T.—Commentaries. I. Ogilvie, Lloyd
John. II. Maxwell, John C., 1947–
BS1151.2.C66 1986   221.7'7   86–11138
ISBN 0–8499–0410–2 (v. OT5)

Printed in the United States of America

5 6 7 8 9 9 AGF 9 8 7 6

Special appreciation to my family
Margaret
Elizabeth
Joel
Deuteronomy 11:18–21

Contents

Editor's Preface

God has called all of His people to be communicators. Everyone who is in Christ is called into ministry. As ministers of "the manifold grace of God," all of us—clergy and laity—are commissioned with the challenge to communicate our faith to individuals and groups, classes and congregations.

The Bible, God's Word, is the objective basis of the truth of His love and power that we seek to communicate. In response to the urgent, expressed needs of pastors, teachers, Bible study leaders, church school teachers, small group enablers, and individual Christians, the Communicator's Commentary is offered as a penetrating search of the Scriptures of the Old and New Testament to enable vital personal and practical communication of the abundant life.

Many current commentaries and Bible study guides provide only some aspects of a communicator's needs. Some offer in-depth scholarship but no application to daily life. Others are so popular in approach that biblical roots are left unexplained. Few offer impelling illustrations that open windows for the reader to see the exciting application for today's struggles. And most of all, seldom have the expositors given the valuable outlines of passages so needed to help the preacher or teacher in his or her busy life to prepare for communicating the Word to congregations or classes.

This Communicator's Commentary series brings all of these elements together. The authors are scholar-preachers and teachers outstanding in their ability to make the Scriptures come alive for individuals and groups. They are noted for bringing together excellence in biblical scholarship, knowledge of the original Hebrew and Greek, sensitivity to people's needs, vivid illustrative material from biblical, classical, and contemporary sources, and lucid communication by the use of clear outlines of thought. Each has been selected to contribute to this series because of his Spirit-empowered ability to

9

help people live in the skins of biblical characters and provide a "you-are-there" intensity to the drama of events of the Bible which have so much to say about our relationships and responsibilities today.

The design for the Communicator's Commentary gives the reader an overall outline of each book of the Bible. Following the introduction, which reveals the author's approach and salient background on the book, each chapter of the commentary provides the Scripture to be exposited. The New King James Bible has been chosen for the Communicator's Commentary because it combines with integrity the beauty of language, underlying Hebrew and Greek textual basis, and thought-flow of the 1611 King James Version, while replacing obsolete verb forms and other archaisms with their everyday contemporary counterparts for greater readability. Reverence for God is preserved in the capitalization of all pronouns referring to the Father, Son, or Holy Spirit. Readers who are more comfortable with another translation can readily find the parallel passage by means of the chapter and verse reference at the end of each passage being exposited. The paragraphs of exposition combine fresh insights to the Scripture, application, rich illustrative material, and innovative ways of utilizing the vibrant truth for his or her own life and for the challenge of communicating it with vigor and vitality.

It has been gratifying to me as Editor of this series to receive enthusiastic progress reports from each contributor. As they worked, all were gripped with new truths from the Scripture—God-given insights into passages, previously not written in the literature of biblical explanation. A prime objective of this series is for each user to find the same awareness: that God speaks with newness through the Scriptures when we approach them with a ready mind and a willingness to communicate what He has given; that God delights to give communicators of His Word "I-never-saw-that-in-that-verse-before" intellectual insights so that our listeners and readers can have "I-never-realized-all-that-was-in-that-verse" spiritual experiences.

The thrust of the commentary series unequivocally affirms that God speaks through the Scriptures today to engender faith, enable adventuresome living of the abundant life, and establish the basis of obedient discipleship. The Bible, the unique Word of God, is unlimited as a resource for Christians in communicating our hope to others. It is our weapon in the battle for truth, the guide for ministry, and the irresistible force for introducing others to God.

A biblically rooted communication of the Gospel holds in unity and oneness what divergent movements have wrought asunder. This commentary series courageously presents personal faith, caring for individuals, and social responsibility as essential, inseparable dimensions of biblical Christianity. It seeks to present the quadrilateral Gospel in its fullness which calls us to unreserved commitment to Christ, unrestricted self-esteem in His grace, unqualified love for others in personal evangelism, and undying efforts to work for justice and righteousness in a sick and suffering world.

A growing renaissance in the church today is being led by clergy and laity who are biblically rooted, Christ-centered, and Holy Spirit-empowered. They have dared to listen to people's most urgent questions and deepest needs and then to God as He speaks through the Bible. Biblical preaching is the secret of growing churches. Bible study classes and small groups are equipping the laity for ministry in the world. Dynamic Christians are finding that daily study of God's Word allows the Spirit to do in them what He wishes to communicate through them to others. These days are the most exciting time since Pentecost. The Communicator's Commentary is offered to be a primary resource of new life for this renaissance.

It has been very encouraging to receive the enthusiastic responses of pastors and teachers to the twelve New Testament volumes of the Communicator's Commentary series. The letters from communicators on the firing line in pulpits, classes, study groups, and Bible fellowship clusters across the nation, as well as the reviews of scholars and publication analysts, have indicated that we have been on target in meeting a need for a distinctly different kind of commentary on the Scriptures, a commentary that is primarily aimed at helping interpreters of the Bible to equip the laity for ministry.

This positive response has led the publisher to press on with an additional twenty-one volumes covering the books of the Old Testament. These new volumes rest upon the same goals and guidelines that undergird the New Testament volumes. Scholar-preachers with facility in Hebrew as well as vivid contemporary exposition have been selected as authors. The purpose throughout is to aid the preacher and teacher in the challenge and adventure of Old Testament exposition in communication. In each volume you will meet Yahweh, the "I AM" Lord who is Creator, Sustainer, and Redeemer in the unfolding drama of His call and care of Israel. He is the Lord who acts, intervenes, judges, and presses His people into the immense challenges and privileges of being a chosen people, a holy nation. And in the descriptive exposition of each passage, the implications of the ultimate revelation of Yahweh in Jesus Christ, His Son, our Lord, are carefully spelled out to maintain unity and oneness in the preaching and teaching of the Gospel.

It is my privilege to introduce you to the author of this commentary on Deuteronomy. John C. Maxwell is Senior Pastor of Skyline Wesleyan Church in Lemon Grove, California. A gifted preacher, Dr. Maxwell offers dynamic leadership in the renewal of the contemporary church.

I was pleased to get to know Dr. Maxwell when we served together on the Planning Committee for the Congress on Biblical Exposition. It was a delight to sense his vision for preaching and his strong commitment to excellence as a communicator and leader.

In writing this commentary, he imitates the model of Deuteronomy. He writes, "I want to do what Deuteronomy itself does: bring the power of the past to bear on the present, with an eye to the future. When this happens, Deuteronomy should come alive and breathe spiritual renewal into the personal histories of its readers." As you use this volume, you will be impressed with how regularly and insightfully Dr. Maxwell does indeed "bring the power of the past to bear on the present." This commentary is full to the brim with contemporary illustrations, anecdotes, quotations, and applications. Biblical passages are clearly interpreted, and then neatly applied through ordered, contemporary principles. In Dr. Maxwell's hands, Deuteronomy addresses our current situation with vigor and relevance.

We often hear today about the vacuum of leadership in our country, and, sadly, in the church as well! Those of us who function as Christian leaders in the church, in business, in government, and in the home, desperately need a biblical vision for leadership. We need to order our God-given responsibilities according to biblical principles.

Deuteronomy is a rich vein from which we may mine gems of leadership. In John Maxwell's hands, the biblical text becomes a guidebook for Christian leaders. Drawing upon his own vast experience, he allows the example of Moses to speak definitively to our generation of leaders. As a communicator of God's Word, you will benefit from the lessons in leadership offered by Deuteronomy—and wisely interpreted by Dr. Maxwell.

At the core, Deuteronomy reveals the relational covenant between God and His chosen people. Its relational and legal principles guide us into deeper intimacy with our Heavenly Father and with our Lord, Jesus Christ. As Dr. Maxwell unfolds these principles, you will feel the text "come alive and breathe spiritual renewal" into your own soul. As a communicator, as a leader, as a spiritual pilgrim, you will discover anew the contemporary significance of Deuteronomy. Indeed, in Dr. Maxwell's own words, "Deuteronomy is relevant to your life today!"

LLOYD J. OGILVIE

Acknowledgments

Never will I forget the day that Lloyd Ogilvie asked me to write the commentary on Deuteronomy for the Communicator's Commentary Series. I felt honored by the invitation, yet humbled by the size of the project. Immediately I sensed the need for strength from God and assistance from friends. Walt Disney once said, "A genius is a person who surrounds himself with better men than he is." I certainly don't claim to be a genius, but I did have the good sense to surround myself with the following people who have surrounded me with the spiritual and emotional support necessary to complete this volume:

Dr. Lloyd Ogilvie—general editor and friend
Professor William Yarchin—Old Testament tutor
Mrs. Barbara Brumagin—administrative assistant
Mrs. Barbara Babby—editor
Mrs. Jan Cantor—typist
The Skyline Wesleyan Church—prayers and continual encouragement

Introduction

Deuteronomy is relevant to your life today! This Old Testament book teaches principles that could determine the success of your Christian walk. It contains the final addresses that Moses delivered to the Israelites at a decisive time in their history: the eve of their emergence into the world as a political power. The merging of the final words of a great leader with the dawning of a new era for the nation Israel creates a sense of anticipation as we read Deuteronomy.

There are crucial times in our lives when we strain to understand what we're hearing. Occasions such as our graduation, ordination, wedding, and other events which represent new chapters in our life's journey compel us to listen carefully to those who have already successfully walked this path.

This week I was called to the hospital bedside of one of my parishioners, a dear Christian brother who has cancer and is courageously facing his approaching death. As he spoke to me, I listened very attentively to what he was saying. Why? Because these are his final words! My own journey will be enriched if I remember them.

In Deuteronomy, a dying leader stands before Israel, a nation about to give birth to a long-awaited promise of God. Moses' words, if heeded, will allow the people of God to reach their potential; if ignored, Israel's dreams will be dissolved. In exhorting the people to do what is right, Moses addresses the following significant issues:

1. Don't Forget God

The nation of Israel's attitude toward God is a major consideration. In various ways, Moses continually warns the people not to forget God. Today, the fundamental question "What place will God have in our country?" is generating scores of church-state cases before the court systems in our land.

The news reports covering the death of school teacher Christa McAuliffe in the 1986 shuttle tragedy again brought this issue to my mind. Much support was given to Christa's students and fellow teachers to help them through the grieving process. Counselors came to the school to listen. The administration scheduled a special closed memorial service and gave time for those who hurt to share with one another. But there was no time specifically set aside for prayer. Ironically, that which could have brought the greatest relief—prayer—is not allowed in the public schools.

2. Care for the Disadvantaged

Deuteronomy deals effectively with the importance of caring for the disadvantaged of the Israelite community. The test of any legal system's respect of the rights of individuals is best reflected in its treatment of society's weakest members.[1] Today, the social needs of the community must be effectively addressed by the Christian community. Recent government belt tightening in areas of social concerns highlights both the need and the opportunity for Christian ministry. How will we respond?

3. No Generation Stands Alone

The messages of Moses are intergenerational in scope. This great leader stands between past and future generations. The Israelites of the preceding years have suffered the consequences of wrong decisions. What will happen to the next generation? Moses impresses on the current generation their responsibility to their children. Deuteronomy interprets the past for the sake of the future. Israel's present position in their journey is a result of past decisions. Their decisions now regarding entry into the promised land and what they teach their children will affect the next generation. Today, we too face issues that will have a direct bearing on our children's future. Nuclear war strategy and ecology are just two of many very important intergenerational concerns about which we must make decisions that will affect our children.

4. Obedience Is Essential to Success in the Christian Journey

Each of Moses' messages revolves around the same command: "Obey." Everything—possession of the land, victory over enemies, prosperity, and enjoyment of life—depends upon Israel's obedience to God. Moses continually asks his people for a positive response to God's leading. He exhorts them to "hear" (50 times), "do," "keep," and "observe" (177 times) "out of a heart of love" (21 times). This is relevant today, since our success as Christians depends on our obedience to God. "If we walk in the light as He is in the light, we have fellowship with one another, and the blood of Jesus Christ His Son cleanses us from all sin" (1 John 1:7).

5. Personal Responsibility for Obedience to God Must Be Accepted

Moses motivates his people to obey God by appealing to their common sense and desire to maintain their own well-being. This appeal is threefold: (1) As a nation they never had it so good (Deut. 4:7, 8); therefore, (2) they are responsible for the well-being of the nation; and (3) an unfaithful response will bring retribution. Deuteronomy is the first book to introduce this subject. In Leviticus, Moses is saying "Don't do wrong, because God says not to." In Deuteronomy he is saying "Don't do wrong, because God will punish you if you do." A transition is made from collective to individual retribution (Deut. 24:16). Today, we are faced with responsibility for our sins both collectively and individually.[2] It is popular to deny this and to insist that we are helpless victims of our circumstances. But Deuteronomy tells us that personal change cannot be effective unless personal responsibility is accepted.

6. Be Open to the Future

The Israelites are marching toward the promised land. Their potential is unlimited, and they are waiting for fulfillment of that potential. But in their as yet unfulfilled condition, many dangers threaten their future. Therefore, Moses constantly exhorts his people to not be afraid because God will be with them. Our twentieth-century walk with God is also a journey with great promise for the future. With modern technology, our generation has reached more people for Christ than ever before. At the same time, Satan does not sit idly by and allow the Good News to be spread without a fight. The only path to victorious Christian living is an absolute, unwavering trust in God.

7. God Acts among His People

By word and event, God continually communicates to His people. Israel's history becomes a theater of God's purposive activity.[3] Moses combines past events which reveal the working of God with fresh exhortation to reveal what God wants in the present. The Old Testament understanding of God is one in which He is always personal, always known by what He does. There is nothing vague about the biblical God. Scripture clearly defines His character and His desire; He even has a name—Yahweh. There is nothing undemanding about His active relationship with His people; it calls for the most strenuous efforts toward obedience and trust in Him alone.[4] The Christian community must again embrace this truth.

8. The Covenant between God and His People Must Be Renewed

The renewal of the covenant between God and His people is an integral part of Deuteronomy, for it sets out the terms of the relationship between God and Israel. This covenant was the constitution of a theocracy. God was King and had claimed His people for Himself out of Egypt; the people, who owed everything to God, were required to submit to Him in a covenant that was based on love. The approaching death of Moses provided the initial basis for the renewal of the covenant. Today, when a crisis of transition comes upon us, we also need to be reminded of God's faithfulness and of our responsibility to obey Him.

THE AUTHOR AND STYLE OF DEUTERONOMY

Deuteronomy has traditionally been regarded by both Christianity and Judaism as the work of Moses. Since the eighteenth century,

20

however, this book has been ascribed to many different dates and authors. After studying various theories concerning the possible dates and authors, I must concur with the traditional view that Moses is the source of virtually everything in Deuteronomy.

Deuteronomy, which means "second law," does not actually contain a distinct second law. Although it repeats some of the legislation of Moses' preceding books, its concern goes beyond law. Its approach is more sermonic than legal. "On this side of Jordan in the land of Moab, Moses began to explain this law . . ." (Deut. 1:5). Yet the first speech of Moses, which immediately follows this verse (1:6–4:40), contains nothing of any specific law. The really distinctive feature of the book is not its treatment of the law per se, but its urgent and appealing preaching style. The book is a commentary on the command, "You shall love the Lord your God with all your heart, with all your soul, and with all your strength" (Deut. 6:5). The language is not that of the law; it is the language of the heart and the conscience.

Moses knows that a national law can never attain its goal so long as it remains a system which is endured reluctantly and only by coercion; it must be founded on the inward assent of the people.[5] Therefore, the emphasis of his words is not to inform but to exhort. Instead of saying "Observe them" (the laws), Moses pleads with the people, "Be *careful* to observe them" (Deut. 4:6). Instead of simply instructing Israel on what action to take, he is saying "Make sure you are doing what you already know to do."

Comparison of Deuteronomy with Leviticus provides a clear contrast in style and purpose even though both books cover much of the same material. Whereas Leviticus is technical, Deuteronomy is human. Leviticus emphasizes *ritual* in worship; Deuteronomy emphasizes *obedience* in worship. Leviticus speaks to the head; Deuteronomy speaks to the heart. In short, Deuteronomy is a series of messages from Moses to his people, appealing for a "higher law."

It is important for each one of us, as communicators, to study the style of Moses' preaching. He displays the ability to take God's law and apply it to the daily affairs and decision-making processes of his people. G. Campbell Morgan said that effective preaching contains truth, clarity, and passion. Moses' messages not only contain the truth and the clarity of the law, but also the passion which stirs his people to obedience.[6] This style of communication has always been used by God to bring about a positive change in the lives of others. It was the "theology of a warmed heart," experienced by George Whitefield and John Wesley, that renewed the church and reformed society in eighteenth-century England. It is the kind of communication that is needed today.

THE VALUE OF DEUTERONOMY

1. Deuteronomy Is Vital to Understanding the Other Old Testament Books

Deuteronomy emphasizes that every person stands under God's judgment. It reflects the principles by which God judges human activities. The Old Testament historical books that follow Deuteronomy are examples of the principles laid down in this great book. In other words, Deuteronomy sets the agenda and criteria for other books. S. R. Driver says, "Deuteronomy became a 'spiritual rallying point' which reaffirmed the fundamental principles which Moses had long ago insisted on—loyalty to Jehovah and repudiation of false gods. It was an endeavor to realize in practice the ideals of the prophets, particularly Hosea and Isaiah, to transform the Judah demoralized by Manasseh into the holy nation pictured in Isaiah's vision and to awaken in it that devotion to God and love for men which Hosea had declared to be the first of human duties."[7]

2. The Message of Deuteronomy Is Relevant Today

Deuteronomy can be the catalyst for spiritual evaluation and renewal of our lives today. It happened in King Josiah's day (2 Kings 22–23). When Hilkiah, the high priest, discovered a law book (probably Deuteronomy), he sent it to be read before the king. Immediately, Josiah realized that curses were inevitable if the people disobeyed God's law. This in itself was a significant insight. Until this time the people thought God's covenant was strictly gracious and in no way affected by their response. Josiah's reaction to Deuteronomy was emphatic, "Go, inquire of the Lord for me, for the people and for all Judah, concerning the words of this book that has been found; for great is the wrath of the Lord that is aroused against us, because our

22

fathers have not obeyed the words of this book, to do according to all that is written concerning us" (2 Kings 22:13). The result was that God gave peace to Judah, and Josiah restored true worship in the land.

It is my prayer that the study of Deuteronomy will bring spiritual renewal within your life. Deuteronomy calls for all of us to . . .

a. Review the past dealings of God in our lives. The word "remember" is continually used by Moses, especially in reference to the deliverance from Egypt. The phrase "Hear, O Israel" is often used in connection with the people of God remembering and obeying Him. Personal revival can also happen in our lives if we heed Moses' admonition to look, to listen, and to obey.

b. Ratify our loyalty to God. The theme of Deuteronomy could be "Don't forget God." A society that tends to go chasing false gods needs Deuteronomy's emphasis on worship of Yahweh and Yahweh alone.

c. Reacknowledge consequences of the choices that are made. In fact, these consequences are personal as well as collective. Blessings follow obedience; curses follow disobedience. Renewal comes into our lives when we feel and express repentance. This only happens when we understand and accept our responsibility to choose.

d. Realize the potential of our lives as Christians. Before us lies "a land of milk and honey." God desires for us to possess the land. His faithfulness makes it a possibility. Our obedience can make it a reality.

THE GOAL OF THIS COMMENTARY

My intention is to explain what Deuteronomy meant to Moses and his people; thus enabling us to more effectively apply it to our own lives today. This quote from G. Ernest Wright beautifully describes my desire:

In its [Deuteronomy's] pages we are not confronted first of all with a series of rational, infallible, theological abstractions, but with the person of the living God and of His Son, our Lord, Jesus Christ. We are also confronted with the activity of men in whom we see ourselves, so that the distance between the biblical generation and our generation is bridged and we become participants in the original history in order to participate rightly in our

23

own. For what is history but the interacting "challenge and response" movement between God and man which God is directing to His own good? The primary means by which God communicates with man is by His acts, which are events of history. The Word leads us, not *away from* history, but *to* history and to responsible participation *within* history.[8]

I want to do what Deuteronomy itself does: bring the power of the past to bear on the present, with an eye to the future. When this happens, Deuteronomy should come alive and breathe spiritual renewal into the personal histories of its readers.

NOTES

1. Dale Patrick, *Old Testament Law* (Atlanta: John Knox Press, 1985), p. 86.

2. John G. Gammie, "The Theology of Retribution in the Book of Deuteronomy," *Catholic Bible Quarterly* 32 (1970).

3. John Bright, *The Authority of the Old Testament* (Grand Rapids: Baker Book House, 1967), p. 130.

4. Elizabeth Achtemeier, *The Old Testament and the Proclamation of the Gospel* (Philadelphia: Westminster Press, 1941), pp. 43–44.

5. W. Eichrodt, *Theology of the Old Testament*, vol. 1 (Philadelphia: Westminster Press, 1961), p. 91.

6. Patrick, *Old Testament Law*, p. 7.

7. Samuel R. Driver, *An Introduction to the Literature of the Old Testament* (Utica, NY: Meridian Pub., 1957), p. 89.

8. G. Ernest Wright, *God Who Acts* (London: SCM Press, 1952), p. 107.

An Outline of Deuteronomy

VIII. Old Law for Succeeding Generations: 6:1–25
    A. Receive the Law Personally: 6:1–5
    B. Teach the Law Continually: 6:6–9
    C. Live the Law Completely: 6:10–19
    D. Explain the Law Historically: 6:20–25
IX. A Chosen People: 7:1–26
    A. Separated to God: 7:1–5
    B. Selected by God: 7:6–11
    C. Successful in God: 7:12–26
X. Remember the Lord's Provision: 8:1–20
    A. Remember the Lord's Blessings When Things Are Bad: 8:1–10
    B. Remember the Lord's Blessings When Things Are Good: 8:11–20
XI. Remember Your Provocation: 9:1–10:11
    A. God's Provisions in Spite of Our Provocation: 9:1–6
    B. Israel's Problems Because of Provoking God: 9:7–24
    C. Moses' Prayer on Behalf of the People: 9:25–10:11
XII. Respond with Total Obedience: 10:12–11:32
    A. Israel Must Obey God Because of His Greatness: 10:12–22
    B. Israel Must Obey God Because of What They Have Seen: 11:1–7
    C. Israel Must Obey God Because of What They Will Receive: 11:8–17
    D. Israel Must Obey God Because of His Blessings on Their Family: 11:18–21
    E. Israel Must Obey God Because of the Victories They Will Accomplish: 11:22–25
    F. Israel Must Obey God Because of the Consequences of Their Choices: 11:26–32
XIII. Regulations Concerning Worship: 12:1–32
XIV. Potential Influences to Idolatry: 13:1–18
    A. Religious Leaders: 13:1–5
    B. Family and Close Friends: 13:6–11
    C. Community Leaders: 13:12–18
XV. Regulations Concerning Mourning and Eating: 14:1–21
    A. Improper Mourning: 14:1–2
    B. Eating: 14:3–21

XVI.   Regulations Concerning Giving: 14:22–15:23
   A.   Giving Support to God's Work: 14:22–29
   B.   Giving Release to Debtors: 15:1–6
   C.   Giving Generously to the Poor: 15:7–11
   D.   Giving Freedom to the Bondservant: 15:12–18
   E.   Sacrifice of Firstborn Animals: 15:19–23
XVII.   Regulations Concerning Feasts: 16:1–17
   A.   The Passover: 16:1–8
   B.   The Feast of Weeks: 16:9–12
   C.   The Feast of Tabernacles: 16:13–17
XVIII.   Regulations Concerning Society: 16:18–19:21
   A.   Administration of Justice: 16:18–17:13
   B.   Principles for Israel's Kings: 17:14–20
   C.   Provision for the Priests and Levites: 18:1–8
   D.   Prohibition of Wicked Customs: 18:9–14
   E.   Another Moses Promised: 18:15–22
   F.   The Cities of Refuge: 19:1–21
XIX.   Regulations Concerning War: 20:1–20
   A.   Preparing the Army Spiritually: 20:1–4
   B.   Preparing the Army Internally: 20:5–9
   C.   Preparing the Approach Externally: 20:10–20
XX.   Regulations Concerning Murder, War, and Family Affair 21:1–23
   A.   Unsolved Murder: 21:1–9
   B.   Female War Prisoners: 21:10–14
   C.   The Firstborn Inheritance Rights: 21:15–17
   D.   The Rebellious Son: 21:18–21
   E.   A Hanged Man: 21:22–23
XXI.   Regulations Concerning Various Issues: 22:1–23:25
   A.   Assisting Your Neighbor: 22:1–4
   B.   Transvestism: 22:5
   C.   Birds: 22:6–7
   D.   Home Safety: 22:8
   E.   Prohibition of Certain Mixtures: 22:9–11
   F.   Tassels: 22:12
   G.   Sexual Morality: 22:13–30
   H.   Admission into the Lord's Assembly: 23:1–8
   I.   Cleanliness in the Camp: 23:9–14
   J.   Escaped Slaves: 23:15–16

CHAPTER ONE

"These Are the Words Which Moses Spoke"

Deuteronomy 1:1-5

Deuteronomy is mainly composed of three messages Moses gives to "all Israel" before he dies. They are sermons of exhortation, strongly admonishing the people to obey God, who has been and will continue to be faithful. They are filled with illustration, instruction, and application. Most important, these messages lead the children of Israel to crossroads at which they must make decisions regarding their future.

The preacher, Moses, stands at a point between the people's past history of disobedience and their potential future obedience. He is the leader. Battles and burdens give birth to his messages. Experience teaches him what to say. After forty years of aimless wandering and unrealized potential, he is compelled to press on in the direction God desires. Forty years of facing failure motivates him to emphasize God's ability to provide success. Samuel Wilberforce said, "Some clergy prepare their sermons; others prepare themselves." Moses is ready on both accounts.

MOSES' FINAL MESSAGES

1:1 These *are* the words which Moses spoke to all Israel on this side of the Jordan in the wilderness, in the plain opposite Suph, between Paran, Tophel, Laban, Hazeroth, and Dizahab.

2 *It is* eleven days' *journey* from Horeb by way of Mount Seir to Kadesh Barnea.

3 Now it came to pass in the fortieth year, in the eleventh month, on the first *day* of the month, *that* Moses spoke to the children of Israel according to all that the LORD had given him as commandments to them,
4 after he had killed Sihon king of the Amorites, who dwelt in Heshbon, and Og king of Bashan, who dwelt at Ashtaroth in Edrei.
5 On this side of the Jordan in the land of Moab, Moses began to explain this law, saying,

Deut. 1:1-5

1. *"The words which Moses spoke"* were *"to all Israel"* (v. 1). We will continually see this phrase in Deuteronomy. The last verse of this great book uses it after Moses' death to describe the impact of Moses' life on the people. The entire congregation has heard the words of their leader and has seen the wonders Moses *"performed in the sight of all Israel"* (Deut. 34:12).

Why is it necessary that *"all Israel"* see and hear? Because God is developing a relationship with the people that will influence succeeding generations. A covenant will be renewed; a land will be possessed; an identity will be given. All the people need to understand and participate in the formation of their nation.

Recently *Review* magazine documented that one-third of all references and quotations in America's political writings come from the Bible. And the book of the Bible most frequently cited by Americans during the founding era of our nation was Deuteronomy.

2. *"The words which Moses spoke"* were at a crucial place. Moses delivers his first message *"on this side of the Jordan in the wilderness"* (v. 1). Verse 5 again emphasizes the location. This sermon is delivered at a place where God's people had previously failed. They are surrounded by reminders of their earlier disobedience to God. Imagine the emotional war raging within their minds. Moses continues to exhort the people because they need assistance in making their decision to cross over into the promised land.

Communicators agree that the most effective way to deliver a message of lasting impact is by visual means. Eighty-nine percent of what we learn is through visual channels, 10 percent through audio, and 1 percent through other senses. This statistic was recently underscored in my own life. Last August after several years of absence, my wife, Margaret, and I returned to the place of our beginning ministry. Immediately, things that were tucked away in our subconscious minds began to surface as we saw old landmarks of special meaning to us. Old relationships, decisions, joys, and heartaches flooded our lives as we recounted those days gone by. The familiar scenes of a place where we once lived would not let us forget the things we experienced there. No doubt this also happened to the Israelites as they listened to Moses *"on this side of the Jordan in the wilderness."*

3. *"The words which Moses spoke"* were from the Lord. *"Moses spoke to the children of Israel according to all that the Lord had given him as commandments to them"* (v. 3).

Moses, like any sensitive spiritual leader, does not dare speak unless God speaks. By ourselves we have nothing to say. Without Him, we cannot speak. Without us, He will not speak. To address a congregation without any assurance that we bring a divine message is the height of arrogance and folly. When we are convinced that God is who He says He is—the light of the world—then we will be compelled to speak.

Amos expressed this well when he said, "The Lord God has spoken! Who can but prophesy?" (Amos 3:8). A similar logic lies behind Paul's statement, "since we have the same spirit of faith, according to what is written, 'I believed and therefore I spoke,' we also believe and therefore speak" (2 Cor. 4:13). The "spirit of faith" to which Paul refers is the conviction that God has spoken. If we are persuaded that God has spoken, like Moses we also must speak.

4. *"The words which Moses spoke"* were after significant victories (v. 4). Moses has already experienced many victories in the wilderness and is anticipating more to come. This expectation fills his sermons with an air of victory. His words, impregnated with hope, are uplifting to a people conscious of their past failures. They need encouragement. They need to see God's hand actively directing their lives. Crossing the Jordan is not a likely prospect until they feel good about their God and themselves.

Every leader understands the value of momentum. When it is positive, people will accomplish the impossible. When it is negative, however, those same people will not accomplish the possible. It is my privilege as a communicator to play the part of David and continually remind my people of the "Goliaths" that God has slain for us.

This brings a spirit of encouragement to the lives of others as they face the giants before them. The extra positive momentum really makes the difference. The largest locomotive in the New York Central system, when standing still, can be prevented from movement by a single one-inch block of wood placed in front of each of the eight driving wheels. That same locomotive, traveling at a hundred miles per hour, can crash through a wall of steel-reinforced concrete five feet thick!

5. *"The words which Moses spoke" were for a specific purpose.* One of my homiletics professors used to repeatedly say, "Preach for a verdict!" Those words continue to echo in my memory as I communicate today. Moses knew the significance of proclaiming truth and asking for a decision. This time as Israel faces the promised land, Moses wants to make sure that they go over and possess it. His message is full of truth, clarity, and passion. It is his final appeal.

I can well remember the first time I asked people to respond to my message with visible signs. Never before had I felt such anxiety. There was a time of awkward silence, punctuated by doubts and questions in my own mind. "Will they or won't they? How long should I wait? What more can I say?" Nothing is more tiring emotionally than trying to lead the listener toward the goal of the presentation. Nothing is more energizing than to witness a positive response. We must always remember that as communicators we don't just teach lessons, we change lives.

Charles L. Allen, in his autobiography *What I Have Lived By*, relates the story of a conductor who was making his last run before retirement. A man asked him how he felt about this final trip on the passenger train. He replied, "It seems like I have spent my life trying to help people get home." Moses would have understood.

CHAPTER TWO

Preparation Commanded for the Promised Land

Deuteronomy 1:6–18

Success occurs when opportunity meets preparation. Moses understood that principle. He knew that tomorrow's success in entering Canaan depended on today's planning. Because of his foresight, the children of Israel began their preparation long before they saw the land.

This portion of Scripture divides itself into four parts, each dealing with a principle necessary for effective preparation.

SEE THE LAND (VISION)

1:6 "The LORD our God spoke to us in Horeb, saying: 'You have dwelt long enough at this mountain.

7 'Turn and take your journey, and go to the mountains of the Amorites, to all the neighboring *places* in the plain, in the mountains and in the lowland, in the South and on the seacoast, to the land of the Canaanites and to Lebanon, as far as the great river, the River Euphrates.

8 'See, I have set the land before you; go in and possess the land which the LORD swore to your fathers—to Abraham, Isaac, and Jacob—to give to them and their descendants after them.'"

Deut. 1:6–8

Helen Keller was once asked, "What would be worse than being born blind?" She replied, "To have sight with no vision."

33

Reflecting on that statement, I realize that the consequences of having sight without vision are much more severe for a leader. For when a leader has no vision, his followers have no direction. Vision is not just an advantage for great spiritual leadership—it's a prerequisite.

William Carey, a pioneer missionary, was able to envision the needs of the whole world, while his fellow preachers were preoccupied with their own little parishes. *Vision has a wide-angle lens.*

Henry Martyn saw India, Persia, and Ardia (a vision of the Muslim world), while the church at home was engrossed in its petty theological squabbles. *Vision sees needs and is not thwarted by problems.*

The contemporaries of A. B. Simpson said that his life work seemed to "push him on alone, while his fellows had nothing to explore." *Vision is compelling.*

David Livingstone exclaimed, "I will go anywhere provided it is forward." *Vision instigates positive action.*

Those who have most powerfully and permanently influenced their generation have been "seers." Men and women of caution have never advanced the kingdom of God. People of vision are willing to take risks, knowing that they are attached to God's rope of security.

Moses was a man with great vision. His name is in the Bible "hall of fame." He was compelled to realize his vision. Hebrews 11:27 states, "By faith he forsook Egypt, not fearing the wrath of the king; for he endured as seeing Him who is invisible."

The emphasis on *"land"* is unusually strong in Deuteronomy. The word occurs almost two hundred times. This passage of Scripture gives two conditions necessary in order for the land to be seen.

1. *The first condition is the faithfulness of the Lord to provide.* Moses begins his message, *"The Lord our God spoke to us in Horeb"* (*v. 6*). He immediately introduces the Lord's interaction with His people. It began with the covenant promise made to Abraham and continues to this point in Israel's life. What God has done in the past He is able to continue in the future. Deuteronomy repeatedly says, "God who is faithful demands that His people *also* be faithful." It is on this basis that the covenant will be renewed. God wants the people to see more than geographical boundaries. He wants them to see His commitment to Abraham and his descendants (v. 8). The Israelites' abil-

ity to see the Promisor will determine their ability to possess the promised land.

2. *The second condition necessary for the land to be seen is the willingness of the people to move.* "You have dwelt long enough at this mountain" (*v. 6*). It's time to move. The formation of the covenant has made of the Israelites a potential nation. Now they must go and possess the land to make it a reality. The dimensions of this land, described in verse 7, are enormous. All of Palestine and Syria are included in this geographical description. This is a larger area than Israel ever possessed, even during the reigns of David and Solomon.[1]

God did not want His people to sit and become satisfied. Their task was to continue moving until they saw and possessed the land.

Phillips Brooks once said, "Sad is that day for any man when he becomes absolutely satisfied with the life that he is leading, the thoughts that he is thinking, and the deeds he is doing. Then there ceases to be a desire to do something greater for God than ever before." Those words apply to this story. God's people were not brought out of Egypt only to remain in the wilderness.

During the Civil War, the Confederate Army was approaching the lines of battle. Night fell, stopping them just a short way from their destination. Quickly they began setting up their tents, preparing for a night's rest. Walking among his soldiers, the commanding officer continually exhorted them, saying, "Don't drive those stakes too deep; we're moving up in the morning." That is what God is saying to Israel. He is telling them not to get comfortable. We could apply this advice to our spiritual lives today. It's too easy to become complacent in our personal journeys with the Lord. It's too easy to settle for less than His best. Like Israel, we need to *"see . . . the land"* and not forget God's plan for us and the potential within us.

SHARE THE LOAD (DELEGATION)

1:9 "And I spoke to you at that time, saying: 'I alone am not able to bear you.

10 'The LORD your God has multiplied you, and here you *are* today, as the stars of heaven in multitude.

11 'May the LORD God of your fathers make you a

thousand times more numerous than you are, and
bless you as He has promised you!
12 'How can I alone bear your problems and your
burdens and your complaints?
13 'Choose wise, understanding, and knowledgeable men from among your tribes, and I will make
them heads over you.'
14 "And you answered me and said, 'The thing
which you have told *us* to do *is* good.'"

Deut. 1:9–14

The inability of some leaders to delegate work is often a big stumbling block to progress. Many leaders fail to delegate because they
have an exaggerated estimate of their own ability—the "no one can
do it as well as I can" attitude. Unfortunately, they fail to recognize
the abilities of their subordinates.

Moses, a great leader, decided to delegate for two reasons. One
was that the load of leadership had become too heavy (vv. 9, 12).
One of the signs that tell us it is time to delegate is missed deadlines.
Obviously, Moses was feeling the pressure, and the only relief would
be in passing some responsibility on to others. The other reason was
that God had *"multiplied"* the people. There were too many to see
in too short a time. God's word to Abraham was being fulfilled:
"'Look now toward heaven, and count the stars if you are able to
number them.' And He said to him, 'So shall your descendants be'"
(Gen. 15:5).

The phrase *"May the Lord God of your fathers"* (v. 11) shows a continuity of relationship from the past, to the present, and on to the
future. The promise of many descendants made to Abraham was
now being realized, and succeeding generations would continue to
multiply. The continuity and responsibility of Israel's successful relationship to God and to the generations that follow is a predominant
thought in Deuteronomy.

Verse 13 describes the kind of leaders needed to fulfill the responsibility of continuing the relationship. The people were to *"choose
wise, understanding, and knowledgeable men from among your tribes."*
These leaders were to be able to comprehend moral qualities and
discern right from wrong. They were to be experienced and of good
reputation among the people. The reaction of the people to Moses'
decision to delegate to others was very positive (v. 14).

SELECT THE LEADERS (LEADERSHIP)

1:15 "So I took the heads of your tribes, wise and knowledgeable men, and made them heads over you, leaders of thousands, leaders of hundreds, leaders of fifties, leaders of tens, and officers for your tribes."

Deut. 1:15

Everything rises and falls on leadership. The best one-word definition that I know for leadership is *influence.* He who thinks he leads but has no one following him is only taking a walk. Leaders affect how their followers think, feel, and respond. All leaders have a degree of influence on others. Moses understood the important role these key leaders would play in the welfare of Israel. Therefore, he carefully outlined for the people the process of selection. A leader should be (1) chosen by the people (v. 13); (2) spiritually qualified (v. 13); (3) approved by the head leader (Moses) (v. 15); and (4) appointed by the head leader according to ability (v. 15).

Moses felt that a leader could be defined as one who knows the way (understanding), goes the way (experience), and shows the way (credibility). He understood that a leader was not necessarily an extraordinary man, but an ordinary man committed to an extraordinary God. Therefore, the selection of men who qualified to fill this role was not a matter to be taken lightly. Personally, I feel that this is an area where the church today often falls sadly short.

After assuming the senior pastorate at Skyline Wesleyan Church in San Diego, my first goal was to disciple the leadership (both professional and lay) within the congregation. This is my most important ministry to the church. Weekly I talk with key men and women sharing with them biblical leadership principles and helping them to apply these truths to their lives and the ones for whom they have responsibility. The results have been overwhelming. Not only am I proclaiming God's word from the pulpit, but it is being modeled in the pew.

Acts 6 also places an important emphasis upon lay leadership. The situation there is very similar to the one facing Moses. The church was growing and the "professional" leadership could not meet all the needs. This problem was settled when the following instructions were given to the congregation: "Therefore, brethren, seek out from

37

among you seven men of good reputation, full of the Holy Spirit and wisdom, whom we may appoint over this business. . . . And the saying pleased the whole multitude. And they chose [seven men] whom they set before the apostles; and when they had prayed, they laid hands on them" (Acts 6:3, 5–6).

This process was very similar to the one Moses used in selecting leaders. It is my conviction that the selection and equipping of qualified leaders within the local congregation will determine its success in its mission more than anything else.

Structure the Leadership (Organization)

1:16 "Then I commanded your judges at that time, saying, 'Hear *the cases* between your brethren, and judge righteously between a man and his brother or the stranger who is with him.

17 'You shall not show partiality in judgment; you shall hear the small as well as the great; you shall not be afraid in any man's presence, for the judgment *is* God's. The case that is too hard for you, bring to me, and I will hear it.'

18 "And I commanded you at that time all the things which you should do."

Deut. 1:16–18

One of my favorite stories on the subject of organization comes from a Charles Schultz "Peanuts" cartoon. Charlie Brown enters the TV room to watch a ball game, but Lucy is watching a romantic movie and the following exchange takes place:

Charlie Brown: Lucy, change the channel.

Lucy (shaking her fist angrily): No, I will not change the channel. Do you see these fingers? When they come together tightly they become a fist. This fist is almost a lethal weapon!

Charlie Brown (looking intently at his own fingers): Why can't you guys ever get organized?

Once Moses identifies the leaders, he organizes them. They are responsible for passing judgment on controversial issues in their

38

communities. Moses exhibits outstanding insight by understanding that decisions must be made at the lowest level possible. To aid in the process, he develops a simple procedure for making wise decisions.

1. Listen Fairly (v. 16)

The judge is to give an impartial hearing to every person who stands before him. Even an alien in conflict with an Israelite is to receive equal treatment under the law. No distinction is made between the *"small"* and the *"great"* (v. 17). The rich and the poor are to be treated equally. Perhaps the possibility of the judges' showing favoritism toward the rich motivated Moses to insert the second step for wise decision-making.

2. Minister Boldly (v. 17)

Decision-making is a job for the courageous. Too many leaders tend to make decisions that are based on general acceptance rather than on rightness. The larger the number of people involved in any given decision, the greater the pressure for conformity. Sometimes the easiest way out is to make no decision. This is the coward's route which can be disastrous to the morale and direction of the followers. A right decision is like a sharp knife that cuts clean and straight. There may be some pain, but the healing process will be free of infection. Indecision is like a dull knife that hacks and tears and leaves ragged edges behind it. If and when the wound heals, an ugly scar will remain as a reminder.

3. Decide Dependently (v. 17)

Moses emphasizes to his leaders that *"the judgment is God's."* This important principle removed the basis and authority of the law from the human arena and placed it firmly in the arena of divine authority.

P. T. Forsyth once said, *"You must live with people to know their problems and live with God in order to solve them."* Moses understood this truth. He recognized that without God he could do nothing.

4. Refer Occasionally (v. 17)

Moses also understood that a leader can give up anything except final responsibility. He said, *"The case that is too hard for you, bring to me, and I will hear it."*

Abraham Lincoln, like Moses, understood the motivation that subordinates receive when the top man is willing to assume responsibility for others. He demonstrated this truth immediately following the Battle of Gettysburg. Lincoln sensed an opportunity to end the war by driving hard against Lee's army as it retreated. A swift, daring attack might do it. As commander-in-chief of the army, he ordered General Meade to pursue. A friendly note in the president's handwriting accompanied the official orders. It said, "The order I enclose is not on record. If you succeed, you need not publish the order. If you fail, publish it. Then, if you succeed, you will have all the credit of the movement. If not, I'll take the responsibility." With that kind of loyalty, Lincoln instilled confidence in his generals. They would go the extra mile for him.

Moses summarizes Israel's preparation for entering the promised land with these words: *"And I commanded you at that time all the things which you should do"* (v. 18). What more could the people ask than a God who is faithful and a leader who is responsible? Now the people must be obedient.

NOTE

1. P. C. Craigie, *Commentary on the Book of Deuteronomy*, New International Commentary on the Old Testament (Grand Rapids: Wm. B. Eerdmans Publishing Co., 1976), p. 95.

CHAPTER THREE

Problems Encountered at the Promised Land

Deuteronomy 1:19–46

THE BEST IS YET TO COME

There is a wonderful life attainable by every person—our "promised land." This life represents God's best for us. Whether or not we reach it depends totally on our obedience to the Lord.

Our "promised lands" never come cheaply! We never accidentally arrive at them, and we always face barriers traveling to them. We may cover the same ground several times and bump into the same obstacle more than once. Only when we've learned to successfully follow God through the twists and turns of life will we be able to quicken our forward pace.

Booker T. Washington said, "Success should be measured not so much by the position one has reached in life as by the obstacles which one has overcome while trying to succeed."

In the Exodus story, success is measured by the arrival of God's people at His place of promise. Certainly obstacles will be encountered and problems will have to be solved, but there will be no joy until the Jordan is crossed. Listen to the story as Moses recollects it.

THE LAND IS SEEN

1:19 "So we departed from Horeb, and went through all that great and terrible wilderness which you saw on the way to the mountains of the Amorites, as the LORD our God had commanded us. Then we came to Kadesh Barnea.

20 "And I said to you, 'You have come to the mountains of the Amorites, which the LORD our God is giving us.

21 'Look, the LORD your God has set the land before you; go up *and* possess *it*, as the LORD God of your fathers has spoken to you; do not fear or be discouraged.'"

Deut. 1:19–21

This was a journey of over a hundred miles across an almost waterless limestone plateau. After days of heat and dust, the prospect of the promised land must have been very inviting. But most important, the journey had been just *"as the Lord . . . had commanded"* (v. 19).

"Then we came to Kadesh Barnea." Kadesh Barnea was on the border of the promised land. They were not in the promised land yet, but they were close. No doubt there was excitement in the camp. At last they were about to realize the promise which had been given hundreds of years before to their father Abraham. The best was yet to come.

Every great accomplishment begins with vision. We have to see it before we can seize it. Our vision is the picture of what we can be one day. Yet Moses realized vision is not enough—it must be combined with venture. Vince Abner said, "It is not enough to stare up the steps; we must step up the stairs." Therefore Moses exhorted the people to *"go up and possess"* the land (v. 21).

This great leader also understood that many people see the obstacles but not the objective. Not wanting this to happen, he added, *"Do not fear or be discouraged."*

All great leaders look beyond the obstacles to the objective. Napoleon saw Italy but not the Alps. George Washington saw the Hessians at Trenton. A man of smaller stature would have seen the Delaware River choked with ice. These men were each committed to a goal. If they had to endure hardships to reach their goals, so be it. Their final destinations were worth the inconvenience of getting there.

Often the Christian community feels that the ability to see an obstacle is the mark of maturity and insight. Usually, problems are the easiest things to see. The sad truth is that many of us look for problems, then use them as an excuse to stay right where we are. God

42

wants men who see beyond the difficulties and who give encouragement to those facing challenges.

THE LAND IS SEARCHED

1:22 "And every one of you came near to me and said, 'Let us send men before us, and let them search out the land for us, and bring back word to us of the way by which we should go up, and of the cities into which we shall come.'

23 "The plan pleased me well; so I took twelve of your men, one man from *each* tribe.

24 "And they departed and went up into the mountains, and came to the Valley of Eshcol, and spied it out.

25 "They also took *some* of the fruit of the land in their hands and brought *it* down to us; and they brought back word to us, saying, '*It is* a good land which the LORD our God is giving us.'"

Deut. 1:22-25

The words of Moses in previous verses have indicated his aggressiveness in desiring to possess the land. The people who lacked this vision suggested practical measures first. They wanted representatives to be sent over first to *"bring back word to us of the way by which we should go up, and of the cities into which we shall come"* (v. 22).

Notice, there is no mention of basing the decision whether to go or stay on the spies' mission. The issue was not whether they should or should not possess the land. God's will had already been expressed: The people were to go forward. The spies were sent to map out the *strategy* for Israel's conquest of the land.

This plan pleased Moses, so he took twelve men, *"one man from each tribe"* (v. 23). The parallel account of this story is recorded in Numbers 13. Verses 1-3 read, "And the Lord spoke to Moses, saying, 'Send men to spy out the land of Canaan, which I am giving to the children of Israel; from each tribe of their fathers you shall send a man, every one a leader among them.' So Moses sent them . . . according to the command of the Lord, all of them men who were heads of the children of Israel."

This added information indicates that while the people might have initiated the plan for sending the spies, Moses consulted with the Lord and received His divine approval. As God's chosen leader he felt the weight of the decision-making responsibility.

The spies entered the promised land by way of *"the Valley of Eshcol"* (v. 24) which is located in the vicinity of Hebron. Even today there are vineyards in this region known for the excellent quality of their grapes. Undoubtedly, the contrast between the barren wilderness and the fertile land that God had chosen for them impressed the twelve spies. Moses recalls that the spies *"took some of the fruit of the land in their hands and brought it down to us; and they brought back word to us, saying, 'It is a good land which the Lord our God is giving us'"* (v. 25).

Numbers 13:26–33 gives more complete details about this event. It is necessary to read this portion of Scripture to understand why the children of Israel did not enter into the promised land, because Deuteronomy 1:25 only gives us the positive message of the spies. Without the passage in Numbers, we would question why the people did not enter Canaan. In the next few pages, we will place a great deal of emphasis upon the Numbers account; a proper understanding of this portion of Deuteronomy cannot be achieved without a parallel study of Numbers. The application of these two passages to our walk with God makes this section one of the most important within the entire book.

> 26 Now they departed and came back to Moses and Aaron and all the congregation of the children of Israel in the Wilderness of Paran, at Kadesh; they brought back word to them and to all the congregation, and showed them the fruit of the land.
>
> 27 Then they told him, and said: "We went to the land where you sent us. It truly flows with milk and honey, and this is its fruit."
>
> *Num. 13:26–27*

These verses from Numbers are basically the same as Deuteronomy 1:25. But notice the change of atmosphere as the spies' report continues in Numbers 13.

> 28 "Nevertheless the people who dwell in the land are strong; the cities are fortified and very

44

large; moreover we saw the descendants of Anak there.

29 "The Amalekites dwell in the land of the South; the Hittites, the Jebusites, and the Amorites dwell in the mountains, and the Canaanites dwell by the sea and along the banks of the Jordan."

30 Then Caleb quieted the people before Moses, and said, "Let us go up at once and take possession, for we are well able to overcome it."

31 But the men who had gone up with him said, "We are not able to go up against the people, for they are stronger than we."

32 And they gave the children of Israel a bad report of the land which they had spied out, saying, "The land through which we have gone as spies is a land that devours its inhabitants, and all the people whom we saw in it are men of great stature.

33 "There we saw the giants (the descendants of Anak came from the giants); and we were like grasshoppers in our own sight, and so we were in their sight."

Num. 13:28-33

These spies had their eyes open. They had discovered a number of obstacles which they reported to the people:

(1) "The people who dwell in the land are strong" (Num. 13:28).

(2) "The cities are fortified and very large" (Num. 13:28).

(3) They would encounter people who had previously given them problems (Num. 13:29).

(4) They saw themselves as weaker than their enemies (Num. 13:31).

(5) They stressed the negative rather than the positive (Num. 13:32).

(6) They saw themselves as inadequate and perceived that their enemies saw them in the same light (Num. 13:33).

There is an oasis of encouragement within this discouraging report. "Then Caleb quieted the people before Moses, and said, 'Let us go up at once and take possession, for we are well able to overcome it'" (Num. 13:30).

Isn't it interesting that Caleb saw the same land as the other ten spies, yet he said go while the others screamed no? Why the difference? We see things not as they are but as *we* are.

Recently I developed a leadership lecture entitled, "Your Problem Is NOT Your Problem." The thesis was that although we all have problems, we do not all respond to them the same way. Examples of this truth are numerous. Some people who stay married have greater problems than others who seek divorce. Some people who are happy have heavier burdens than others who are sad. It is a major mistake when we focus on the problems instead of the possibilities!

This is what happened with the spies. Ten saw the barriers; two saw the blessings. Ten saw giants; two saw God. Ten saw fortified cities and their faith crumbled; two possessed faith and saw the fortified cities crumble. Two said, "The best is yet to come"; ten said, "The best is not to come."

THE REBELLION OF THE PEOPLE

1:26 "Nevertheless you would not go up, but rebelled against the command of the LORD your God;

27 "and you complained in your tents, and said, 'Because the LORD hates us, He has brought us out of the land of Egypt to deliver us into the hand of the Amorites, to destroy us.

28 'Where can we go up? Our brethren have discouraged our hearts, saying, "The people *are* greater and taller than we; the cities *are* great and fortified up to heaven; moreover we have seen the sons of the Anakim there."'

29 "Then I said to you, 'Do not be terrified, or afraid of them.

30 'The LORD your God, who goes before you, He will fight for you, according to all He did for you in Egypt before your eyes,

31 'and in the wilderness where you saw how the LORD your God carried you, as a man carries his son, in all the way that you went until you came to this place.'

32 "Yet, for all that, you did not believe the LORD your God,

46

33 "who went in the way before you to search out a place for you to pitch your tents, to show you the way you should go, in the fire by night and in the cloud by day."

Deut. 1:26-33

Verses 27, 28, and 29 highlight the reasons the children of Israel *"nevertheless . . . would not go up"* (v. 26).

(1) They forgot the *past* (v. 27).
(2) They were discouraged by the *present* (v. 28).
(3) They were fearful of the *future* (v. 29).

They Forgot the Past (vv. 27, 30-33)

How could they forget where they had been and what God had done? Hadn't they cried to be delivered from Egypt? How could they forget the words of Aaron, on behalf of God, to Pharaoh: "Let My people go" (Exod. 7)? How could they have forgotten the plagues (Exod. 7–10)? How could they have forgotten the passover (Exod. 11–13)? How could they have forgotten the miraculous Red Sea crossing (Exod. 14–15)? How could they have forgotten the bitter waters made sweet, or the bread from heaven, or the water from the rock, or the victory over the Amalekites (Exod. 15–17)?

I am amazed when I read such expressions as: "If only we had died in the land of Egypt!" (Num. 14:2); "Would it not be better for us to return to Egypt?" (Num. 14:3); "Let us select a leader and return to Egypt" (Num. 14:4). Moses' supply of patience must have been nearing the "Empty" mark. He must have been thinking, "Will they ever learn?"

It is interesting to note that God gave Israel a leader to take them out of Egypt. Now they want to select a leader to take them back into Egypt. God gives us leaders to stretch us. We are more comfortable with leaders who will satisfy us. And so were the children of Israel.

Moses tries to remind his people of God's past blessings (vv. 30–33). Observe the following phrases that show God as the One who prepared the way for them. *"The Lord your God, who goes before you, He will fight for you, according to all He did for you in Egypt before your eyes"* (v. 30). God is doing His great works before their eyes!

Not only did they see His works in Egypt, but also *"in the wilderness where you saw how the Lord your God carried you, as a man carries his son, in all the way that you went until you came to this place"* (v. 31). God cannot carry those who refuse to go forward with Him. We cannot sense God's power until we have attempted the impossible. For it is then that He manifests His greatness.

Moses continues, *"[God] went in the way before you to search out a place for you to pitch your tents, to show you the way you should go, in the fire by night and in the cloud by day"* (v. 33).

What was the response of the people after the many blessings of God? Moses sums it up in verse 32. *"Yet, for all that, you did not believe the Lord your God."*

Recently, one of our Sunday school teachers said to me, "Pastor, my greatest challenge in teaching children is to instill within their lives the spirit of gratitude." Most church leaders, especially in America, could echo this statement. It seems the more we receive, the more we take for granted.

Moses found out that God's blessings do not automatically produce grateful hearts. As far as the Israelites were concerned, the glorious past was immediately negated by the discouraging present. In their fears, they forgot their God and His blessings.

They Were Discouraged by the Present (v. 28)

C. H. Spurgeon, one of the most outstanding preachers in history, said,

> Before any great achievement, some measure of depression is very usual. . . . Such was the case when I first became a pastor in London. My success appalled me, and the thought of the career which seemed to open up, so far from elating me, cast me into the lowest depth, out of which I uttered my misery and found no room for a *gloria in excelsis*. Who was I that I should continue to lead so great a multitude? I would betake me to my village obscurity or emigrate to America and find a solitary nest in the backwoods where I might be sufficient for the things that were demanded of me. It was just then that the curtain was rising on my life's work . . . this depression comes over me whenever the Lord is preparing a larger blessing for my ministry.

This was Israel's finest hour! Their fathers had died dreaming of the promised land. They had told the story of God's covenant with Abraham thousands of times over. They had prayed often for this hour. Yet, when it came, Moses says, *"Nevertheless you would not go up."* Why? They became discouraged over the report of the spies. *"Where can we go up? Our brethren have discouraged our hearts, saying, 'The people are greater and taller than we; the cities are great and fortified up to heaven; moreover we have seen the sons of the Anakim there'"* (v. 28).

Now that the spies have discovered and presented the obstacles (Num. 12), another question arises: Why did ten of the spies bring back such a discouraging report?

a. Perhaps they thought this project was bigger than their God. Certainly, God had blessed them in the past, but never before had they faced such a challenge. It is significant that in the detailed Numbers 13 account of the spies' report, there is no mention of God. They had allowed their problems to get between them and God. He was no longer in their field of vision. Facts without faith and goals without God can be very intimidating.

b. Maybe it was fear of the unknown that caused the spies to be negative. History is full of "experts" who have made discouraging remarks to explorers, scientists, and inventors, telling them, "It can't be done."

In 1490 Queen Isabella and King Ferdinand of Spain commissioned a royal committee to look into Christopher Columbus's scheme to find a new and shorter route to the fabled Indies. The committee, an impressive panel of experts headed by Spain's leading geographer and scholar, examined Columbus's plans and presented its findings to the king and queen. Columbus's plan, they wrote, could not be accomplished. Quite impossible. Fortunately, Isabella, Ferdinand, and, more important, Columbus himself ignored the experts, and the Nina, the Pinta, and the Santa Maria set sail. Consequently, a flat world was found to be globular, and "nonexistent" new lands were discovered.

History abounds with tales of experts who said positively that things could not be done—and were proved wrong.

There was an impressive array of scientific wizards who poohpoohed the airplane. Stuff and nonsense, they said. An opium-induced fantasy! A crackpot idea!

One of America's influential scientific journalists hurried into print to say that "time and money is being wasted on aircraft experimentation." One week later in a bumpy field at Kitty Hawk, North Carolina, the Wright brothers taxied their crackpot idea down a homemade runway and launched the human race into the air. Even after that, the journalists continued to snipe at the airplane.

Marshal Foch, Supreme Commander of the Allied Forces in France during World War I, watched an air display and remarked, "All very well for sport, but it is no use whatsoever to the Army."

Thomas Edison, an outstanding genius and inventor of the light bulb, the gramophone, and endless bits and pieces of pure wizardry, is on record as having said that the talking picture would never catch on. Nobody, he said, would pay to listen to sounds coming from a screen.

He also tried to persuade Henry Ford to abandon his work on the fledgling motor car. "It's a worthless idea," he told the young Ford. "Come and work for me and do something really worthwhile."

Inventors and educated friends told Benjamin Franklin to leave alone all that foolish experimenting with lightning. It was a waste of time, they said.

Madame Curie was urged to forget the scientifically impossible idea of radium.

Laurence Olivier was earnestly advised by a sincere theatrical expert to give up plans for a career in the theater because he just did not have what it takes.

Like Moses, Caleb, and Joshua, many other leaders of uncommon courage have stepped forth, only to hear the crowd say, "It can't be done."

c. Could it be that the ten spies had expectations of the promised land that were not realistic? Did the negative leaders not expect opposition? Were they looking for easy access into the land?

Perhaps we can compare the ten negative and the two positive spies with the amateur and the experienced sculptor. The amateur was hitting his mallet against his chisel without any apparent effect. The stone would not chip and he soon became frustrated and discouraged. The expert sculptor was also hitting his mallet against his chisel and, like the amateur, there was no apparent effect. But the expert did not become discouraged.

The difference in reaction lay in the expectations of the two people. The goal of the amateur was to chip the stone; each blow that did not produce a chip was regarded as a failure. The goal of the expert was more realistic; all he wanted to do with each blow was to weaken the structure of the stone, so that a chip would eventually break off. He regarded each of his blows as a success.

The Israelites' response to the discouraging report was staggering. Immediately after the "we can't do it" speech, we read, "So all the congregation lifted up their voices and cried, and the people wept that night" (Num. 14:1).

They Were Fearful of the Future (v. 29)

Moses saw the people's fear and said, *"Do not be terrified, or afraid of them"* (v. 29). This great leader of Israel sensed a need for courage when he sent the spies into Canaan.

The Numbers account says:

> Then Moses sent them to spy out the land of Canaan, and said to them, "Go up this way into the South, and go up to the mountains, and see what the land is like: whether the people who dwell in it are strong or weak, few or many; whether the land they dwell in is good or bad; whether the cities they inhabit are like camps or strongholds; whether the land is rich or poor; and whether there are forests there or not. *Be of good courage. And bring some of the fruit of the land."* Now the time was the season of the first ripe grapes.
> *Num. 13:17–20.*

Moses realized there would probably be difficulties in Canaan. He acknowledged to the spies that the people who lived in the land might be strong and many, that the cities might be fortified, and that the land might be poor.

Therefore, he exhorted the spies to "be of good courage. And bring some of the fruit of the land." No doubt, Moses felt that upon seeing the fruit of the promised land, the people would be encouraged to possess it.

This did not happen. Fear became the dominant emotion of the camp. And nothing is more challenging than trying to motivate fearful people. Notice the results of their fears in Numbers 13 and 14.

51

a. The spies' report was negative (Num. 13:28–29, 31–33).

b. The good things did not relieve their fears (Num. 13:27).

c. Caleb's positive report did not relieve their fears (Num. 13:30).

d. Their fears caused them to exaggerate the negative (Num. 13:32–33).

e. The ten spies' fear affected many people (Num. 14:1).

f. Fear caused the congregation to turn against their leaders (Num. 14:2, 10).

g. Fear perverted the people's understanding of the nature of God (Num. 14:3).

h. Fear encouraged them to backslide (Num. 14:4).

i. Fear focused their attention on people instead of on God (Num. 14:9).

The remarkable thing about fearing God is that when we fear Him, we fear nothing else; whereas if we do not fear God, we fear everything else. This is what happened to Israel.

W. Clement Stone, a multimillionaire insurance tycoon, discovered two principles which can unlock the secret of overcoming fear: First, go where you don't want to go. Second, do what you don't want to do. Too bad he could not address the congregation of Israel at this time in their lives! They were looking into the future and crossing their bridges before they got to them.

Someone once said that if an ocean liner could think and feel, it would never leave its dock; it would be afraid of the thousands of huge waves it would encounter. It would fear all of its dangers at once, even though it had to meet them only one wave at a time.

Who caused this fear and panic to run rampant throughout the camp? The leadership! Remember that in the selection of the spies, "the Lord spoke to Moses saying, 'Send men to spy out the land of Canaan, which I am giving to the children of Israel; from each tribe of their fathers you shall send a man, every one a leader among them.' So Moses sent them from the Wilderness of Paran according to the command of the Lord, all of them men who were heads of the children of Israel" (Num. 13:1–3).

These "leaders" flunked the positive leadership test which consists of taking individuals and groups from where they are to where they could be. In every age there comes a time when the leadership must come forth and meet the needs of the hour. There is no potential leader who does not eventually find his time. Tragically, however, there are times when no leader arises for that hour.

The ten spies' failure as positive leaders was twofold. First, they failed to see their responsibilities, both to God and to the people. Their response to God should have been obedience and trust, regardless of circumstances. Nowhere in the Scripture do we read that the spies had permission to decide whether to go or to stay. Their mission was to be a fact-finding one that would determine the best way to enter the promised land. "Let us send men before us, and let them search out the land for us, and bring back word to us of the way by which we should go up, and of the cities into which we shall come" (Deut. 1:22). They were not to provide options; they were to obey. Throughout Deuteronomy the need for *obedience to God* will continually confront the children of Israel.

The spies, except for Caleb and Joshua, also failed in their responsibility to the people. They were bad examples to others. They became fearful; therefore the people became fearful. They saw problems; therefore the people saw problems. They were intimidated; therefore the people were intimidated. As leaders rise or fall, so do their followers. The congregation could not go any farther than its leaders were willing to go.

Albert Schweitzer said, "Example is not the main thing influencing others—it is the *only* thing."

When Benjamin Franklin wished to interest the people of Philadelphia in street lighting, he didn't try to persuade them by just talking about it. He hung a beautiful lantern on a long bracket in front of his home. He kept the glass highly polished, and every evening at the approach of dusk, he carefully lit the wick. People saw the light from a distance, and when they walked in its light, they found that it helped them to avoid sharp stones on the pavement. Others placed lights at their homes, and soon Philadelphia recognized the need for street lighting.

Leadership is influence. The spies influenced people to disobey God. They caused them to murmur and rebel. They kept them from reaching their dream and God's best for their lives. No wonder "the congregation lifted up their voices and cried and the people wept that night" (Num. 14:1). The ten spies failed to see their responsibility.

The spies' second failure as positive leaders was in failing to see the results of disobedience. This truth will be seen in the next passage of Scripture (Deut. 1:34–40). Needless to say, a great majority of the people suffered as a result of following these men who disobeyed God.

As the children of Israel sat there at Kadesh Barnea, the promised land lay right before them. The land that signified growth and happiness, blessing and beauty, fruit and fulfillment was just ahead. Certainly the best was yet to come!

Often leaders who are responsible for bringing people "into the land" fail God and the people. Instead of encouraging, they discourage. Instead of leading the way, they lead the stay. Dreams are dashed. Continual murmuring replaces high morale. The "best is yet to come" is erased. Now, the best is *not* yet to come.

The Response of the Lord

1:34 "And the LORD heard the sound of your words, and was angry, and took an oath, saying,

35 'Surely not one of these men of this evil generation shall see that good land of which I swore to give to your fathers,

36 'except Caleb the son of Jephunneh; he shall see it, and to him and his children I am giving the land on which he walked, because he wholly followed the LORD.'

37 "The LORD was also angry with me for your sakes, saying, 'Even you shall not go in there.

38 'Joshua the son of Nun, who stands before you, he shall go in there. Encourage him, for he shall cause Israel to inherit it.

39 'Moreover your little ones and your children, who you say will be victims, who today have no knowledge of good and evil, they shall go in there; to them I will give it, and they shall possess it.

40 'But *as for* you, turn and take your journey into the wilderness by the Way of the Red Sea.'"

Deut. 1:34–40

This section of Scripture gives insight into the various responses that the Lord gave on the day of Israel's rebellion.

1. *The present adult generation will not enter the promised land* (v. 35). Principle: Disobedience causes us to forfeit the best that God has for us. This truth will continue to be demonstrated throughout Deuteronomy.

2. *Caleb, who followed the Lord completely, will enter the promised land* (v. 36). Principle: Obedience allows us to receive the best God has for us.

Recently, I preached a message entitled, "See It. Say It. Seize It!" The message was taken from Joshua 14:6–13, where Caleb receives the land he had spied out for Moses forty-five years earlier. Notice how Caleb became more bold as "he wholly followed the Lord."

"I was forty years old when Moses the servant of the Lord sent me from Kadesh Barnea to spy out the land, and I brought word back to him as it was in my heart" (Josh. 14:7).

"And Joshua blessed him, and gave Hebron to Caleb the son of Jephunneh as an inheritance" (Josh. 14:13).

This passage describes the fulfillment of God's response to Moses during the rebellion of the children of Israel. Caleb saw the land, spoke about it from his heart, and seized it to fulfill the promise of God.

3. *Moses, the leader, will not enter the promised land* (v. 37). Principle: Leaders are ultimately responsible for the decisions of their people. Moses' identification with his people meant that he also accepted with them the penalty for their failure to obey. This incident took place before the time when Moses presumptuously struck the rock with his rod and was told he would not enter the promised land (Num. 20:10–12).

The rewards of leadership come when the followers respond positively to the challenges and grow as a result of them. The responsibility of leadership comes when the followers respond negatively to the challenges and draw back as a result. The leader is united with his people whether their response is positive or negative.

4. *Joshua, the next leader, will enter the promised land* (v. 38). Principle: God depends on leaders to bring others into the promised land. In this situation, God changed leaders to accomplish this purpose. This leadership transfer will be discussed more fully in Chapter 26.

God tells Moses to model leadership for Joshua, to *"encourage him"* (v. 38). Moses will do this for the next forty years. Is it any wonder that Joshua would rise to be a great leader?

5. *The children of the disobedient parents will enter the promised land* (*v. 39*). Principle: God can turn a victim into a victor! The parents had used their children as an excuse to rebel against the Lord's command. It is ironic that the little ones, who were weak, would be able to conquer and possess the land, while those who were strong would not.

The reason the covenant between God and His people must be renewed in Deuteronomy is that God's people had become disobedient and had lost His promise for one generation. Moses is reminding a new generation that this renewal is both a warning and a blessing. The warning is that each generation is held responsible for obedience to God. The blessing is that each generation has a new hope for God's best, regardless of the disobedience of previous generations.

THE REACTION OF THE PEOPLE

1:41 "Then you answered and said to me, 'We have sinned against the LORD; we will go up and fight, just as the LORD our God commanded us.' And when everyone of you had girded on his weapons of war, you were ready to go up into the mountain.

42 "And the LORD said to me, 'Tell them, "Do not go up nor fight, for I *am* not among you; lest you be defeated before your enemies."'

43 "So I spoke to you; yet you would not listen, but rebelled against the command of the LORD, and presumptuously went up into the mountain.

44 "And the Amorites who dwelt in that mountain came out against you and chased you as bees do, and drove you back from Seir to Hormah.

45 "Then you returned and wept before the LORD, but the LORD would not listen to your voice nor give ear to you.

46 "So you remained in Kadesh many days, according to the days that you spent *there.*"

Deut. 1:41–46

The children of Israel jump out of the frying pan into the fire. Things get worse because of their blatant rebellion. Four truths stand tall as God's people react in a wrong way.

1. *Repentance is more than words.* Their cry, *"We have sinned against the Lord,"* rings hollow when their actions are exhibited. Repentance means to turn away from our ungodly ways. No longer do we walk the wicked path. The fruit of repentance is a change of behavior.

They still were filled with unbelief. They disbelieved God's threats. And they still were filled with self-will. They did not ask, *"Will God permit us?"* but arrogantly exclaimed, *"We will go up and fight."*

2. *Delayed obedience is disobedience.* The test of obedience is a willingness to do what God requires at the time He requires it and not when it is convenient for us.

A distraught pilot, experiencing trouble landing his plane, listened as the control tower radioed instructions. "But there is a pole there," the pilot objected. The answer came back, "You take care of the *instructions* and we'll take care of the *obstructions.*" What good advice for the Israelites. They were allowing the obstructions to bog them down.

Because of their disobedience to God, they *"wept before the Lord, but the Lord would not listen to your voice nor give ear to you"* (v. 45). This passage reminds me of a passage from Proverbs:

> 24 Because I have called and you refused,
>   I have stretched out my hand and no one
>   regarded,
> 25 Because you disdained all my counsel,
>   And would have none of my rebuke,
> 26 I also will laugh at your calamity;
>   I will mock when your terror comes,
> 27 When your terror comes like a storm,
>   And your destruction comes like a whirlwind,
>   When distress and anguish come upon you.
> 28 Then they will call on me, but I will not
>   answer;
>   They will seek me diligently, but they will not
>   find me.
>   *Prov. 1:24–28*

3. *A false security brings defeat.* The people failed to understand the covenant. In the beginning they would not trust God because the

task was too big. Now they trust their weapons and the task is small. They did not see God as their provider and protector, nor were they ready to go up when God commanded. They were only willing to go when *"everyone of you had girded on his weapons of war"* (v. 41).

Contrast their attitude with that of David, the great warrior-king who said, "Some trust in chariots, and some in horses; / But we will remember the name of the Lord our God" (Ps. 20:7).

On what do we rely for security? Throughout the centuries, man has attempted to build walls of security around his possessions. A classic example is the Great Wall of China. It was started by the Emperor Shih Huong-ti, a merciless and ruthless tyrant. By brute force he had defeated feudal war lords and created an empire for himself.

And then, as always happens, he started worrying that someone might do to him what he had done to them, so he decided to wall his country off completely from the rest of the world.

The emperor began to build the Great Wall in 228 B.C., and eventually it stretched across the entire northern border of the country. It is built of bricks, stones, and mud, and has high towers every several hundred feet—twenty thousand towers in all. It took hundreds of thousands of men over fifteen years to build the wall.

Finally the wall was completed and the empire, at the cost of thousands of lives, was seemingly secure. However, with the death of the emperor, the empire fell apart. Ironically, it was not overthrown by invaders, but by rebellion from within.

That old story is not a new story. In trying to remain secure within "false walls," the Israelites were soundly defeated. Verse 44 says that the Amorites *"chased you as bees do, and drove you back."* Every man had weapons, yet they were unprotected on the battlefield.

4. *Rebellion wears many masks.* Rebellion wears the mask of inconsistency. Yesterday the Israelites would not go up to possess the land. Today they will.

It wears the mask of stubbornness. They refused to listen to Moses or his message from God.

It wears the mask of arrogance. They *"presumptuously went up into the mountain"* (v. 43). They displayed an attitude of insolence toward God.

The mask of rebellion comes off in verse 45 when the defeated children of Israel *"returned and wept before the Lord, but the Lord would not listen."*

CHAPTER FOUR

Potential Lost at the Promised Land

Deuteronomy 2:1–15

A GOAL IS LOST AND A GENERATION IS LOST

2:1 "Then we turned and journeyed into the wilderness of the Way of the Red Sea, as the LORD spoke to me, and we skirted Mount Seir for many days.

2 "And the LORD spoke to me, saying:

3 'You have skirted this mountain long enough; turn northward.

4 'And command the people, saying, "You *are about* to pass through the territory of your brethren, the descendants of Esau, who live in Seir; and they will be afraid of you. Therefore watch yourselves carefully.

5 "Do not meddle with them, for I will not give you *any* of their land, no, not so much as one footstep, because I have given Mount Seir to Esau *as* a possession.

6 "You shall buy food from them with money, that you may eat; and you shall also buy water from them with money, that you may drink.

7 "For the LORD your God has blessed you in all the work of your hand. He knows your trudging through this great wilderness. These forty years the LORD your God *has been* with you; you have lacked nothing."'

8 "And when we passed beyond our brethren, the descendants of Esau who dwell in Seir, away from the road of the plain, away from Elath and Ezion

59

Geber, we turned and passed by way of the Wilderness of Moab.

9 "Then the LORD said to me, 'Do not harass Moab, nor contend with them in battle, for I will not give you *any* of their land *as* a possession, because I have given Ar to the descendants of Lot *as* a possession.'"

10 (The Emim had dwelt there in times past, a people as great and numerous and tall as the Anakim.

11 They were also regarded as giants, like the Anakim, but the Moabites call them Emim.

12 The Horites formerly dwelt in Seir, but the descendants of Esau dispossessed them and destroyed them from before them, and dwelt in their place, just as Israel did to the land of their possession which the LORD gave them.)

13 "'Now rise and cross over the Valley of the Zered.' So we crossed over the Valley of the Zered.

14 "And the time we took to come from Kadesh Barnea until we crossed over the Valley of the Zered *was* thirty-eight years, until all the generation of the men of war was consumed from the midst of the camp, just as the LORD had sworn to them.

15 "For indeed the hand of the LORD was against them, to destroy them from the midst of the camp until they were consumed."

Deut. 2:1–15

"Then we turned and journeyed into the wilderness" (*v. 1*). This is one of the saddest statements in the Bible. Dreams are dashed as the people turn their backs on the land of promise. A vision vanishes as their leader Moses turns with them. Notice in Deuteronomy 1:43–46 the continual use of the second person *"you."* Chapter 2 opens with the first person *"we."* Moses did not take part in Israel's rebellion against God, but now, as their leader, he must walk with them into the wilderness.

This section of Scripture fills the reader with two emotions. First, there is a sense of waste. A goal—the promised land—and a generation of warriors is lost. The saddest words ever penned are these: "What might have been." Now the children of Israel turn away from a dream to die. In one of his songs, singer-songwriter Mac Davis says, "There is nothing to do but bury a man when his dreams are gone." That could have been said of the Israelites. Men who were skilled warriors were walking in land they could not even possess (vv. 5, 9). Instead of living in a land that flowed with milk and honey they were wandering in a desert where they had to buy food and water from the residents of the land (v. 6). The hand of the Lord which was to have destroyed the enemy in Canaan was instead destroying the people of promise (vv. 14–15). What a terrible waste! Elton Trueblood summarized this story in one sentence: "To make your life small when it could be great is sin and heresy."

These people wandering in the wilderness are like the unfinished statues sculpted by Michelangelo. Of the forty-four he attempted, only fourteen were completed. Those statues that were completed, such as *Moses, The Pietà,* and *David* have become famous. But the thirty he did not finish are interesting too. You can see some of them in a museum in Florence, Italy—huge chunks of marble from which he sculpted only an elbow or the beginning of a wrist. One shows the leg, the thigh, the knee, the calf, the foot, even the toes. But the rest of the body is locked in stone; it will never come out. Another reveals a head and shoulders, but the arms and hands are still frozen inside. Is this not also what happened to Moses and his people? They lived and died without ever coming out of themselves. They never realized the potential hidden within.

There is a charming little story about a Japanese artist who painted a picture on a fairly large canvas. Down in one corner of the canvas was a tree and on its limbs were some birds. But the rest of the canvas was bare. When the artist was asked if he was going to paint something more to fill the rest of the canvas, he replied, "Oh no, I have to leave room for the birds to fly."

The canvas of the wilderness leaves no room for the descendants of Abraham to "fly." They can only wait. They will circle but not soar; they will sit but not sing. They are in a holding pattern. Though God equipped them to be eagles, they will not use their wings. There is no room in the wilderness.

The second thing that strikes me when reading these verses centers around the faithfulness of God during the desert years. The key statement in describing this truth is in verse 7. *"For the Lord your God has blessed you in all the work of your hand. He knows your trudging through this great wilderness. These forty years the Lord your God has been with you; you have lacked nothing."*

The people who had insulted God by not trusting Him wanted for nothing! The Lord gave them food, clothing, and protection. He knew their path in the wilderness and for forty years He took care of them.

The words of "How Firm a Foundation" seem appropriate in this setting:

> Fear not, I am with Thee; O be not dismayed,
> For I am thy God, and will still give thee aid;
> I'll strengthen thee, help thee; and cause thee to stand,
> Upheld by My righteous, omnipotent hand.

Areas of God's Faithfulness in Deuteronomy 2:1–15

1. God is faithful in speaking to His people (vv. 1–2). Notice that it was when the people *"turned and journeyed into the wilderness"* that the Lord spoke. God is still communicating with His people even though they have rebelled against Him. His interest in their welfare remains strong.

2. God is faithful in guiding His people (v. 3). Throughout this section of Scripture, God is continually guiding the people. Even the wandering has a sense of purpose. A Christian's life is in the hands of God as a bow and arrow are in the hands of an archer. God is aiming at something the saint cannot see; He stretches and we strain, and at times we say I cannot stand any more. But God goes on stretching until His purpose is accomplished—then He lets the arrow fly. God has a purpose in every zig-zag of Israel's journey.

3. God is faithful to other nations (vv. 5, 6, 9). Here we see God's power over peoples and nations other than Israel. Deuteronomy allows us at various times to see God's faithfulness to other nations besides Israel. This sovereignty should have encouraged the Israelites to enter their land of promise. If God would honor Edom's (v. 5) and also Moab's (v. 9) right to possess their land, how much more would He honor Israel's right to possess Canaan.

Another reason for the command to leave Edom and Moab alone is that God does not want Israel to settle down and covet land that is not theirs. He will not let them settle for less than His promise to them!

4. God is faithful in blessing His people (v. 7a). Forty years of faithful blessing bestowed on an unfaithful people! This is one of many examples that underscore the words of Richard C. Halverson. "There is nothing you can do to make God love you more. There is nothing you can do to make God love you less. His love is unconditional, impartial, everlasting, infinite, and perfect!"

5. God is faithful in knowing about His people (v. 7b). He also knew about other nations. I remember Dr. Donald Snow's saying, "You may not know where God is, but He always knows where you are." Yes, Israel, God sees you *"trudging through this great wilderness."*

> There is an Eye that never sleeps,
> Beneath the wind at night.
> There is an Ear that never shuts,
> When sinks the beam of light.
> There is an Arm that never tires,
> When human strengths decay.
> There is a Love that never fails,
> When earthly loves decay.
> George Matheson

The Wilderness of Moab was to the east of the Dead Sea. It was named after one of Lot's sons (Gen. 19:37). Because the land had been allocated *"to the descendants of Lot as a possession,"* the Israelites were not to *"contend with them in battle"* (v. 9).

The *"Emim"* were giants whose name meant "terrors" or "dreaded ones" (vv. 10–11). The Horites were non-Semitic people who lived in scattered groups in Palestine, Syria, and Mesopotamia. They occupied Seir before Esau drove them out. The explanatory notes (vv. 10–12) leave the impression that no enemy is invincible. If the Moabites could drive out the people of Emim who were *"great and numerous and tall"* and if Esau's descendants could expel the Horites, then surely God could give Canaan to Israel, regardless of the opposition.

The crossing over of the Valley of the Zered (v. 13) marks a new beginning for Israel. A revived spirit and a new freedom begin to fill the camp. During the past thirty-eight years an entire generation has been dying out. The *"men of war [were] consumed from the midst of the camp, just as the Lord had sworn to them"* (v. 14).

6. God is faithful in disciplining His people. These *"men of war"* did not die a natural death from old age; it was the direct action of the Lord that hastened their end (vv. 14–15). Jude 5 refers to this incident. *"But I want to remind you, though you once knew this, that the Lord, having saved the people out of the land of Egypt, afterward destroyed those who did not believe."*

This is just one of the New Testament examples illustrating that it is possible for men to receive the greatest of privileges and yet fall into a terrible calamity. In teaching the parable of the faithful servant and the evil servant, Jesus said, "For everyone to whom much is given, from him much will be required; and to whom much has been committed, of him they will ask the more" (Luke 12:48).

The children of Israel had been given deliverance from the oppression of Egypt. God had committed to them the promised land. Yet, because they *"rejected authority"* (Jude 8), they were consumed in the wilderness.

This possibility of falling into calamity haunted Paul (1 Cor. 10:5–12) and the writer of the Epistle to the Hebrews (3:18–4:2). Dr. Johnstone Jeffrey tells of a great man who absolutely refused to have his life story written before his death. His reason? "I have seen too many men fall out on the last leg."

I enjoy collecting books written by or about John Wesley. He and his followers were particularly concerned about "dying well." Dr. John Whitehead's account of John Wesley's last days points out the importance of finishing life victoriously. In the message recorded at Wesley's funeral, Dr. Whitehead notes that as Wesley lay dying, his friends entered his room and inquired about his spiritual health. Then they spent time praising God for victory at the close of his life.

It was Wesley himself who warned: "Let, therefore, none presume on past mercies, as if they were out of danger." In other words, never take God for granted.

The author of the Epistle to the Hebrews says, "Therefore, since a promise remains of entering His rest, let us fear lest any of you seem to have come short of it. For indeed the gospel was preached to us as well as to them; but the word which they heard did not profit them, not being mixed with faith in those who heard it" (Heb. 4:1, 2).

An entire generation lost everything at the door of the promised land because of their disobedience. What a waste. "You ran well. Who hindered you from obeying the truth?" (Gal. 5:7).

CHAPTER FIVE

Principal Events Outside the Promised Land

Deuteronomy 2:16–3:29

THE KINGS ARE DEFEATED AND DELIVERED

In 2:16–23 the children of Israel begin to move into Ammon.

2:16 "So it was, when all the men of war had finally perished from among the people,

17 "that the LORD spoke to me, saying:

18 'This day you are to cross over at Ar, the boundary of Moab.

19 'And *when* you come near the people of Ammon, do not harass them or meddle with them, for I will not give you *any* of the land of the people of Ammon *as* a possession, because I have given it to the descendants of Lot *as* a possession.'"

20 (That was also regarded as a land of giants; giants formerly dwelt there. But the Ammonites call them Zamzummim,

21 a people as great and numerous and tall as the Anakim. But the LORD destroyed them before them, and they dispossessed them and dwelt in their place,

22 just as He had done for the descendants of Esau, who dwelt in Seir, when He destroyed the Horites from before them. They dispossessed them and dwelt in their place, even to this day.

23 And the Avim, who dwelt in villages as far as Gaza—the Caphtorim, who came from Caphtor, destroyed them and dwelt in their place.)"

Deut. 2:16–23

The death of the defeatists who had trembled at the report of the spies and refused to enter the land now makes possible the resumption of the journey and the fulfillment of God's promise.

As Israel crosses the border into Ammon they are again forbidden to harass the people to whom God has given the land. The two daughters of Abraham's nephew Lot bore children by their father. One son became the father of the Moabites and the other was the father of the Ammonites (Gen. 19:36–38). Therefore, Israel had an ancient kinship link with these people.

Verses 20–23 are explanatory notes. The people called *"Zamzummim"* at one time were *"great and numerous and tall. . . . But the Lord destroyed them"* (v. 21). The meaning of the word *"Zamzummim"* can probably explain God's wrath. It means *"to murmur and meditate,"* which implies demon worship and communication with evil spirits. Therefore, *"the Lord destroyed them."*

Moses' story changes direction as his people are about to engage in conflict with King Sihon.

> 2:24 "'Rise, take your journey, and cross over the River Arnon. Look, I have given into your hand Sihon the Amorite, king of Heshbon, and his land. Begin to possess *it*, and engage him in battle.
>
> 25 'This day I will begin to put the dread and fear of you upon the nations under the whole heaven, who shall hear the report of you, and shall tremble and be in anguish because of you.'
>
> 26 "And I sent messengers from the Wilderness of Kedemoth to Sihon king of Heshbon, with words of peace, saying,
>
> 27 'Let me pass through your land; I will keep strictly to the road, and I will turn neither to the right nor to the left.
>
> 28 'You shall sell me food for money, that I may eat, and give me water for money, that I may drink; only let me pass through on foot,
>
> 29 'just as the descendants of Esau who dwell in Seir and the Moabites who dwell in Ar did for me, until I cross the Jordan to the land which the LORD our God is giving us.'
>
> 30 "But Sihon king of Heshbon would not let us pass through, for the LORD your God hardened his

spirit and made his heart obstinate, that He might deliver him into your hand, as *it is* this day.

31 "And the LORD said to me, 'See, I have begun to give Sihon and his land over to you. Begin to possess *it,* that you may inherit his land.'

32 "Then Sihon and all his people came out against us to fight at Jahaz.

33 "And the LORD our God delivered him over to us; so we defeated him, his sons, and all his people.

34 "We took all his cities at that time, and we utterly destroyed the men, women, and little ones of every city; we left none remaining.

35 "We took only the livestock as plunder for ourselves, with the spoil of the cities which we took.

36 "From Aroer, which *is* on the bank of the River Arnon, and *from* the city that *is* in the ravine, as far as Gilead, there was not one city too strong for us; the LORD our God delivered all to us.

37 "Only you did not go near the land of the people of Ammon—anywhere along the River Jabbok, or to the cities of the mountains, or wherever the LORD our God had forbidden us."

Deut. 2:24–37

This Scripture confronts us with the issue of war. Is there such a thing as a justified war? For centuries Christian theologians and laymen alike have grappled with this issue. In a State of the Union address in the early 1960s, President John F. Kennedy said that each day was drawing mankind nearer to the hour of maximum danger. By the end of 1980 the editors of the *Bulletin of Atomic Scientists,* who use a twenty-four-hour "doomsday clock" to represent the entire span of human history, moved the hands to four minutes until midnight. The escalating nuclear arms race led them to make this change. They reasoned that if an atomic war were to take place, the total destruction of mankind would be inevitable.

God instructs Moses to begin possessing the land and to engage King Sihon in battle (v. 24). We suppose that this war was fought for no other reason than that the Lord commanded it. Therefore, let's ask ourselves the question, When is war justified?

1. *A war is justified when there is a rejection of reasonable demands.*

There is something to be learned from the message that Moses sent to King Sihon:

It was *peaceable* (v. 26). Even though the Lord prepared Moses for future conflict with this king, Moses' message contained *"words of peace."* Israel's leader wanted to exhaust peaceful means before resorting to force.

It was *courteous* (v. 27). No spirit of arrogance can be detected here. The king's people will experience no inconvenience since the children of Israel *"will keep strictly to the road, and . . . will turn neither to the right nor to the left."*

It was *generous* (v. 28). Moses' offer to buy food and water demonstrates that there is no thought of plundering the land. In fact, this could have been a very profitable arrangement for King Sihon.

It was *trustworthy* (v. 29). Israel's past dealings with the people of Edom (Seir), Moab, and Ammon proved their ability to pass through land without plundering it. They had a track record worthy of trust.

It was *necessary* (v. 29). They were on their way to possess the land that God had promised Abraham. They could only reach that land by traveling through King Sihon's territory. The request certainly was reasonable!

2. *A war is justified when a nation is deprived of its natural rights.* The patriarch Jacob had acquired by purchase and inheritance much of the land of Canaan. Now that they are released from Egyptian bondage, the people are ready to claim their ancestral lands.

3. *A war is justified when God commands it.* In His government of the earth, God takes responsibility for the outbreak and conduct of war. Although others may differ, it is my understanding from Scripture that God Himself assumes responsibility for what has happened on earth. What He has not directly caused, He has divinely permitted.

Sihon rejected the proposal of Moses and was hostile toward Israel (vv. 30–32). The unyielding spirit of the king must be attributed to his own stubbornness, for God never compels a man to be bad. The Lord only confirmed what was already in Sihon's heart. Like Pharaoh in Exodus, his heart was already set against the people of Israel. This verse reflects a part of the Hebrew theology of history. Man is free and responsible for his own actions, but the actions of all men are set within the sphere of history, and God is the Lord of history. The Old Testament steadily refuses to see any inconsistency between human freedom and divine sovereignty. Because the ancient Hebrews ascribed all causality to God, it was both natural and proper for them to see the response of Sihon in the light of the larger activity of God.[1]

Israel's first victory is a result of God's direct intervention. The warriors have all died in the wilderness. Now God is their only hope of victory. Notice the phrasing: *"I have given into your hand Sihon the Amorite . . . and his land"* (v. 24). *"This day I will begin to put the dread and fear of you upon the nations under the whole heaven, who shall hear the report of you, and shall tremble and be in anguish because of you"* (v. 25). *". . . that He might deliver him into your hand"* (v. 30). *"See, I [God] have begun to give Sihon and his land over to you"* (v. 31). *"And the Lord our God delivered him over to us"* (v. 33). *"The Lord our God delivered all to us"* (v. 36).

This victory was complete. The details given in verses 33-35 are in accord with the laws for a holy war (Deut. 20:10-18). One aspect of a holy war was the total destruction of all booty, including towns, people, and flocks (Josh. 6:21; 7:20-21). In some cases the destruction was only partial, and certain items were reserved for the use of the people. But once Israel crossed the Jordan, the law was applied rigidly (Deut. 7:24-26; 13:16, 17; Josh. 6:17-19).

This practice raises theological issues about God's character. We must distinguish the difference between principle and practice. The principle here is that God was to be Israel's only sovereign. Anything that stood in the way of His divine purpose was removed. Further, the wickedness of the Canaanite nations offended His holiness and opposed His sovereignty. This practice of complete destruction was not a form of fanaticism; it affirmed not only the lordship of Yahweh over Israel and her history, but also His judgment on wicked nations. In the holy war, God accomplished purposes of both redemption and judgment.

As Christians we must still accept the principles of divine redemption and divine judgment in history, along with the total sovereignty of God over our whole life. However, the application of this principle in today's society is very difficult.[2]

Deuteronomy 3:1-11 gives the account of Israel's next military success over Og king of Bashan.

3:1 "Then we turned and went up the road to Bashan; and Og king of Bashan came out against us, he and all his people, to battle at Edrei.

2 "And the LORD said to me, 'Do not fear him, for I have delivered him and all his people and his land into your hand; you shall do to him as you did to Sihon king of the Amorites, who dwelt at Heshbon.'

3 "So the LORD our God also delivered into our hands Og king of Bashan, with all his people, and we attacked him until he had no survivors remaining.

4 "And we took all his cities at that time; there was not a city which we did not take from them: sixty cities, all the region of Argob, the kingdom of Og in Bashan.

5 "All these cities *were* fortified with high walls, gates, and bars, besides a great many rural towns.

6 "And we utterly destroyed them, as we did to Sihon king of Heshbon, utterly destroying the men, women, and children of every city.

7 "But all the livestock and the spoil of the cities we took as booty for ourselves.

8 "And at that time we took the land from the hand of the two kings of the Amorites who *were* on this side of the Jordan, from the River Arnon to Mount Hermon

9 "(the Sidonians call Hermon Sirion, and the Amorites call it Senir),

10 "all the cities of the plain, all Gilead, and all Bashan, as far as Salcah and Edrei, cities of the kingdom of Og in Bashan.

11 "For only Og king of Bashan remained of the remnant of the giants. Indeed his bedstead *was* an iron bedstead. (*Is* it not in Rabbah of the people of Ammon?) Nine cubits *is* its length and four cubits its width, according to the standard cubit."

Deut. 3:1-11

These verses are almost an exact repetition of Numbers 21:33–35. Bashan was an area northeast of Galilee and was rich in forests and pastures. Many years later, the prophet Amos referred to them. Notice how God encourages Moses and the people in verse 2. He assures them that He will be the deliverer, and He reminds them of their previous victory over Sihon, thus building their confidence. The sequence of the account of the battle with Og in verse 3 is significant. The military success was seen as the Lord's. God's action is referred to first: *"So the Lord our God also delivered into our hands Og king of Bashan, with all his people."* Israel's action is secondary: *"And we attacked him until he had no survivors remaining."*

Destruction was total. Sixty cities fell. They *"were fortified with high walls, gates, and bars"* (v. 5). Moses is saying, "The cities in Canaan were walled high with gates and bars and we were fearful. Look, God is giving us victory over those type of cities today and He will still do that after you cross the Jordan."

Moses' mention of victory over King Og is also meaningful because Og was a giant whose bed was nine by four cubits. A cubit measures from the elbow to the tip of the middle finger, approximately eighteen inches. Again Moses remembers the report of the spies concerning the giants that dwelt in Canaan. If God could help them defeat Og, then He could help them defeat other giants!

My friend, Lon Woodrum, wrote an amusing poem about Og and his bed.

Bed of Og

While browsing through the Bible once
I ran across the queerest thing:
A Bashanite of giant height
Upon his nation's throne was king.
His name was Og.

There is no record whether he
Was dull or smart or sour or gay.
He had a bedstead made of iron—
That's all the Bible has to say
About this Og.

He must have used a lot of room!
They laid a tapeline on his bed;
From side to side it was six feet wide
And fifteen feet from foot to head.
Some man, this Og!

71

I wonder, was he cruel or kind?
A gentleman or snooty cad?
And did he have a smile or frown?
A bedstead made of iron he had!
That's all we know.

I hope when I have lived my life
And gone the common way of man,
The folks will find I've left behind
Something for memory better than
Old Og's iron bed!

I'd rather be remembered by
One gentle, friendly word I've said,
One smile I've worn or song I've sung
Than by a fifteen-foot iron bed
Like poor old Og!

The children of Israel are finally becoming victorious in battle. There are some important lessons we can learn concerning successful warfare from Deuteronomy 2:16–3:11.

Secrets of Success in Battle

1. God promises to help stimulate our endeavors, but not to supplant them. The formula was simple: "God delivered . . . so we defeated" (2:33). "God also delivered into our hands . . . and we attacked" (3:3). Our spiritual battles are to be a cooperative effort. Paul encourages us in our battle with temptation by saying, "No temptation has overtaken you except such as is common to man; but *God is faithful,* who will not allow you to be tempted beyond what you are able, but with the temptation will also make the way of escape, *that you may be able to bear it"* (1 Cor. 10:13).

2. God's initial action should be followed with prompt obedience. "See, *I have begun* to give Sihon and his land over to you. *Begin* to possess it, that you may inherit his land" (2:31). God clears the way for us and expects us to follow immediately. Remember, delayed obedience is disobedience.

3. The destruction of false security is often the preparation for true security. It wasn't until after "all the men of war had finally perished

72

from among the people" that the Israelites engaged in war. In order to demonstrate His supreme power, God had to eliminate anything that could give His people a false sense of security. So the temptation to trust in the veterans and their military ideas must first be removed.

Throughout the Scriptures we are reminded that God desires the glory in the lives of His children. Therefore, God chooses the weak to accomplish great things. Paul teaches that we also must choose to rely on the resources of God.

> For you see your calling, brethren, that not many wise according to the flesh, not many mighty, not many noble, are called. But *God has chosen* the foolish things of the world to put to shame the wise, and God has chosen the weak things of the world to put to shame the things which are mighty; and the base things of the world and the things which are despised God has chosen, and the things which are not, to bring to nothing the things that are, that no flesh should glory in His presence. But of Him you are in Christ Jesus, who became for us wisdom from God—and righteousness and sanctification and redemption—that, as it is written, "He who glories, let him glory in the Lord." And I, brethren, when I came to you, did not come with excellence of speech or of wisdom declaring to you the testimony of God. *For I determined* not to know anything among you except Jesus Christ and Him crucified. I was with you in weakness, in fear, and in much trembling. And my speech and my preaching were not with persuasive words of human wisdom, but in demonstration of the Spirit and of power, that your faith should not be in the wisdom of men but in the power of God.
>
> *1 Cor. 1:26–2:5*

4. *One success encourages another.* "*You shall do to him as you did to Sihon king of the Amorites, who dwelt at Heshbon*" (Deut. 3:2). "*And we utterly destroyed them, as we did to Sihon king of Heshbon*" (v. 6). God was creating a winning atmosphere to prepare His people for their most important battle, the crossing of the Jordan.

Another example of this is David's confidence when explaining to King Saul why he was willing to face Goliath.

Then David said to Saul, "Let no man's heart fail because of him; your servant will go and fight with this Philistine." And Saul said to David, "You are not able to go against this Philistine to fight with him; for you are but a youth, and he a man of war from his youth." But David said to Saul, "Your servant used to keep his father's sheep, and when a lion or a bear came and took a lamb out of the flock, I went out after it and struck it, and delivered the lamb from its mouth; and when it arose against me, I caught it by its beard, and struck and killed it. Your servant has killed both lion and bear; and this uncircumcised Philistine will be like one of them, seeing he has defied the armies of the living God." Moreover David said, *"The Lord, who delivered me from the paw of the lion and from the paw of the bear, He will deliver me from the hand of this Philistine."* And Saul said to David, "Go, and the Lord be with you!"

1 Sam. 17:32–37

5. *The art of war is not as important as the art of faith.* The experience of Israel's war veterans had not produced victory but fear. The inexperience in warfare of a new generation that had faith in God produced victory! All human efforts become vain if they are not grounded upon faith in God.

THE LAND IS POSSESSED AND DIVIDED

3:12 "And this land, *which* we possessed at that time, from Aroer, which *is* by the River Arnon, and half the mountains of Gilead and its cities, I gave to the Reubenites and the Gadites.

13 "The rest of Gilead, and all Bashan, the kingdom of Og, I gave to half the tribe of Manasseh. (All the region of Argob, with all Bashan, was called the land of the giants.

14 "Jair the son of Manasseh took all the region of Argob, as far as the border of the Geshurites and the Maacathites, and called Bashan after his own name, Havoth Jair, to this day.)

15 "Also I gave Gilead to Machir.

16 "And to the Reubenites and the Gadites I gave from Gilead as far as the River Arnon, the middle of the river as *the* border, as far as the River Jabbok, the border of the people of Ammon;

17 "the plain also, with the Jordan as *the* border, from Chinnereth as far as the east side of the Sea of the Arabah (the Salt Sea), below the slopes of Pisgah."

Deut. 3:12–17

This section reads like a real-estate deed. Moses was allowed to lead the start of the conquest and he supervised the first distribution of land. The conquered territory east of the Jordan was divided among Reuben, Gad, and half the tribe of Manasseh.

A question is often raised concerning whether the east side of the Jordan was part of the promised land. If it was not, we can understand why Moses tried to make peace with Sihon (2:26). On the west side of the Jordan, the children of Israel were to exterminate their enemies. The land that is conquered must be occupied. Two and one-half tribes chose to live on the east side of the river. History teaches us that when the other tribes had settled into Canaan, Reuben, Gad, and half the tribe of Manasseh returned to the other side of the Jordan. They took little part in the national life of Israel and soon completely lost their inheritance. They appear to have been absorbed by the nations which they were supposed to overcome. Is there a lesson to all of us in this story? Are there future problems in our spiritual lives which may cause us to stop short of the total will of God?

THE PEOPLE ARE COMMANDED AND DIRECTED

2:18 "Then I commanded you at that time, saying: 'The LORD your God has given you this land to possess. All you men of valor shall cross over armed before your brethren, the children of Israel.

19 'But your wives, your little ones, and your livestock (I know that you have much livestock) shall stay in your cities which I have given you,

20 'until the LORD has given rest to your brethren

as to you, and they also possess the land which the LORD your God is giving them beyond the Jordan. Then each of you may return to his possession which I have given you.'

21 "And I commanded Joshua at that time, saying, 'Your eyes have seen all that the LORD your God has done to these two kings; so will the LORD do to all the kingdoms through which you pass.

22 'You must not fear them, for the LORD your God Himself fights for you.'"

Deut. 3:18–22

Three phrases in verses 18–29 point to the outstanding leadership of Moses. Sandwiched between these phrases are tasks that give us insight into the effectiveness of this great man. An outline is given below so the overview can be clearly seen.

Tasks of a Leader

I. *"I commanded you"* (*v. 18*)
  A. Moses reminds his people of their potential (v. 18)
  B. He resolves current problems to achieve it (v. 19)
  C. He requires a commitment to establish it (vv. 19–20)
II. *"I commanded Joshua"* (*v. 21*)
  A. Moses reviews past triumphs God has given (v. 21a)
  B. He reassures about future assistance from God (v. 21b)
  C. He refuses to fear because of God's protection (v. 22)
III. *"Then I pleaded with the Lord"* (*v. 23*)
  A. Moses recognizes God's greatness (v. 24)
  B. He longs for the promised land (v. 25)
  C. He accepts God's will (vv. 26–27)
  D. He relinquishes leadership with a positive attitude (v. 28)

The following is an elaboration of the above outline.
I. *"I commanded you"* (*v. 18*).
  A. Moses reminds his people of their potential. *"Then I commanded you at that time."* Moses' exhortation to possess the promised land came at a crucial time. When two and a half tribes decide to stay on the east side of the Jordan, their

leader points to the other side and encourages them not to stop short of God's best for their lives.

A great leader is always asking his people to give up at any moment what they are, in order to receive all that they can become. Moses reminds the Israelites of what they can become. This issue is not "can they?" but "will they?" By reminding the people that this land is promised and given by God, Moses is helping them measure their potential not by what they see in themselves, but by what they see in God for them.

B. Moses resolves current problems to help Israel achieve her potential (vv. 18–19). All successful leaders have the ability to solve problems so that their goals can be achieved. Moses demonstrates his problem-solving skills in verses 18–19.

When I am faced with a problem, I ask six questions that help me determine a solution. So did Moses.

1. What is the problem?

Moses realized that the two and a half tribes who now possessed their land would have a tendency to become satisfied and want to settle down without possessing the promised land.

2. What is the background?

This situation is even more difficult in light of Israel's past failures to cross the Jordan. Past failures breed fear of continued failures. At this time a conquering faith is needed to replace a cowardly fear.

3. What do we want to achieve?

For forty years the goal has been for Israel to get out of Egypt, through the wilderness, and into Canaan. The pressure of taking the final step is being felt by the people of God.

4. What are the possible answers?

Option 1: They can stop short of their goal.

Option 2: The other nine and a half tribes can enter Canaan and try to possess the land.

Option 3: All twelve tribes can enter and possess the land, and then the two and a half tribes can return to the east side.

5. What is the best answer?

It would be best for all the tribes to enter Canaan and do battle together until they all have a place to live.

6. Why not try the best solution?

Moses does. The men who have already been given land are to *"cross over . . . before your brethren"* (v. 18). They are reminded that they are related (*"brethren"*) and encouraged to model (by crossing first) a commitment to the tribes that had yet to possess their land. In all respects the nation had to act as a group under Yahweh. Community responsibility is an important aspect of Old Testament thinking. In later times, after the initial stages of the conquest, the eastern tribes sometimes came under severe criticism for failing their western brethren.

C. Moses requires a commitment to establish all the tribes in Canaan (vv. 19–20). The commitment of the eastern tribes was twofold. First, they were to leave their families and possessions and go fight with the other tribes. Craigie says, "The now deceased rebellious generation had used their children as an excuse for the disobedience (Deut. 1:39); the new generation had obeyed the Lord and their obedience meant that now they could leave their families in the security of their newly acquired towns."[3] The explanatory note of Moses, *"(I know that you have much livestock)"* (v. 19) gives insight into the reason that these particular tribes wanted to dwell on the eastern side of the Jordan. It was a land well suited to the raising of cattle.

The second commitment made by the eastern tribes is expressed in verse 20. They must stay in battle with their brethren until the land is possessed and the people are at peace.

II. *"I commanded Joshua"* (v. 21).

A. Moses reviews past triumphs because of God's faithfulness. *"Your eyes have seen all that the Lord your God has done to these two kings"* (v. 21). Throughout Deuteronomy, Moses continually cites the past blessings of God to encourage present decisions and actions. He knows that refocusing their attention will bring a positive response.

B. Moses realizes future assistance because of God's faithfulness. *"So will the Lord do to all the kingdoms through which you pass"* (v. 21). Moses' faith is strengthened because of past successes. Here he tells Joshua that victory is assured as the children of Israel pass into enemy territory. Joshua knows that the people need to *"pass through"* the land in order to occupy it. The Lord underlines this truth in Joshua 1:3: "Every place that the sole of your foot will tread upon I have given you, as I said to Moses."

C. Moses refuses to fear because of God's faithfulness (v. 22). The words of Moses, *"The Lord your God . . . fights for you,"* represent a major theme in Deuteronomy's historical prologue (1:30; 2:24–25, 31, 33, 36; 3:2–3; 20:4). The first attempt to cross the Jordan was characterized by fear. As Moses transfers his leadership duties to Joshua he emphasizes the necessity of a strong faith, a positive response to what God has said. Notice in verses 21 and 22 Moses' continual focus on God's ability: *". . . the Lord your God has done . . . so will the Lord do. . . . The Lord your God Himself fights for you."* Israel's leader for forty years is exhorting his people not to leave God out of the picture. Promised lands without God are impossible! F. B. Meyer said, "Unbelief puts our circumstances between us and God. Faith puts God between us and our circumstances." Moses knew that if the people could see nothing but God they would begin to learn that God is enough!

MOSES IS FORBIDDEN TO SEE THE PROMISED LAND

III. *"Then I pleaded with the Lord"* (v. 23).
The third section of the outline continues under this section.

> 3:23 "Then I pleaded with the LORD at that time, saying:
> 24 'O Lord GOD, You have begun to show Your servant Your greatness and Your mighty hand, for what god *is there* in heaven or on earth who can do *anything* like Your works and Your mighty *deeds*?
> 25 'I pray, let me cross over and see the good land beyond the Jordan, those pleasant mountains, and Lebanon.'

26 "But the Lord was angry with me on your account, and would not listen to me. So the Lord said
to me: 'Enough of that! Speak no more to Me of this
matter.

27 'Go up to the top of Pisgah, and lift your eyes
toward the west, the north, the south, and the east;
behold *it* with your eyes, for you shall not cross over
this Jordan.

28 'But command Joshua, and encourage him and
strengthen him; for he shall go over before this people, and he shall cause them to inherit the land which
you will see.'

29 "So we stayed in the valley opposite Beth Peor."

Deut. 3:23–29

A. Moses recognizes God's greatness (v. 24). Moses' prayer is
filled with pathos and personal intimacy. The phrase *"Lord
God"* is used only twice in Deuteronomy and on both occasions it appears in a prayer of Moses (3:24; 9:26). This title is
commonly used in the context of prayer. Abraham used it in
his prayer regarding the covenant of the Lord (Gen. 15:2, 8).
Joshua will use it in a prayer of desperation during the early
period of the conquest (Josh. 7:7–9).

Moses has witnessed forty years of God's miraculous intervention in the lives of his people. This experience had
demonstrated God's power not only to the Hebrews but also
to other nations. God is now seen as the ruler of all govern-
ments. At the beginning of the exodus, Moses had sung,
"Who is like You, O Lord, among the gods? / Who is like You,
glorious in holiness, / Fearful in praises, doing wonders?"
(Exod. 15:11). Now forty years later Moses is still in awe at
the wondrous majesty of God!

B. Moses reaches out toward his goal (v. 25). This great leader
longed to see that good land beyond the Jordan. The portion
chosen by the two and a half tribes could not satisfy his
heart; he wanted to plant his feet on the true inheritance of
God's people. Perhaps Moses was motivated to make this request because God had recently given the people victories
over the two kings. False hopes began to rise within this
warrior leader and he felt that perhaps God would allow him

to finish the work that he had begun. But his desire is not to be granted.

C. Moses rests on God's will (vv. 26–27). Verses 26–27, where God denies Moses' request, have personally gripped me more than any others in this chapter. Probably my sensitivity is heightened because of my own position of leadership. I can feel with Moses as he pleads with God to allow him the privilege of completing the promise of God to his people.

Six things stand out in verses 26 and 27. The first is *the intimacy between God and Moses*. "*But the Lord was angry with me.*" The word "*angry*" perhaps can be more accurately translated "furious." This strong reaction from God illustrates the intimacy between the two of them. Is it not true that many times our strongest emotions, whether positive or negative, are directed toward those we love most? Is there not an intimacy in our circle of loved ones that allows us to be more open and honest? In this conversation with God, Moses' use of the word "*angry*" expresses his heaviness of heart. It also indicates his intimacy with God.

But Moses' boldness in making his request to his Friend is met by God's disappointment and anger. Is it not also true that the ones we love the most often give us our greatest pleasures as well as our biggest disappointments? Is there not a higher level of expectation from those with whom we spend a great deal of time? No leader has ever been more intimate with God than Moses. Exodus 33 gives an account of Moses' meetings with the Lord. Many verses in that chapter give insight into God's special relationship with His chosen leader. The apex of them all is verse 11, "So the Lord spoke to Moses face to face, as a man speaks to his friend." Moses reminded the people in Deuteronomy 5:5 that he "stood between the Lord and you at that time, to declare to you the word of the Lord." Now Moses stands before the congregation with a message of the Lord's anger.

The second thing that stands out is *the responsibility of Moses* (or of any leader) *to obey God regardless of outside pressures.*

We must remember two things when considering God's decision not to allow Moses to enter into Canaan. Moses disobeyed the Lord's command; he was under a lot of pressure from his people when he disobeyed. We only need to look back at previous events in Moses' life to see that these things are true. However, the responsibility of leaders in every age is to act with integrity and according to God's law—even in the face of dissent and rebellion. The value of a leader is not only in what he can do but in what pressures he or she can withstand.

Throughout Deuteronomy we are continually admonished to be totally obedient. God's word gives special attention to strategic men who paid a heavy price for their disobedience. Adam was driven out of paradise; Aaron was stripped of his priestly robes; Moses was sternly refused entrance into Canaan; Saul was deprived of his kingdom—all for neglecting to obey God. In this day of independence, in which self-expression and personal opinion are highly valued, as God's children we must walk in submission to Him. Our only responsibility is to be obedient to Him, regardless of the outside pressure.

The third thing that stands out in verses 26–27 is *the disqualification of Moses' request to enter Canaan.* "The Lord . . . would not listen to me. So the Lord said to me: 'Enough of that! Speak no more to Me of this matter.'" The Hebrew wording implies that Moses had been extremely persistent in his request. Moses' tenacious nature, when channeled in the right direction, made him a great leader. His request was motivated by a natural desire. Neither his persistence nor his natural desire were wrong. But there is a sense in which Moses' vision had slightly lost its focus. This vision of the promised land had turned into a consuming passion to set foot in the land. The focus of the vision had slipped from the Lord of the promise to the promise itself. This shift in focus is what made Moses' request wrong. It was the Lord Himself who was to remain the true promise and vision of Moses.

How easy it is to get wrapped up in the gift and forget the Giver. Moses' joy should have sprung from the fact that the land was about to be possessed and that God's promises were true. The psalmist understood this principle when he said, "Delight yourself also in the Lord, / And He shall give you the desires of your heart. / Commit your way to the Lord, / Trust also in Him, / And He shall bring it to pass" (Ps. 37:4–5). Was Moses' delight in God or in the land? Which was he committed to?

The transparency of Moses to his people is the fourth thing that stands out. This great leader does not hide from them the fact that the Lord has refused to grant his request. He admits that the Lord was angry with him and refused to hear him—not only refused to allow him to cross the Jordan, but called upon him to appoint his successor. All of this is from Moses' own lips!

This is the man whom God had elevated and called to lead the children of Israel out of bondage; his rod had made the land of Egypt tumble; he spoke to God face-to-face. Now he stands before his people confessing that he has sinned, and God has not granted his request.

Does this lower Moses in our estimation? No, it raises him immensely. It is encouraging to see him meekly accept God's answer. It is inspiring to watch him act unselfishly toward the man who was to succeed him in his high office, the man who was to accomplish what Moses had dreamed of for forty years. With beautiful self-effacement he steps down from his elevated position, throws his mantle over the shoulders of his successor, and encourages him to discharge faithfully the duties of that high office which he himself had to give up.

I have found that the most effective communicators are those who are open and honest before their people. At a church growth conference for church leaders from my denomination across America, I preached a sermon entitled "Flops, Failures, and Fumbles." This forty-five-minute sermon was a chronicle of the mistakes that I had made in previous years in the ministry. I must have communicated effectively, because the response was overwhelming. Hundreds of pastors made new commitments to "roll up their sleeves" and try again. Their reaction seemed to be "If God can use Maxwell when he has made that many mistakes, He can certainly use me!"

Moses' transparency with his congregation demonstrates his humility and his desire to teach them a lesson in obedience. If God will not allow His chosen leader to enter the promised land because of disobedience, what consequences will the children of Israel suffer if they are reluctant to follow God?

The fifth thing that stands out is *the privilege that God gives His chosen leader.* "Go up to the top of Pisgah, and lift your eyes toward the west, the north, the south, and the east; behold it with your eyes." If Moses could not touch it, he could at least get a glimpse of the longed-for land. Moses, who early in his life "forsook Egypt, not fearing the wrath of the king; for he endured as seeing Him who is invisible" (Heb. 11:27), will close his ministry seeing the land promised to Abraham.

The sovereignty of God is the sixth thing that stands out in these verses. *"For you shall not cross over this Jordan"* was not the answer Moses wanted to hear. Wasn't the pressure on him almost unbearable? Didn't he deserve another chance? Wouldn't it make sense for the man who had paid such a heavy price leading the children of God through the wilderness to be able to end his ministry with a reward? Yes, a thousand times yes—in man's eyes. But "'My thoughts are not your thoughts, / Nor are your ways My ways,' says the Lord. / 'For as the heavens are higher than the earth, / So are My ways higher than your ways, / And My thoughts than your thoughts'" (Isa. 55:8–9).

Perhaps the following thoughts were behind God's no to His chosen leader. (1) God will not let sin go unpunished. (2) Because he was a leader, Moses was an example and therefore must be disciplined. (3) God needed to underscore the importance of total obedience. (4) The people were relying too much on Moses. (5) A new leader was needed for the battles ahead.

From verses 26 and 27 we not only receive understanding about the relationship between God and Moses, but we can also develop a checklist of questions to ask ourselves when God says no to us.

Am I in intimate communication with God?

Am I responsible for this situation?

Is my request appropriate?

Will I share this experience with others?

Have I counted my blessings?

Will I accept the sovereignty of God?

    D. Moses relinquishes leadership with a positive attitude (v. 28). *"'But command Joshua, and encourage him and strengthen him; for he shall go over before this people, and he shall cause them to inherit the land which you will see.' So we stayed in the valley opposite Beth Peor"* (vv. 28, 29). It is the responsibility of Moses to *"encourage . . . and strengthen"* Joshua. The transfer of leadership is an important theme in Deuteronomy. It has already been mentioned three times (1:38; 3:21, 28). By bringing this subject up so often, Moses was not only encouraging Joshua, but he was giving him his blessing and his approval as the next leader.

NOTES

1. P. C. Craigie, *Commentary on the Book of Deuteronomy*, New International Commentary on the Old Testament (Grand Rapids: Wm. B. Eerdmans Publishing Co., 1976), p. 117.

2. J. A. Thompson, *Deuteronomy: An Introduction and Commentary*, Tyndale Old Testament Commentary Series, ed. D. J. Wiseman (Downers Grove, IL: Inter Varsity Press, 1975), pp. 96–97.

3. Craigie, *Commentary*, p. 124.

CHAPTER SIX

Past Incidents Interpreted for Entry into the Promised Land

Deuteronomy 4:1–40

RESPOND APPROPRIATELY TO GOD'S LAW

4:1 "Now, O Israel, listen to the statutes and the judgments which I teach you to observe, that you may live, and go in and possess the land which the LORD God of your fathers is giving you.

2 "You shall not add to the word which I command you, nor take from it, that you may keep the commandments of the LORD your God which I command you.

3 "Your eyes have seen what the LORD did at Baal Peor; for the LORD your God has destroyed from among you all the men who followed Baal of Peor.

4 "But you who held fast to the LORD your God *are* alive today, every one of you.

5 "Surely I have taught you statutes and judgments, just as the LORD my God commanded me, that you should act according *to them* in the land which you go to possess.

6 "Therefore be careful to observe *them;* for this *is* your wisdom and your understanding in the sight of the peoples who will hear all these statutes, and say, 'Surely this great nation *is* a wise and understanding people.'

7 "For what great nation *is there* that has God *so* near to it, as the LORD our God *is* to us, for whatever *reason* we may call upon Him?

8 "And what great nation *is there* that has *such*

statutes and righteous judgments as are in all this
law which I set before you this day?"

Deut. 4:1-8

The first three chapters of Deuteronomy are filled with examples
of God's direct involvement and intervention in Israel's past history.
In chapter 4 Moses exhorts the people to remember from past experience that God blesses obedience. He wants them to experience
future success by recalling past victories.

The introductory *"now"* of this chapter refers to Moses' preceding
speech. It is preparatory to the appeal to obey, as though he is saying, "And now, in light of God's acts of deliverance, you should obey
His commandments."

Deuteronomy 4 is a miniature sermon on the covenant and the
law. This law forms the basis of the covenant relationship. An understanding of the law, its nature and purpose, is expanded here, so that
the people's obedience will be based on comprehension. This law is
not simply a written code to be framed and hung on the wall. It
is presented to the people for the purpose of education and application. The life of the Hebrew nation would depend on the law, not in
a totally legalistic sense, but in the sense that the law was the basis
of the covenant wherein lay Israel's close relationship to their God.[1]

Therefore Moses exhorts, *"Now, O Israel, listen to the statutes and
the judgments which I teach you to observe."* The observation and application of the commandments will accomplish two things. (1) Israel
will receive full enjoyment of life (vv. 1–4). (2) Israel will be different and draw other nations to God (vv. 5–8).

Israel's Full Enjoyment of Life (vv. 1–4)

Full enjoyment of life was based on full obedience to God's law.
This included listening, observing, and doing in order to reach full
potential and possess the land of promise (v. 1). It also meant that
Israel must not *"add to the word"* (as the Pharisees would later do),
thereby weakening it, nor should they *"take from it"* to accommodate
the weakness of human nature (v. 2).

Using a poignant illustration from their own history, Moses refers
to the incident at Baal Peor when their very lives depended on total
obedience to God's law. Numbers 25 tells this story of spiritual and

physical adultery committed by the Israelites with the Moabite followers of Baal. As a result of their disobedience, over twenty-four thousand Israelites died. Those who were obedient to God's commands lived (v. 4).

The Difference That Would Draw Others to God (vv. 5-8)

The law and obedience to it are required to make Israel morally and spiritually unique among all other nations. Israel's strength would not be in military might or human skills. Other nations not comprehending the beauty of obedience would marvel at Israel's wisdom and understanding. It was not by learned discussion or arguments that their wisdom was to be displayed but by childlike, unquestioning obedience. All the wisdom was in the statutes and judgments of God, not in their own thoughts or reasonings (vv. 5–6). The profound and marvelous providence of God as revealed in His word was what the nations were to see and admire.

Moses made two deductions about the law that was given to Israel (vv. 7–8). First, God's law given to Israel pointed to an intimate relationship between Him and the descendants of Abraham. This type of kinship existed in no other religion. Second, God's law, which surpassed all other laws in righteousness, should be the pride of Israel. Obedience to this great law was Israel's only hope for success and for the drawing of other nations to God.

Forty-two times in the Bible we read that the blessings of God are contingent on our obedience. One of the many examples is Psalm 25:10. "All the paths of the Lord are mercy and truth, / To such as keep His covenant and His testimonies." Too many Christians use the "dip and skip" method of Christian living. They dip into His promises and skip His commands. This type of living did not please God in the day of Moses and it does not please Him now.

REMEMBER DILIGENTLY GOD'S BLESSINGS

4:9 "Only take heed to yourself, and diligently keep yourself, lest you forget the things your eyes have seen, and lest they depart from your heart all the days of your life. And teach them to your children and your grandchildren,

10 *"especially concerning* the day you stood before the LORD your God in Horeb, when the LORD said to me, 'Gather the people to Me, and I will let them hear My words, that they may learn to fear Me all the days they live on the earth, and *that* they may teach their children.'

11 "Then you came near and stood at the foot of the mountain, and the mountain burned with fire to the midst of heaven, with darkness, cloud, and thick darkness.

12 "And the LORD spoke to you out of the midst of the fire. You heard the sound of the words, but saw no form; *you* only *heard* a voice.

13 "So He declared to you His covenant which He commanded you to perform, the Ten Commandments; and He wrote them on two tablets of stone.

14 "And the LORD commanded me at that time to teach you statutes and judgments, that you might observe them in the land which you cross over to possess."

Deut. 4:9–14

Two expressions continually used in Deuteronomy are seen in verse 9. *"Take heed"* is found four times in this chapter alone (vv. 9, 15, 19, 23). *"Lest you forget"* is a constant reminder throughout Deuteronomy that the people must remember God's saving acts on behalf of Israel. These acts were the foundation of Israel's claim to be God's people and the basis on which God challenged Israel to enter into His covenant.

When writing his Gospel, John said, "And truly Jesus did many other signs in the presence of His disciples, which are not written in this book; but these are written that you may believe that Jesus is the Christ, the Son of God, and that believing you may have life in His name" (John 20:30–31). The manifestation of God's works within the lives of man, whether in the Old Testament or the New, is an appeal for man to enter into a new relationship with God.

Religious education consisted of remembering the experiences with God in the past, and also of teaching the children these remembered truths. Deuteronomy lays great stress on the parents' responsibility for their children's spiritual education. Failure either to remember God's blessing or to teach these truths to their children would mean spiritual disaster for Israel.

The parents were especially to tell about God's interaction with them at Horeb. Hearing about this experience would encourage the children to *"learn to fear [God] all the days they live on the earth"* (v. 10). It would open the door for them to acknowledge His sovereignty and then *reverence* Him. This reverence would be expressed in their worship and obedience. The "fear of the Lord" is one of the dominating thoughts of the Old Testament. It is a God-given response which enables a man to reverence God's person, to obey His commandments, and to hate evil (Prov. 8:13; Jer. 32:40; Heb. 5:7–8). It is the beginning of wisdom (Ps. 111:10), the secret of uprightness, and the whole duty of man (Eccles. 12:13). It is given as one of the characteristics of the Messiah (Isa. 11:2, 3). God's people in every age are urged to cultivate and walk in fear of the Lord (Ps. 34:11; Jer. 2:19; Acts 9:31; 10:2; Eph. 5:21; Phil. 2:12). In Deuteronomy the verb *"fear"* occurs in 4:10; 5:29; 6:2, 13, 24; 8:6; 10:12, 20; 14:23; 17:19; 28:58; 31:12, 13.[2]

Worship is an intelligent and loving response to the revelation of God. It is the adoration of His name and His works. Therefore, acceptable worship is impossible without teaching. For this reason the parents were to make known the *works* of the Lord so that succeeding generations could make known the *name* of the Lord. Worship becomes paltry if our knowledge of God is poor, and our knowledge of God will be poor if our teaching is inadequate. But when the word of God and His acts are expounded in their fullness, and the congregation begins to catch a glimpse of the glory of the living God, they bow down in solemn awe and joyful wonder before Him. That has been God's desire for His children throughout the ages.

The following events happened at Horeb as recorded in Deuteronomy 4:10–14. (1) The people came together to hear the words of the Lord. (2) The mountain burned to the sky, causing thick darkness and clouds. (3) The Lord spoke to the people from the fire. (4) The people heard God but did not see Him. (5) God also wrote the Ten Commandments *"on two tablets of stone."*

The covenant is identified with the law in verse 13. This can be harmful. Undue emphasis on the external, statutory nature of the compact can push the spiritual bond between God and His people into the background. This could cause us to think that God asked only for obedience to laws. He did require obedience, but the covenant was more than law, it was a relationship. Deuteronomy preserves the balance between law and relationship by its constant emphasis on the extraordinary grace of God at the exodus and in the wilderness. The response to these acts of God is love. Our primary relationship to God should be a warm, complete devotion to Him personally. If we possess this kind of love, we will be completely and obediently loyal to Him. Laws need to be written inwardly—on the heart—or the gospel will be lost in law (Jer. 31:31–34). Covenant as a purely juridical institution encouraged them to keep the outward forms of obedience, while neglecting the deeper, inner relationships to God which alone made for true community and obedience.[3] Moses' point in Deuteronomy 4 is that the keeping of the covenant is obedience to the law, and the keeping of the law is the Ten Commandments.

REJECT CONTINUALLY ANY OTHER GODS

4:15 "Take careful heed to yourselves, for you saw no form when the LORD spoke to you at Horeb out of the midst of the fire,

16 "lest you act corruptly and make for yourselves a carved image in the form of any figure: the likeness of male or female,

17 "the likeness of any animal that *is* on the earth or the likeness of any winged bird that flies in the air,

18 "the likeness of anything that creeps on the ground or the likeness of any fish that *is* in the water beneath the earth.

19 "And *take heed*, lest you lift your eyes to heaven, and *when* you see the sun, the moon, and the stars, all the host of heaven, you feel driven to worship them and serve them, which the LORD your God has given to all the peoples under the whole heaven as a heritage.

20 "But the LORD has taken you and brought you out of the iron furnace, out of Egypt, to be His people, an inheritance, as you are this day.

21 "Furthermore the LORD was angry with me for your sakes, and swore that I would not cross over

the Jordan, and that I would not enter the good land which the LORD your God is giving you as an inheritance.

22 "But I must die in this land, I must not cross over the Jordan; but you shall cross over and possess that good land.

23 "Take heed to yourselves, lest you forget the covenant of the LORD your God which He made with you, and make for yourselves a carved image in the form of anything which the LORD your God has forbidden you.

24 "For the LORD your God *is* a consuming fire, a jealous God.

25 "When you beget children and grandchildren and have grown old in the land, and act corruptly and make a carved image in the form of anything, and do evil in the sight of the LORD your God to provoke Him to anger,

26 "I call heaven and earth to witness against you this day, that you will soon utterly perish from the land which you cross over the Jordan to possess; you will not prolong *your* days in it, but will be utterly destroyed.

27 "And the LORD will scatter you among the peoples, and you will be left few in number among the nations where the LORD will drive you.

28 "And there you will serve gods, the work of men's hands, wood and stone, which neither see nor hear nor eat nor smell.

29 "But from there you will seek the LORD your God, and you will find *Him* if you seek Him with all your heart and with all your soul.

30 "When you are in distress, and all these things come upon you in the latter days, when you turn to the LORD your God and obey His voice

31 "(for the LORD your God *is* a merciful God), He will not forsake you nor destroy you, nor forget the covenant of your fathers which He swore to them."

Deut. 4:15–31

Moses is concerned that once the Israelites dwell in Canaan, they will find the temptation of idolatry irresistible (vv. 15–19, 23–26).

God's children had a profound experience of God's presence at Mount Sinai (Horeb), yet they *"saw no form"* (v. 15). The reality of God's presence could never be doubted since they heard His voice and sensed His awesome presence in the fire. Yet the danger of turning a spiritual experience into a physical representation was a distinct possibility. In fact, this had already happened in the golden calf incident, so Moses has reason to be concerned. He warns them to *"take careful heed"* not to do that again (vv. 15–19).

Their greatest temptation would be to make an image like themselves, *"male or female"* (v. 16). Since they perceived God as personal it would seem natural to make Him in human likeness. Deuteronomy 4:15–19 gives us an understanding of why idolatry is contrary to Hebrew theology. Man cannot be a complete representation of God since He is transcendent. Any attempt to represent God in an idol would be an attempt to undermine His transcendence. There is no way man can limit God!

When Moses lists the forms of graven images prohibited (vv. 16–19), his sequence is the opposite of the creation sequence of Genesis 1:2–4a: male and female, beast and animal, creeping things, bird, fish, and heavens. For the Israelites to abandon their Lord and to engage in idolatry would be to reverse His will for their lives. It would equal the undoing of God's creation.[4]

The forms of idolatry that Moses warns against are hero worship (v. 16), animal worship (vv. 17–18), and nature worship (v. 19). The first two forms take place when man makes an image. The last, nature worship, is a more subtle danger, that of taking something within the created universe and making it an object of divine worship.

Paul teaches in Romans 1:22–23 that men "became fools, and changed the glory of the incorruptible God into an image made like corruptible man." The result of this type of action is a degraded intellect, misplaced affections, and degenerate morals (Rom. 1:24–32). The Israelites could not afford to corrupt themselves through idolatry (Deut. 4:16)—the consequences would be too severe.

Aside from the fact they would corrupt themselves, another reason that Israel was to denounce all forms of idolatry was that God had chosen them to be His people (v. 20). They were *"taken . . . out of Egypt."* This phrase is mentioned about twenty times in Deuteronomy. We can sense the pressures the people encountered in Egypt when Moses describes that experience as being an *"iron furnace."* God brought them out of this terrible place *"to be His people, an inheritance."* The fact that Israel is a chosen people is repeatedly stated in Deuteronomy (i.e., 7:6; 14:2; 26:18). Other Old Testament Scriptures address the fact that Israel was God's inheritance, His own unique possession (Ps. 28:9; 33:12; 68:9; 78:62–71; 79:1; 94:14; Joel 2:17; 3:2; Mic. 7:14, 18).

Moses again laments that he is forbidden to enter into the promised land (vv. 21–22). There is a sadness and finality in the words of this great leader as he says, *"But I must die in this land, I must not cross over the Jordan"* (v. 22). Moses warns the people not to forget their covenant with the Lord, lest they suffer the consequences (vv. 23–27). He knew firsthand that *"God is a consuming fire, a jealous God"* (v. 24). As a consuming fire, God purifies what is precious and destroys what is worthless. As a jealous God, He intensely covets righteousness among His people and His own prominence in their lives.

Moses anticipates the negative effects that prolonged enjoyment and blessings will have on the people. Israel will tend to forget the demands of the covenant and turn to idolatry. When that happens, the people will (1) *"utterly perish,"* (2) be separated from the land, (3) be scattered among other nations, and (4) *"be left few in number among the nations where the Lord will drive you"* (vv. 26–27).

Heaven and earth are called to witness against Israel's unfaithfulness. In contrast to the fickleness of God's people these witnesses were permanent and unchanging. These judgments were fulfilled in the Assyrian and Babylonian captivities, and perhaps in the dispersion of Israel after they rejected Jesus.

It is interesting that the context of verse 25 indicates that Israel's extended period of comfort will give rise to the idolatry which will result in God's judgments on them. When the families are settled, satisfaction creeps into their lives. The result? They will forget God. No wonder Phillips Brooks said, "Sad is that day when we are satisfied with the thoughts we are thinking, the lives we are living, the dreams we are dreaming, until there ceases to be forever knocking at the door of our souls a desire to do something greater for God." Sidney J. Harris expressed the same concern. "Our real enemies," he said, "are the people who make us feel so good that we are slowly, inexorably, pulled down into the quicksand of smugness or self-satisfaction." Moses is not going to be Israel's enemy. He is passionately warning them not to become self-satisfied when they settle down in the land of their dreams.

An old, familiar story by an unknown author comes immediately to mind and seems to apply well to the situation of Israel at that time.

> An old Vermont farmer was talking with a young neighbor. The young man was complaining because the devil's paintbrush (that bright but destructive weed) was ruining his hay crop. "Fertilize your land, my boy, fertilize your land," said the old man. "I've noticed that the devil's paintbrush is like lots of folks. It can't stand prosperity."

A life of ease has ruined too many people. Hannibal of Carthage had conquered the conquerors. He had even routed the Roman legions. But victory was not to remain his. One winter, battle was suspended and Hannibal and his army settled back to wait out the weather in Capua, a city of luxury. These few months in luxury were enough to destroy his army; they lost their will to fight. Their winter of ease made them an easy target for defeat in the spring.

Moses realizes that the battles on the other side of the Jordan will be met with honor and victory. But he fears a complacent attitude will set in when things are going along well. It is then that Israel will be prone to forget God. And when that happens, God's people will encounter persecution (vv. 26–27) and emptiness (v. 28). This will motivate them to again *seek the Lord your God, and you will find Him if you seek Him with all your heart and with all your soul"* (v. 29). As they seek God in their distress, they will find Him to be merciful. *"He will not forsake you nor destroy you, nor forget the covenant of your fathers which He swore to them"* (v. 31).

One feature of God's covenant with Israel that differed from the usual political treaties of that day was the provision that a rebel could repent, return, and be forgiven. The prospect of beginning a new life of obedience and blessing was promised to these chosen people. In ancient political treaties, rebellion was seldom treated with mercy, even if the offending party repented. But God's nature is vastly different from that of human rulers. His mercy is equal to His might.

E. Stanley Jones made an important point when he said, "Anything less than God will let you down." He went on to reason that anything less than God is not rooted in eternal reality and is destined to fail.[5] Is that not what Moses is saying? Israel will try other gods but will be sorely disappointed. Then, after much trouble, she will return to God, who is faithful and never disappoints.

REFLECT INWARDLY THAT GOD CHOSE YOU

4:32 "For ask now concerning the days that are past, which were before you, since the day that God created man on the earth, and *ask* from one end of heaven to the other, whether *any* great *thing* like this has happened, or *anything* like it has been heard.

33 "Did *any* people *ever* hear the voice of God speaking out of the midst of the fire, as you have heard, and live?

34 "Or did God *ever* try to go *and* take for Himself a nation from the midst of *another* nation, by trials, by signs, by wonders, by war, by a mighty hand and an outstretched arm, and by great terrors, according to all that the LORD your God did for you in Egypt before your eyes?

35 "To you it was shown, that you might know that the LORD Himself *is* God; *there is* none other besides Him.

36 "Out of heaven He let you hear His voice, that He might instruct you; on earth He showed you His great fire, and you heard His words out of the midst of the fire.

37 "And because He loved your fathers, therefore He chose their descendants after them; and He brought you out of Egypt with His Presence, with His mighty power,

38 "driving out from before you nations greater and mightier than you, to bring you in, to give you their land *as* an inheritance, as *it is* this day.

39 "Therefore know this day, and consider *it* in

your heart, that the LORD Himself *is* God in heaven above and on the earth beneath; *there is* no other.

40 "You shall therefore keep His statutes and His commandments which I command you today, that it may go well with you and with your children after you, and that you may prolong *your* days in the land which the LORD your God is giving you for all time."

Deut. 4:32–40

Israel's hope rests not only on the mercy of God (vv. 29–31) but also on the fact that they were chosen by Him (vv. 32–40). This section of Scripture is one of the most beautiful in Deuteronomy because it focuses on God instead of on the people. The theme here is that God communicates with His chosen people. Verses 32–38 deal with *how* God communicates and verses 39–40 deal with *why* He does.

In sum, (1) by pointing to His past blessings, God communicates convincingly. (2) By reminding Israel of their privileges, He communicates personally. (3) He deals with them in such a way that they know that He alone is God and beside Him there is no other. If they pay attention to what He says, He promises that it will *"go well with"* them and future generations.

God communicates convincingly, by pointing to His past blessings. Moses considers all of past history when he asks *"whether any great thing like this has happened, or anything like it has been heard"* (v. 32). He gives examples of God's revelation (v. 33) and of His choosing and delivering Israel (v. 34). They had heard God's voice and lived. They had seen God's miraculous signs and witnessed their own deliverance from Egypt. What nation before had ever been chosen, delivered, protected, and had revealed to them by sight and sound that God had special plans for them? None!

God communicates personally, by reminding Israel of their privileges. Here are some of the phrases that demonstrate how God spoke to Israel in a personal way: *"To you it was shown"* (v. 35); *"He let you hear His voice"* (v. 36); *"He brought you out of Egypt"* (v. 37); *". . . to bring you in . . ."* (v. 38); *"Consider it in your heart"* (v. 39); *"You shall therefore keep His statutes"* (v. 40).

This great God remembers His love and His promise to their

fathers. He rescues them from Egyptian bondage and reveals Himself to them continually.

God communicates authoritatively, so that they would *"know that the Lord Himself is God"* (v. 35) and would consider in their hearts that *"there is no other"* God (v. 39). Their knowledge of God stemmed from God's revelation of Himself in word and in deed. The two primary sources of this knowledge were the exodus and events in the Sinai. These incidents formed the framework of their belief. The result of their keeping God's statutes and commandments was *"that it may go well with you and with your children after you, and that you may prolong your days in the land which the Lord your God is giving you for all time"* (v. 40).

The words, *"that it may go well with you"* occur eight times in Deuteronomy, undoubtedly to emphasize the motive for obedience (4:40; 5:16; 6:3–18; 12:25, 28; 19:13; 22:7). The idea that righteousness lengthens life and sin shortens it is common in the Old Testament (Prov. 3:1–2, 5–16; 10:27).

Howard Nogle, a friend of mine, was spending some time with his grandson, Chris. During their few days together, Howard tried to teach him Micah 6:8: "He has shown you, O man, what is good; / And what does the Lord require of you / But to do justly, / To love mercy, / And to walk humbly with your God?"

As Chris was getting the verse down pat, a thought struck him. "But Grandpa," he said, "I don't quite understand. It would be hard to be humble—*walking with God!*" What an outstanding concept of the greatness of God for a seven-year-old!

Moses would have been pleased to have heard his people respond in such a way. He did not want them to be ungrateful for the continual blessings and faithfulness of God. For if Israel ever lost the spirit of gratitude to God or failed to pass it on to succeeding generations, they would be spiritually, morally, and physically in trouble.

NOTES

1. P. C. Craigie, *Commentary on the Book of Deuteronomy,* New International Commentary on the Old Testament (Grand Rapids: Wm. B. Eerdmans Publishing Co., 1976), p. 129.

2. J. A. Thompson, *Deuteronomy: An Introduction and Commentary,* Tyndale Old Testament Commentary Series, ed. D. J. Wiseman (Downers Grove, IL: Inter Varsity Press, 1975), pp. 104–5.

3. G. Ernest Wright, *God Who Acts* (London: SCM Press, Ltd., 1952), p. 99.

4. Victor P. Hamilton. *Handbook on the Pentateuch* (Grand Rapids: Baker Book House, 1982), p. 397.

5. E. Stanley Jones, *Abundant Living* (Nashville: Abingdon Press, Festival Books, 1976), p. 39.

CHAPTER SEVEN

Old Law for a New Generation

Deuteronomy 4:41–5:33

INTRODUCTION TO THE MESSAGE

Verses 41–43 serve as a transition between Moses' first and second addresses to his people. The theme of this passage is the value of life, a theme underscored in preceding and succeeding chapters of Deuteronomy.

> 4:41 Then Moses set apart three cities on this side of the Jordan, toward the rising of the sun,
> 42 that the manslayer might flee there, who kills his neighbor unintentionally, without having hated him in time past, and that by fleeing to one of these cities he might live:
> 43 Bezer in the wilderness on the plateau for the Reubenites, Ramoth in Gilead for the Gadites, and Golan in Bashan for the Manassites.
>
> *Deut. 4:41–43*

Three cities were appointed east of the Jordan to provide safety for the person who inadvertently committed manslaughter (19:1–13). In nomadic societies the possibility of blood revenge acted as a restraint on men. In settled, more civilized societies there were proper legal procedures for the trial of such persons, but until these procedures were established provisions such as those given here were necessary.

> 4:44 Now this *is* the law which Moses set before the children of Israel.

100

45 These *are* the testimonies, the statutes, and the judgments which Moses spoke to the children of Israel after they came out of Egypt,

46 on this side of the Jordan, in the valley opposite Beth Peor, in the land of Sihon king of the Amorites, who dwelt at Heshbon, whom Moses and the children of Israel defeated after they came out of Egypt.

47 And they took possession of his land and the land of Og king of Bashan, two kings of the Amorites, who *were* on this side of the Jordan, toward the rising of the sun,

48 from Aroer, which *is* on the bank of the River Arnon, even to Mount Sion (that is, Hermon),

49 and all the plain on the east side of the Jordan as far as the Sea of the Arabah, below the slopes of Pisgah.

Deut. 4:44-49

The lengthy section of Deuteronomy which comprises Moses' second message (4:41–26:19) is the core of the book. Several chapters will divide this message into manageable sections.

"Moses set before the children of Israel" (v. 44) God's instruction. If they were going to prosper individually and nationally they must obey the covenant. These *"testimonies, . . . statutes, and . . . judgments"* were originally given three months after the Israelites *"came out of Egypt"* (v. 45). (See Exod. 20:1–17; 21–23.) Deuteronomy is, therefore, not a new covenant but the renewal of a previous one.

THE TEN COMMANDMENTS RECEIVED

5:1 And Moses called all Israel, and said to them: "Hear, O Israel, the statutes and judgments which I speak in your hearing today, that you may learn them and be careful to observe them.

2 "The LORD our God made a covenant with us in Horeb.

3 "The LORD did not make this covenant with our fathers, but with us, those who *are* here today, all of us who *are* alive.

101

4 "The LORD talked with you face to face on the mountain from the midst of the fire.

5 "I stood between the LORD and you at that time, to declare to you the word of the LORD; for you were afraid because of the fire, and you did not go up the mountain. *He* said:

6 'I *am* the LORD your God who brought you out of the land of Egypt, out of the house of bondage.

7 'You shall have no other gods before Me.

8 'You shall not make for yourself a carved image—any likeness *of anything* that *is* in heaven above, or that *is* in the earth beneath, or that *is* in the water under the earth;

9 you shall not bow down to them nor serve them. For I, the LORD your God, *am* a jealous God, visiting the iniquity of the fathers upon the children to the third and fourth *generations* of those who hate Me,

10 but showing mercy to thousands, to those who love Me and keep My commandments.

11 'You shall not take the name of the LORD your God in vain, for the LORD will not hold *him* guiltless who takes His name in vain.

12 'Observe the Sabbath day, to keep it holy, as the LORD your God commanded you.

13 Six days you shall labor and do all your work,

14 but the seventh day *is* the Sabbath of the LORD your God. *In it* you shall do no work: you, nor your son, nor your daughter, nor your male servant, nor your female servant, nor your ox, nor your donkey, nor any of your cattle, nor your stranger who *is* within your gates, that your male servant, and your female servant, may rest as well as you.

15 And remember that you were a slave in the land of Egypt, and the LORD your God brought you out from there by a mighty hand and by an outstretched arm; therefore the LORD your God commanded you to keep the Sabbath day.

16 'Honor your father and your mother, as the

LORD your God has commanded you, that
your days may be long, and that it may be
well with you in the land which the LORD
your God is giving you.

17 'You shall not murder.

18 'You shall not commit adultery.

19 'You shall not steal.

20 'You shall not bear false witness against your
neighbor.

21 'You shall not covet your neighbor's wife; and
you shall not desire your neighbor's house,
his field, his male servant, his female servant,
his ox, his donkey, or anything that *is* your
neighbor's.'

22 "These words the LORD spoke to all your assembly, in the mountain from the midst of the fire, the
cloud, and the thick darkness, with a loud voice; and
He added no more. And He wrote them on two
tablets of stone and gave them to me."

Deut. 5:1-22

The Ten Commandments: Love's Evidence

"If you love Me, keep My commandments" (John 14:15).

"He who has My commandments and keeps them, it is he who
loves Me. . . . He who does not love Me does not keep My words"
(John 14:21, 24).

I never read the bumper sticker "Christians aren't perfect, just
forgiven" without a tinge of uneasiness. If that statement is a cop-
out for irresponsible Christianity, then its truth becomes diminished. While the Gallup Poll indicates that there has been a great
upsurge in conservative religion in this country—evangelical de-
nominations are on the increase in this country—at the same time
immorality, abortion, and homosexuality also are on the rise. Spirituality is up, but morality is down.

The problem arises when Christians lack understanding of God's
grace and therefore show little evidence of it in their lives. In other
words, some Christians have misunderstood the end of God's grace,
which is the fulfillment of the law.

Could part of our misconception of grace and law be because we do not understand that this law was given twice, and therefore reflects a twofold purpose?

The Ten Commandments were written by God on tablets of stone and given to Moses at Mount Sinai. Moses came down from the mountain and found that the Israelites were a rebellious and stiff-necked people. They had already broken many of those Ten Commandments. In his anger, Moses smashed to pieces the tablets of stone. By so doing, he illustrated the first purpose of the law. Because the law is an external force, it can do nothing to change lives; all the law accomplished was to reveal sin. This was the apostle Paul's experience in Romans 7 and also in Galatians. This too was the experience of both Augustine and Luther.

But, there was another reason for the law. We find this in Moses' words in Deuteronomy 10:1–5:

> "At that time the Lord said to me, 'Hew for yourself
> two tablets of stone like the first, and come up to Me
> on the mountain and make yourself an ark of wood.
> And I will write on the tablets the words that were on
> the first tablets, which you broke; and you shall put
> them in the ark.' So I made an ark of acacia wood,
> hewed two tablets of stone like the first, and went up
> the mountain, having the two tablets in my hand. And
> He wrote on the tablets according to the first writing,
> the Ten Commandments, which the Lord had spoken
> to you in the mountain from the midst of the fire in
> the day of the assembly; and the Lord gave them to
> me. Then I turned and came down from the mountain,
> and put the tablets in the ark which I had made; and
> there they are, just as the Lord commanded me."
>
> *Deut. 10:1–5*

The second time the Ten Commandments were written they were placed in a box, the ark of the covenant, and the ark was placed inside the tabernacle, in the Holy of Holies. The tabernacle was a visual aid for man, symbolizing that God, by means of sacrifice, wanted to take up residence in the deep recesses of man's heart and spirit. The law's location in the tabernacle illustrated the fact that it was not only written on tablets of stone, but was to be written in the hearts of men. In this sense, the law portrays the responsible

lifestyle of a believer whose heart is changed by grace.[1] The observance of the Ten Commandments is the natural outcome of deliverance from bondage. When the law is written in the human heart,
man will want to obey (Jer. 31:33–34; Heb. 10:16–17). Obedience to
the first four commandments is the evidence of our love toward
God. Obedience to commandments five through ten is evidence of
our love for our fellow man.

Moses calls *"all Israel"* together and repeats three words that continually appear in Deuteronomy. These words are *"hear"* (used over
thirty times), *"learn"* (seven times), and *"observe"* (almost one hundred times). Each of these words demands a response of obedience
from the people of God (v. 1).

Although these commandments were given at Horeb to a previous
generation, Moses makes clear to the people that they are to obey
them. *"The Lord did not make this covenant with our fathers, but with
us, those who are here today, all of us who are alive"* (v. 3). God gave
these commandments to the people directly (v. 4). He spoke to them
as a man would speak to his friends, yet at the same time He visibly
manifested His glory.

The fact is stressed that the Horeb event did not only concern
Israel's ancestors but was for Israel in every age. It was the responsibility of every Israelite in every generation to identify with Israel's
ancestors and through collective memory and faith to participate in
their experience of God's deliverance. There is an emphasis on the
covenant relationship between God and His people that transcends
the boundaries of time.

Moses was not the creator of these commandments, only the mediator. Now, as at Horeb, he stands before his people with a message
from their God (v. 5). As he prepares to exhort the people concerning
the commandments, he first reminds them that their God is a personal one; Israel was never expected to believe, obey, and love
a *distant,* impersonal God. Second, Moses tells the people that this
personal God has delivered them from bondage (v. 6). God is not
saying to His people, "When you love Me supremely, I will redeem
you out of Egypt." He is saying, "I have delivered you, now therefore
yield to Me." Israel has for centuries had a master. In Egypt it was a
cruel taskmaster, Pharaoh. Now God is wanting His rightful place as
Master of their lives.

Verse 6 is crucial to understanding not only the first commandment but also the other nine. The Ten Commandments were given to a people already redeemed to enable them to express love for and have fellowship with a holy God. The Decalogue was never given to enable them to achieve justification, for that has always been granted through faith (Gen. 15:6; Rom. 4). These commands demanded a response of obedience, not because that would somehow allow them to accumulate credit in the sight of God, but because the grace of God, experienced in the liberation of Egypt, demanded evidence of man's gratitude and love.

The giving of the Ten Commandments to Israel may be the only time in history when a newly formed nation received a complete code of laws all at one time. These commandments are the foundation of the covenant relationship. They are the heart of the message of Deuteronomy. Therefore, extra space is given in this commentary to their significance to Moses' generation and to ours as well.

The First Commandment (v. 7)

"You shall have no other gods before Me" (v. 7). Had the children of Israel not seen the heavy hand of God on Pharaoh in Egypt? Had they not been aware of His presence guiding them across the wilderness? Had they not heard His voice at Mount Sinai? They could appreciate Moses' rhetorical questions:

> "Did any people ever hear the voice of God speaking out of the midst of the fire, as you have heard, and live? Or did God ever try to go and take for Himself a nation from the midst of another nation, by trials, by signs, by wonders, by war, by a mighty hand and an outstretched arm, and by great terrors, according to all that the Lord your God did for you in Egypt before your eyes? To you it was shown, that you might know that the Lord Himself is God; there is none other besides Him."
>
> *Deut. 4:33–35*

Israel had seen and known the works of God. The issue was that they needed to declare Yahweh as the only God. He would tolerate no rivals. The phrase *"before Me"* can be translated in the following ways: "near by Me," "at My side," "against Me," "in defiance of Me," or "to My detriment." Any of these would express that Yahweh stood alone. There were no others. The same principle of divine sovereignty found application in other areas as well—in the food laws (14:3-21), the sanctions against idolatry (13:1-18), the injunction to destroy pagan sanctuaries (7:5; 12:3), and the laws of separation (7:3-4).

Moses understood that living in Canaan would tempt God's people to make room for other gods in their lives. When they started settling in the land they would naturally assume an agricultural way of life. Before long the novelty of farming would wear off and they would discover that agriculture and religion were closely related. For the Canaanite farmer, the role of the fertility gods was at least as important as the necessary tasks of plowing the field and planting the seed. The Hebrews, however, would have to learn to farm using the Canaanite farmers' tools but not their gods of fertility. They must learn that Yahweh is not only the God of history but also of nature. The people of God had known Him in the exodus, but would they also find Him in their new lifestyle? The challenge was this: In spite of new experiences and blessings, they must remember that the key to their love relationship with God was loyalty.[2]

This commandment calls for a life dominated by a relationship with God. The principle remains the same today. God must control every area of our lives. He must dominate our checkbook and fill our calendar. For whatever our heart is obsessed with, that is our god. It could be a relationship or an ambition. The first commandment says to us, "Do not say you love God and then allow your heart to go after other gods." Love is loyal, first and foremost.

When General Booth, the founder of the Salvation Army, was asked what had been the secret of his success, he replied, "From the day I got the poor of London on my heart and a vision for what Jesus Christ would do for them, I made up my mind that God should have all of William Booth there was; and if anything has been achieved, it is because God has had all the adoration of my heart, all the power of my will and all the influence of my life." William Booth was a man whose heart was obsessed with God. He had no higher loyalty; he understood the principle of love.

The Second Commandment (vv. 8–10)

"You shall not make for yourself a carved image" (v. 8). Images of other gods are not prohibited, since the people are already forbidden by the first commandment to worship other gods. This law deals with images intended to represent God Himself.

Many devout people have misinterpreted this command, understanding it to mean that God is forbidding art. In fact, God instructed the Israelites to make images of cherubim and seraphim to beautify the tabernacle. God is not against image-making; rather He is against image-making for the purpose of idolatry, because such idolatry is based on a lie, making it evil. The lie says, "Life comes through imitation." The ancient Near Eastern man believed that if he could capture the image of his god through engraving, painting, or whatever, he could manipulate the god to his own purposes. He also thought if he could imitate the acts of a god, he could capture the life of that god.

The transition from worshiping God to worshiping an idol is very easily made. The purpose of an image is to remind us of God, and our intention is to look at the image and more readily focus our thoughts on God. What happens, though, is that slowly the image ceases to represent God and itself becomes the object of worship.

We can observe this transition in the Old Testament. Fiery serpents attacked the children of Israel while they were in the wilderness (Num. 21:4–9). God instructed Moses to make a bronze serpent and set it on a pole; those who were bitten would be healed when they looked at the bronze serpent. Centuries later we see the bronze serpent making another brief appearance. But this time we find Hezekiah breaking the serpent in pieces because the people were burning incense to it (2 Kings 18:1–4). The bronze serpent was no longer God's tool; it had become the people's god.

To keep this type of thing from happening, language alone would have to serve as the medium through which God represented Himself. If all other means of representation were forbidden, man could not impose his own limitations on his conception of God.

The practice of idolatry resulted in God's *"visiting the iniquity of the fathers upon the children to the third and fourth generations of those who hate Me"* (v. 9). This is not meant to breed fatalism. In the book of Ezekiel we read, "The word of the Lord came to me again, saying,

'What do you mean when you use this proverb concerning the land of Israel, saying: "The fathers have eaten sour grapes, / And the children's teeth are set on edge"? As I live,' says the Lord God, 'you shall no longer use this proverb in Israel'" (Ezek. 18:1-3). This proverb underscores what Moses is saying—the real danger of idolatry is that when one generation makes idolatrous choices, it becomes very easy for the next generation to go a step further with idolatry.

An example of this would be Solomon's giving his heart to foreign women and their gods. His sons continued to develop his idolatrous choices and the result was a divided kingdom.

Now notice the other side of the coin—God's grace (v. 10). To those who love God and show evidence of that love by keeping His commandments, He will show mercy. So if we put an end to idolatry in our own lives and give God our whole hearts, the action resulting from our obedience will have a positive impact forever.

In the early part of my ministry I was touched by a book entitled *No Rival Love*. It is the account of Abraham's close walk with God. He was obedient to the point of offering his only son Isaac as a sacrifice. The result of his obedience? God, even in this generation, is still answering promises He made to Abraham.

The Third Commandment (v. 11)

"You shall not take the name of the Lord your God in vain" (v. 11). During my junior-high years my father and I enrolled in a Dale Carnegie course. The first and most important thing I learned was this: The sweetest sound a person ever hears is his or her own name. The third commandment reminds us of the importance of the manner in which we use God's name. It says that the way we use God's name is an indication of our relationship with Him. This commandment is very broad; there are many ways in which we can take the Lord's name in vain.

We can attach God's name to our causes, thus manipulating others by our use of His name. This is an arrogant form of deceit.

The original meaning of this verse is literally, "You shall not lift up the name of Yahweh unto vanity." To "lift up," means to invoke God's name in taking an oath. In other words, when we take an oath, we are calling upon God as a witness to confirm the truth of our word. God is saying, "Do not call upon My name to confirm the truth of your word when it is a vain, worthless, empty cause." To attach God's name to emptiness is to misuse it. An example of this is found in Ezekiel 13:1–9 where some prophets were ascribing their own inspirations to the Lord when, in fact, they had not gotten a word from the Lord. In the New Testament Jesus said in the Sermon on the Mount, "Don't be so arrogant as to attach my name to what you think you can do. Just make your yes, yes and your no, no; anything beyond that is evil" (paraphrase of Matt. 5:33–37).

The point is, do not use God's name to support your program. That is presumptuous. God has revealed His name in His character; do not use the name to support your plans. James (4:13–15) teaches us that our lives are a vapor; and we don't know what tomorrow is going to bring or whether we can confirm our word or not. God is not a genie we can summon from a bottle to help us get what we want. He is Lord! Ray Stedman says, "God does not intervene in our lives to take sides; He comes to take over, so move over!"

In Moses' day the name of a person or a god was considered to contain certain powers. Therefore, Balak, the Moabite king, attempted to employ Balaam for the purpose of magically cursing the Israelites in the name of the Lord (Num. 22–24). This third commandment strictly prohibits man from attempting to harness God's power for personal ends or for a worthless idea.[3] Any attempt to manipulate God for personal ends is wrong.

Although the preceding paragraphs may specify the main reason we should not take God's name in vain, here are some other possibilities that are also forbidden:

Scoffing at God's name or His works or any other sacred thing rightfully related to Him is forbidden.

Profanity—the use of God's name for every trifling occasion or in an anti-God manner—is prohibited.

Hollowness or empty formality in the professed worship of God is forbidden. When we sing God's praises from a vacant heart or pray without devotion, we are using His name in vain.

This commandment can also be broken if we make a vow to God and then do not fulfill it. When we commit ourselves to obey God and then are disobedient, we are in violation of this commandment.

Notice that God will confront us when we break this law, *"for the Lord will not hold him guiltless who takes His name in vain"* (v. 11). In the case of idolatry, our choice affects future generations.

When *can* we invoke the name of Yahweh? Only when we are lifting up His holy character or cause. We should always use His name in a manner consistent with His character.

The Fourth Commandment (vv. 12–15)

"Observe the Sabbath day, to keep it holy" (v. 12). This commandment concerns the Sabbath. When Moses wrote about the Sabbath in Exodus he used a different rationale than he does here in Deuteronomy. Exodus 20:11 says, "For in six days the Lord made the heavens and the earth, the sea, and all that is in them, and rested the seventh day. Therefore the Lord blessed the Sabbath day and hallowed it."

In Exodus, Moses says that Israel is to sanctify the seventh day as a day of rest. The rationale? As they entered into the promised land, they were to demonstrate visually that they were related to the Maker of the universe, who by His spoken word created the heavens and the earth in six days. Because God rested from His work, they were to rest from theirs.

Many times I have been asked by people in my congregations, "Why did God rest? Was He tired?" No, the reason had nothing to do with fatigue. After the sixth day the heavens and earth were complete and perfect. Seven is the number of perfection. Therefore, God sat back on the seventh day to appreciate the finished results of His creation. So the purpose of the Sabbath was to give the Israelites time to reflect, not on their works, but on God's works. They were then to find refreshment in knowing that their physical needs were supplied not by their toil, but by the God who had created the universe and had given them life.

Deuteronomy 5:15 gives a different rationale for keeping the Sabbath: *"And remember that you were a slave in the land of Egypt, and the Lord your God brought you out from there by a mighty hand and by an outstretched arm; therefore the Lord your God commanded you to keep the Sabbath day."*

Here, Moses is teaching the Israelites that what was true of creation is also true of redemption. Just as the spoken word of God made possible physical life, it also became the vehicle through which He met the Israelites' spiritual needs. By His word God set them free from Egypt; He rescued them from slavery so they could enjoy the fruits of blessing in their new inheritance. All the feasts of redemption in Israel had Sabbaths so that they could be reminded that every blessing of redemption did not come from the people's toil, but from God. Therefore, rest and enjoyment come by reflecting on God's finished work, not ours.

This viewpoint differs from that of some Sabbatarians, who imply that the reason for the Sabbath is that God is a killjoy, that He is against enjoyment and in favor of solemnity. No, God approves of enjoyment and merriment, but the only way Israel could enjoy life was to know it was a gift from God.

Both in Exodus and Deuteronomy, Moses teaches us that the principle of the fourth commandment on the need for time to reflect upon God's glorious work never changes. Yet it is interpreted differently from one generation to another. Therefore, the immediate application of this commandment might differ from one time and place to another. The meaning of the commandment to the Israelites in the newly formed theocracy will be different than its meaning to modern men who live under a form of technocracy. But the principle remains the same and continues to be valid.

Although Jesus came to fulfill the law and not to destroy it, His statement (Mark 2:27–28) that "the Sabbath was made for man, and not man for the Sabbath" removed the law forever from the unwholesome restrictions of the Pharisees. Our keeping of Sunday is not an observance of the seventh day but of the first, as in the nature of a new commandment based on a new covenant. Nevertheless, it fulfills the old commandment. The principle—the importance of setting aside a day of rest to reflect on God's glorious work and our dependence on Him—remains the same. Notice how the application progresses from Exodus to the time of the early church.

Exodus • We are created in God's image and dependent on Him for our physical life.

Deuteronomy • We are rescued from slavery and dependent on God for our spiritual liberation.

New Testament • We are redeemed through our identification with the risen Christ who works within us a new creation (2 Cor. 5:17), recalling the first creation and the creation of the people of Israel.

Paul says this commandment was "a shadow of things to come, but the substance is of Christ" (Col. 2:16–17).

Hebrews tells us, "There remains therefore a rest for the people of God. For he who has entered His rest has himself also ceased from his works as God did from His" (Heb. 4:9–10).

So what does the Sabbath mean today? Jesus Christ is the Word of God who brought forth the created universe; He is also the Redeemer who rescued us from spiritual bondage. He granted everything to us, "every spiritual blessing in the heavenly places" (Eph. 1:3). His work is done—"It is finished!"

And what is our responsibility? We need to stop and meditate on Him. We need to take time to reflect on His work, not ours; that is what will give us joy in life. The Sabbath is not a day—it is a life-changing attitude. By reflecting on who He is and what He has done, our spirits will be so refreshed that when we return to our workaday world and all of its pressures, we can continue to rest in Him. That is the Sabbath.[4]

The first four commandments deal with our responsibility to love God. We are to give Him our whole heart, flee idolatry, honor His name, and rest in Him, enjoying His finished work. If we don't take these responsibilities to heart, not only will our relationship with God be messed up, but also our relationships with one another—which brings us to the last six commandments, dealing specifically with our responsibility to others. Again, the word *responsibility* is used to emphasize our choice in determining our relationships with God and our fellow-man. A right relationship with God depends on a right relationship with others. The fifth commandment falls between these two relational truths and deals specifically with the family situation. The family is not only the center of the most intimate relationships, but it's the core of the covenant community.

The Fifth Commandment (v. 16)

"Honor your father and your mother, as the Lord your God has commanded you, that your days may be long, and that it may be well with you in the land which the Lord your God is giving you" (v. 16). The first relational responsibility an Israelite had was to his parents. In Hebrew life, parents had a twofold role. First, they were the authors, sustainers, and protectors of the child's physical life. Second, they were the guardians of the child's spiritual life. Parents passed down the teachings of the Torah from generation to generation. They, as

God's representatives, were responsible for training and teaching the Torah in the home; as a result, respect was due them.

Children honored parents by having a receptive spirit to their teaching of the word of God. This is the intent of Proverbs 1:8 where the father tells his son, "My son, hear the instruction of your father, / And do not forsake the law of your mother." Why? Because it was not their teaching, but God's. The parents were God's representatives, so a child who honored his parents honored God. To dishonor them was to dishonor God.

The responsibility of the child is to listen and obey. The responsibility of the parent is to model God's truth by example and instruction. This is not easy. Charles Spurgeon, perhaps the greatest of all English preachers, said, "With children we must mix gentleness with firmness. They must not always have their own way, but still they must not always be thwarted. If we never have headaches through rebuking them, we shall have plenty of heartaches when they grow up. Be obeyed at all cost, for if you yield your authority once, you will hardly get it again." Good parenting requires a lot of energy. Being the father of two creative children, I can appreciate this comment from a brother to his sister, "I don't understand it—every time Mom gets worn out, I have to take a nap!"

This commandment takes on an extra dimension in the New Testament. Many Gentiles were converted from a pagan background. For all practical purposes, therefore, they had two sets of parents. Honor was due not only the physical parents but also the new spiritual ones who cared for and nurtured them as spiritual babies in the word of God. This is our basis for supporting spiritual teachers and overseers. "Obey those who rule over you, and be submissive, for they watch out for your souls, as those who must give account. Let them do so with joy and not with grief, for that would be unprofitable for you" (Heb. 13:17). Spiritual parents are to be obeyed not because of their depth of wisdom and knowledge, but because they represent God, who is all wisdom and knowledge.

There is a promise given to the children of Israel, conditional upon their obedience to their parents. Both in Exodus and Deuteronomy, Moses says that obedient children will be rewarded with longevity. In Deuteronomy 5:16 Moses adds yet another reward of obedience: ". . . that it may be well with you in the land which the Lord your God is giving you." This is another example of Moses' strong tendency in

Deuteronomy to elaborate on the Exodus material. This book is not just a repetition of the law but an urgent appeal to God's children to obey the law.

Because of the close parallel between Deuteronomy 5:16 and 4:40, we can assume that the basic issue in this commandment was the continuity of the covenant. Parents were responsible for teaching their children the covenant, and the result was that both children and parents would prosper in the land and see the fulfillment of the covenant promise of God.[5]

The Sixth Commandment (v. 17)

"You shall not murder" (v. 17). This commandment has often been misinterpreted to mean that all forms of human life-taking are wrong, including war and capital punishment. There are five different Hebrew words which describe the taking of a human life. The word used in this commandment is one which means to take an innocent life either by criminal intent or through negligence. This includes premeditated murder and murder done in anger or revenge, but it also includes manslaughter through negligence. We are not to be negligent when it comes to human life. We are to protect life because man is made in the image of God and therefore life is sacred. In later chapters we will see instances in which the people are commanded to take precautions to safeguard lives. They were asked to build fences around their roofs, which were used as open balconies, so that human life would not be endangered. Also, open pits had to be covered to avoid the possibility of accidents.

Today this commandment is continually being broken. What about abortion? Far from promoting human life, abortion is the most terrible manifestation of negligence toward human life. Carl Henry has said, "A land of a million abortions will not be spared by a million Bibles whose moral imperatives go unheeded." Max Hellstern says, "If you totalled all the battle deaths suffered by U.S. troops in all the wars we've fought—from Lexington and Concord to Beirut and Grenada—and then doubled that figure, you would still have a figure smaller than the total number of unborn babies legally aborted in the U.S. in 1983."

To fulfill this commandment in our society, there are a number of areas where we need to be more conscientious. We should make sure our automobiles are safe. Our houses and streets should have adequate lighting. Safety belts should always be fastened. The environment should be protected and kept clean. Harmful drugs should be abolished. This is not legalism; it is promotion of human life. The implication of this commandment is that my neighbor or my employee has a right to life, and my responsibility is to promote that life by not endangering it through my own negligence or criminal intent while he is in my care. In both Testaments, the path toward obedience and fulfillment of the law is characterized as a path of love toward God and toward our fellow man (Deut. 6:4–5; Rom. 13:9–10).

The Seventh Commandment (v. 18)

"You shall not commit adultery" (v. 18). This commandment deals only with the sin of adultery. (Other matters relating to sexual behavior will be dealt with in Deut. 22–25.) In Exodus 20:17, the prohibition against covetousness lists first the neighbor's house and then his wife, along with other properties, as things not to be coveted. In Deuteronomy 5:21, the wife's position is placed *before* all possessions. There is a tendency in Deuteronomic law to humanize certain laws. Proverbs 5–7 illustrate this commandment. The father says, "Son, if you commit adultery, you are stupid! If you steal from your neighbor, you can pay restitution seven times and he will forgive you, but if you violate his wife, you have so damaged him and her that you can't do anything to appease him. You're taking your life in your hands when you commit adultery, son." He tells his son that rather than commit adultery he should cultivate a love relationship with his own wife. That advice would be well taken in today's society.

We are now living in a generation and culture that continually disobeys this commandment. In 1910 one out of every ten marriages in the U.S. ended in divorce; in 1940 it was one out of every six; by 1948 it was one out of every four and a half; by 1980 it was one out of two; and in some parts of the country it is now one out of one. Many of these marriage failures are due to infidelity. This sin is flaunted across the TV screen many times a day. The word "adulterer" has been replaced by the more glamorous word "playboy." The attitude toward faithfulness in a marriage relationship can be summed up in the modern song which asks, "What's forever anymore?"

The sin of adultery is singled out more than any other illicit sexual behavior because it has to do with unfaithfulness. The binding commitment of faithfulness between two persons in marriage was similar to the covenant relationship itself. The crime of adultery was the social equivalent to the religious crime of idolatry. Either offense of unfaithfulness could not be permitted by a God who was faithful. Faithfulness in every area of life was expected of the Israelites. It was to become a distinctive feature of the nation because it was a distinctive feature of their God.

The Eighth Commandment (v. 19)

"You shall not steal" (v. 19). This commandment is the foundation of our economic system. It recognizes the fact that man has a right to work, earn, save, and own.

In the simple story of the Good Samaritan there are three possible philosophies of wealth (Luke 10:30–37).

The first philosophy could be expressed by the statement: "What belongs to my neighbor belongs to me and I will take it." This is aggressive stealing. It was vividly demonstrated by the thieves who robbed and beat the man traveling to Jericho. No one would question the injustice of this act. But what about robbing a man of his good name? Shakespeare in *Othello* said, "He that filches from me my good name / Robs me of that which not enriches him, / And makes me poor indeed." And what about failure to give your employer an honest day's work? Taking what doesn't belong to you, whether it is tangible or intangible, is aggressive stealing.

"What belongs to me is mine and I will keep it" expresses the second philosophy, held by both the priest and the Levite. This is stealing by withholding from others. Jesus tells us about such a man in Luke 12:16–21. This rich farmer decided to build bigger barns so he could store more crops for himself. Saving is a virtue, but it can become a spiritual liability if done for the wrong reasons. Every resource that I possess carries with it a corresponding obligation to use it as a good steward should.

"What belongs to me belongs to others and I will share it" expresses the third philosophy. The Good Samaritan understood what the priest and the Levite did not comprehend. Deuteronomy 24:19 says, "When you reap your harvest in your field, and forget a sheaf

117

in the field, you shall not go back to get it; it shall be for the stranger, the fatherless, and the widow, that the Lord your God may bless you in all the work of your hands." And Deuteronomy 24:12 teaches, "If the man is poor, you shall not keep his pledge overnight." The principle is that we should not take advantage of someone else's misfortunes.

This commandment not to steal really deals with manipulation of another person for one's own gain. Wouldn't it be wonderful if those of us who are creditors would extend a helping hand to those less fortunate?

The Ninth Commandment (v. 20)

"You shall not bear false witness against your neighbor" (v. 20). Just as the sixth commandment threw a guard around human life, the seventh around purity, the eighth around the rights of property and labor, so this ninth commandment guards a person's reputation. The immediate relevance of this command would be in relation to giving a testimony about someone in a court of justice. Since the evidence given against the defendant in a case determined his future, it was vital that all evidence be truthful. This is expanded in Deuteronomy 19:15–21.

In the context of gossiping, this commandment is probably broken more than any other. Sadly enough, the less some people know, the more anxious they are to tell. This point is illustrated by one gossip's comment to another, "There's something I must tell you before I find out it isn't true!"

Gossip is the lowest level of communication. It is devious, often cloaking itself in spirituality. Gossips may assume a self-righteous attitude, saying, "I don't mean to gossip about him but . . ." and off they go. Sometimes this gossip takes the form of false sympathy, as in, "Isn't it too bad that Mr. Wrong beats his wife?" Very often this "religious gossip" sneaks into the prayer circle. We can usually recognize it—"O Lord, please help Mrs. Wrong to stop running around on Mr. Wrong even though he's sneaking out with Mrs. Bad." The Old Testament story in which Noah's son speaks wrongly of his father's drunkenness teaches us that the one who talks about another's sin is worse than the one who actually commits the sin. Of the seven things that God hates in Proverbs 6:16–19, three relate to the tongue.

The Tenth Commandment (v. 21)

"You shall not covet your neighbor's wife; and you shall not desire your neighbor's house, his field, his male servant, his female servant, his ox, his donkey, or anything that is your neighbor's" (v. 21). The first nine commandments deal with outward actions. They can be seen, therefore judged. This commandment deals with inner motives. If this last commandment were kept, the first nine would never be broken. We cannot deal with the outward actions without first dealing with our own hearts. In other words, adultery never "just happens." It begins when a person allows himself or herself to feed on his or her own lust. People slander others because they are jealous and malicious. Murderers permit anger to well up inside before they strike. An outward sin was never committed that did not first begin with an inward thought.

To *"covet"* means to jealously want what someone else has—to desire something that we have no right to possess. The word *"covet"* is used in the first clause of verse 21. In the second clause a synonym meaning "to strongly desire" is used.

Satan would like us to think that the only way to rid ourselves of wrong strong desires is to yield to them. God says that if we yield, we will find ourselves in a state of conflict. "Where do wars and fights come from among you? Do they not come from your desires for pleasure that war in your members? You lust and do not have. You murder and covet and cannot obtain. You fight and war. Yet you do not have because you do not ask. You ask and do not receive, because you ask amiss, that you may spend it on your pleasures" (James 4:1–3).

Like many of us, the apostle Paul harbored wrong desires. But his approach to controlling them was all wrong. Romans 7 gives the transparent account of his failure. Paul would read the tenth commandment, *"You shall not covet,"* and would resolve to mend his ways. But the harder he tried, the worse things became.

The psalmist struggled with the same desires as Paul, and he found the key to success. Instead of trying to control his sinful desires, he channeled them toward God and took His word deep into his heart.

Teach me, O Lord, the way of your statutes,
And I shall keep it to the end.

Give me understanding, and I shall keep Your law;
Indeed, I shall observe it with my whole heart.
Make me walk in the path of Your commandments,
For I delight in it.
Incline my heart to Your testimonies,
And not to covetousness.
Turn away my eyes from looking at worthless things,
And revive me in Your way.
Establish Your word to Your servant,
Who is devoted to fearing You.
Turn away my reproach which I dread,
For your judgments are good.
Behold, I long for Your precepts;
Revive me in Your righteousness.

Ps. 119:33–40

We will never find satisfaction and enjoyment by feeding our own desires. The only one who can meet our deepest desires is God Himself. We need to feed on Him. Jesus teaches this principle in Matthew 6:33, "Seek first the kingdom of God and His righteousness, and all these things shall be added to you." Paul's emphatic advice is "Put on the Lord Jesus Christ, and make no provision for the flesh, to fulfill its lusts" (Rom. 13:14).

In conclusion, we find that our neighbor has a right to his life, his home, his possessions, and his reputation. As a Christian, I have not fulfilled my responsibility to my neighbor until I have upheld these rights in my heart. The high expectation of this commandment makes us aware of our inability to keep God's law perfectly. This awareness throws us into the arms of our faithful God to supply us with grace and mercy.

THE TEN COMMANDMENTS REVERED

5:23 "So it was, when you heard the voice from the midst of the darkness, while the mountain was burning with fire, that you came near to me, all the heads of your tribes and your elders.

24 "And you said: 'Surely the LORD our God has shown us His glory and His greatness, and we have heard His voice from the midst of the fire.

120

We have seen this day that God speaks with man; yet he *still* lives.

25 'Now therefore, why should we die? For this great fire will consume us; if we hear the voice of the LORD our God anymore, then we shall die.

26 'For who *is there* of all flesh who has heard the voice of the living God speaking from the midst of the fire, as we *have*, and lived?

27 'You go near and hear all that the LORD our God may say, and tell us all that the LORD our God says to you, and we will hear and do *it.*'

28 "Then the LORD heard the voice of your words when you spoke to me, and the LORD said to me: 'I have heard the voice of the words of this people which they have spoken to you. They are right *in* all that they have spoken.

29 'Oh, that they had such a heart in them that they would fear Me and always keep all My commandments, that it might be well with them and with their children forever!

30 'Go and say to them, "Return to your tents."

31 'But as for you, stand here by Me, and I will speak to you all the commandments, the statutes, and the judgments which you shall teach them, that they may observe *them* in the land which I am giving them to possess.'

32 "Therefore you shall be careful to do as the LORD your God has commanded you; you shall not turn aside to the right hand or to the left.

33 "You shall walk in all the ways which the LORD your God has commanded you, that you may live and *that it may be* well with you, and *that* you may prolong *your* days in the land which you shall possess."

Deut. 5:23–33

The awesome display of God's greatness and glory motivated the children of Israel to ask God to allow Moses to be the mediator between Him and them (vv. 23–27). The fact that they had encountered God and remained alive was a miracle in itself. God, in His infinite wisdom, saw fit to grant this request. So Moses is now placed in a unique position as a mediator—he alone stands between

God and Israel. He is not in this position because of his merit or ambition, but because of divine approval and congregational appointment. It is only because God called Moses to this position that he will be able to fulfill it. The calling of the congregation gives him the right to expect their loyalty. The people promise Moses that they will hear and do as he commands. This is the ideal situation for anyone given the responsibility of leadership.

The theme of oneness continues. The repetition of the Ten Commandments had impressed on Israel the idea of divine law. Not only is there one law, there is also only one mediator. This singular position belongs to Moses.

The elevation of Moses to preeminence is indicated further by Moses' use of *"our God"* and *"your God."* In Deuteronomy 1–4, his use of *"our God"* is frequent. In his second message Moses says *"your God"* almost exclusively (approximately 250 times). Observing this insight, Robert Polzin says, "Moses, at chapter 5, leaves off speaking to his audience as a fellow Israelite, and henceforth (apart from 5:2 and 6:4) speaks only from the viewpoint of his role as teacher."[6] His role previously has been that of a pastor. He experienced things with his flock. Now, with God's insistence that Moses cannot go over into Canaan, his role changes to that of preacher. He can no longer show them, he must send them. This chapter, like many others in Deuteronomy, closes with a demand for obedience.

God's words as recorded in verse 29 are some of the most moving within the entire book of Deuteronomy. Here the reader can sense the yearning of God's heart as He expresses His wish for Israel. The relationship that He yearns for is (1) not compulsory—*"Oh, that they had such a heart in them that they would fear Me . . ."* (2) continuous—*". . . and always keep all My commandments . . ."* (3) forever—*". . . that it might be well with them and with their children forever!"*

NOTES

1. Brian Morgan, *Discovery Papers Catalogue* no. 3817 (November 7, 1982).

2. P. C. Craigie, *Commentary on the Book of Deuteronomy*, New International Commentary on the Old Testament (Grand Rapids: Wm. B. Eerdmans Publishing Co., 1976), p. 148.

3. Ibid., pp. 155–56.

4. Morgan, *Discovery Papers*.

5. Craigie, *Commentary*, p. 158.

6. Robert Polzin, *Moses and the Deuteronomist: A Literary Study of Deuteronomic History* (New York: Seabury Press, Inc., 1980).

CHAPTER EIGHT

Old Law for Succeeding Generations

Deuteronomy 6:1–25

RECEIVE THE LAW PERSONALLY

6:1 "Now this *is* the commandment, *and these are* the statutes and judgments which the LORD your God has commanded to teach you, that you may observe *them* in the land which you are crossing over to possess,

2 "that you may fear the LORD your God, to keep all His statutes and His commandments which I command you, you and your son and your grandson, all the days of your life, and that your days may be prolonged.

3 "Therefore hear, O Israel, and be careful to observe *it,* that it may be well with you, and that you may multiply greatly as the LORD God of your fathers has promised you—'a land flowing with milk and honey.'

4 "Hear, O Israel: The LORD our God, the LORD *is* one!

5 "You shall love the LORD your God with all your heart, with all your soul, and with all your strength."

Deut. 6:1–5

Moses again exhorts Israel to obey the commandments of the Lord (4:1; 5:1; 6:1). There are four reasons why the law had preeminence: (1) Obedience meant that Israel would live; (2) obedience would protect the people from God's displeasure; (3) Israel would be respected as a wise people by other nations when they obeyed

God's laws; (4) the law of God was unique for its high spiritual quality. Is it any wonder that Moses would repeatedly exhort the people to be obedient to God's law?

The result of obedience to God is that we will *"fear the Lord"* which will help us keep His commandments. We can sense two strong emotions, fear and love, as we read this chapter. *"Fear the Lord"* is mentioned in verses 2, 13, and 24; and *"love the Lord,"* the greatest of all commandments, is mentioned in verse 5. Though they at first seem contradictory, these two emotions are closely related. Fear must stem from respect and reverence for the Creator God; it must produce within us total awe of His sovereign lordship. It requires the knowledge that God first loved us and has our interests at heart. God has a right to command our love, and He does. Unfortunately, that is not always enough. Fear that arises from a sense of awe can be the motivation for love. The keeping of His commandments is a tangible expression of our obedience to God through fear and love.

The phrase, *"Hear, O Israel, and be careful to observe it, that it may be well with you"* (v. 3) is found often in Deuteronomy (5:16, 29; 6:18, 24). It carries out Moses' recurring theme, "obey, and be blessed." The blessing lies before the children of Israel. Moses, in describing the richness of the blessing, calls it the "land flowing with milk and honey" (11:9; 26:9; 27:3; 31:20).

Verse 4 is a classic statement of the biblical doctrine of monotheism. The idea of oneness in Deuteronomy 5 (one law, one mediator) is perpetuated in Deuteronomy 6 (one Lord).

It follows that since there is only one God, He should be loved completely. Verse 5 is central to the book of Deuteronomy—indeed, to the entire Bible! This command to love is paramount because the whole book is concerned with the renewing of the covenant, which demanded an obedience made possible only by a response of love to God. E. W. Nicholson said, "It is in a very real sense true to say that the entire book is a commentary on the command which stands at the beginning: 'You shall love the Lord your God . . .'" He goes on to say that a national law can never attain its goal as long as it is effected only by compulsion. It must be founded on the inward assent of the people.[1]

Saint Augustine gave interesting advice when he said, "Love God, then do as you please." If we love God sufficiently to want to do what is pleasing in His sight, then we need never worry about our conduct, because things which will not please God will not please us. If we lack love for God, all the rules in the world will not keep us true to Him. The law tells us what to do; love gives the power to do it.

This exhortation to love God is found ten times in Deuteronomy and nowhere else in the Pentateuch. It is the Shema, the basic and essential creed of Judaism. It is used to open every Jewish service and it is the first Scripture that every Jewish child commits to memory. Jesus said Deuteronomy 6:5 is the first and greatest commandment (Matt. 22:38). This love of God involves the total person: *"heart, . . . soul, and . . . strength."* The *"heart"* was regarded as the seat of the mind and will; it controlled the emotions. The Hebrew word for *"soul"* is more difficult to define, but it seems to refer to the source of life and vitality, or even to one's *"being."* The two terms *"heart"* and *"soul"* indicate that we are to love God with unreserved devotion. We are also to love with all our might, or *"strength."* The people of Israel are to exhibit a love which dominates their emotions, directs their thoughts, and is the dynamic of their actions. This degree of love will be evident to God and to others.

A few years ago I read the following:

> The sign said honk if you love Jesus; so I honked,
> and a policeman arrested me for disturbing
> the peace in a quiet hospital zone.
> The sign said smile if you love Jesus;
> so I smiled all day long,
> And people thought I was a staff worker
> for Jimmy Carter.
> The sign said wave if you love Jesus;
> so I waved with both hands;
> And lost control of my car,
> And crashed into the back of a Baptist bus.
> Oh God—
> If I cannot honk,
> or smile,
> or wave,
> How will Jesus know that I love him?

Deuteronomy 6:5 gives us the answer.

TEACH THE LAW CONTINUALLY

6:6 "And these words which I command you today shall be in your heart.

7 "You shall teach them diligently to your children, and shall talk of them when you sit in your house, when you walk by the way, when you lie down, and when you rise up.

8 "You shall bind them as a sign on your hand, and they shall be as frontlets between your eyes.

9 "You shall write them on the doorposts of your house and on your gates."

Deut. 6:6-9

Jesus said, "'You shall love the Lord your God with all your heart, with all your soul, and with all your mind.' This is the first and great commandment" (Matt. 22:37-38). This command, given by Moses and underscored by Jesus, must be diligently taught and observed.

A person must experience the love this commandment requires before he or she can teach it to others. Notice the preeminence of the heart in the words of both Moses and Jesus. They want to make sure that external actions (such as talking, binding, and signs) are not substituted for the inner experience.

There's an old saying, "Be careful what you set your heart on for it might come true!" History surely proves this true. Thomas Edison fell in love with invention, Henry Ford fell in love with motor cars, Kettering fell in love with research, and the Wright brothers fell in love with airplanes. Their "hearts" controlled their time, energy, direction, and output. And look at the results! Love is the most powerful force in the world: want power (the heart) is the strongest impetus for will power (the head).

Recently I read about seventy-eight-year-old Aleida Huissen of Rotterdam, who had been smoking for fifty years. For most of that time she had been trying to give up the habit, but not until recently had she succeeded. The secret? Seventy-nine-year-old Leo Jansen proposed marriage but refused to go through with the wedding until Aleida gave up smoking. Aleida said, "Will power never was enough to get me off the habit. Love made me do it."

When this great commandment is cradled in our hearts, it will be obvious in our conversations and actions. St. Augustine was asked, "What does love look like?" He replied, "It has hands to help others. It has feet to hasten to the poor and needy. It has eyes to see the misery and want. It has ears to hear the sighs and sonnets of men. That is what love looks like." Place truth in the heart and it will spring forth outwardly. Truth cannot be taught until it is first received by the teacher.

This commandment is not automatically transferred from one genera-tion to another. Deuteronomy attaches the importance and responsi-bility of teaching to the family (4:9; 6:7, 20–25; 11:19). This educating must be done in a diligent manner. The home is to be the center for conserving and propagating truth. Home is where life makes up its mind. Moses understood that the greatness of the nation Israel de-pended upon the teaching of the commandments in the home. As a nation, we need desperately to apply this truth ourselves.

A man who had served as a chaplain for many years at a state penitentiary said, "Out of seventeen hundred convicts, I found only one who had been brought up in a home where they had a family altar, and that man was later found innocent of the crime with which he had been charged."

Socrates asked, "Fellow citizens, why do you turn and scrape ev-ery stone to gather wealth and take so little care of your children to whom one day you must relinquish it all?"

The instruction from the parents to the children was not to be a "lesson," but a continual way of life. Truth was to be communi-cated when they sat, as they walked, after they lay down at night, and when they arose in the morning (v. 7). A variety of methods is given to help parents saturate their children with these important commandments. They were to experience them (v. 6); talk about them (v. 7); exhibit them (v. 8); write them (v. 9); and, most impor-tantly, model them.

Interpreting literally the words of verse 8, the custom of Orthodox Jewish men has been to copy four sections from the law (Exod. 13:1–10; 13:11–16; Deut. 6:4–9; 11:13–21) and put these passages in leather cases on straps and bind them to their left arms and on their foreheads during morning prayers. They also put Deuteronomy 6:4–5 and 11:13–20 in a metal or glass case and affixed it to the right-hand doorpost of every entrance to their homes. When Jesus censured the Pharisees, He did so not because they wore the phylacteries, but because they ostentatiously displayed them. They exalted the trappings of religion over the condition of the heart.[2]

Every generation faces the temptation to judge man and his religion by his outward actions. God reminded the prophet Samuel that "the Lord does not see as man sees; for man looks at the outward appearance, but the Lord looks at the heart" (1 Sam. 16:7).

LIVE THE LAW COMPLETELY

6:10 "So it shall be, when the LORD your God brings you into the land of which He swore to your fathers, to Abraham, Isaac, and Jacob, to give you large and beautiful cities which you did not build,

11 "houses full of all good things, which you did not fill, hewn-out wells which you did not dig, vineyards and olive trees which you did not plant—when you have eaten and are full—

12 "*then* beware, lest you forget the LORD who brought you out of the land of Egypt, from the house of bondage.

13 "You shall fear the LORD your God and serve Him, and shall take oaths in His name.

14 "You shall not go after other gods, the gods of the peoples who *are* all around you

15 "(for the LORD your God *is* a jealous God among you), lest the anger of the LORD your God be aroused against you and destroy you from the face of the earth.

16 "You shall not tempt the LORD your God as you tempted *Him* in Massah.

17 "You shall diligently keep the commandments of the LORD your God, His testimonies, and His statutes which He has commanded you.

18 "And you shall do *what is* right and good in the sight of the LORD, that it may be well with you, and that you may go in and possess the good land of which the LORD swore to your fathers,

19 "to cast out all your enemies from before you, as the LORD has spoken."

Deut. 6:10–19

Moses understood that Israel, once they settled in Canaan, would have difficulty living totally for God. Unfortunately, there often exists a negative correlation between God's favor and our gratitude. In verses 10 and 11, Moses describes the blessings God will give to His people. Notice his poetic preaching style in verses 10–11 as he declares that God will give them:

"large and beautiful cities	*which you did not build"*
"houses full of all good things	*which you did not fill"*
"hewn-out wells	*which you did not dig"*
"vineyards and olive trees	*which you did not plant"*

These blessings can lead to Israel's downfall. Notice the relationship between *"when you have eaten and are full"* (v. 11) and *"then beware, lest you forget the Lord"* (v. 12).

Isn't it true that serious thinking must precede genuine thanking? To not think about God's blessings is to not be thankful to God. Moses knew this could happen. So did the apostle Paul, who said, "Although they knew God, they did not glorify Him as God, nor were thankful, but became futile in their thoughts, and their foolish hearts were darkened" (Rom. 1:21).

The Perils of Prosperity

Moses speaks effectively in this section on the tendency for abundance to beget arrogance. He exposits this truth several other times in Deuteronomy. In his song to the people, Moses said, "But Jeshurun grew fat and kicked; / You grew fat, you grew thick, / You are obese! / Then he forsook God who made him, / And scornfully esteemed the Rock of his salvation" (Deut. 32:15). With our limited vision, we often fail to see our spiritual inadequacies when we have no other needs. Self-reliance replaces God-reliance.

Forgetting the Lord is the first peril to which prosperity leads us (vv. 12–13). It was at the height of David's prosperity that he committed his greatest act of unfaithfulness (2 Sam. 11). Nothing dulls our sensitivity to God like independence. There is much truth in the thought that adversity has more benefits than prosperity. Adversity introduces a person to himself; prosperity intoxicates him.

The story of the prodigal son is an excellent illustration of the effects of prosperity and adversity on a person. During his prosperity the son did not think of father and home; he was consumed with the pleasures of the flesh. When he lost all his wealth and friends, he "came to himself" and remembered what was important. Moses, knowing the perils of prosperity, warns the children of Israel not to forget God.

In verse 13 there is a three-step formula for not forgetting God. (1) *"Fear the Lord."* Our independent nature causes us to stray from God, thus obstructing our worship of Him. To prevent this from happening, we need to have a reverent fear of God. This is not the kind of fear that intimidates, causing us to withdraw, but rather the kind that causes us to appreciate the power of God. It creates within us a desire to draw near for security and strength. It causes finite man to cleave to an infinite God. (2) *"Serve Him."* The visible evidence of our fearing the Lord will be our service to Him. One of the first signs of our forgetting God is our lack of service and ministry to God and others. (3) *"Take oaths in His name."* Strength is supplied to those willing to openly declare themselves to be on the Lord's side. Instead of making a name for themselves in Canaan, Moses wants the people's declaration and action to be associated with God—he wants them to make a name for God.

Compromise is another peril of prosperity (vv. 14-15). The temptation to accept other gods is going to face Israel. Their exposure to new cultures will place options before them that could lead to idolatry. They must remember that the first commandment given to them forbids the worship of other gods.

Verse 15 tells of the consequences of breaking this commandment. The *"anger of the Lord"* will be aroused and He will destroy the people because *"the Lord your God is a jealous God among you."* This means He is zealous to protect what belongs to Him alone. He permits no rivalry that might detract from His glory. When He reminds the people that He dwells among them, it is partly to inspire fear by reason of His presence and partly to remove their ingratitude.

Once settled in Canaan, Israel will find it easier to adapt to, rather than change, their new surroundings. The result will be disastrous. Their fate will be that of the Civil War soldier Paul Harvey recently told about. Thinking to play it safe, this soldier dressed himself in a blue coat and gray pants and tiptoed onto the field of battle. He got shot from both directions. Unfortunately, he didn't live to find out what a high price disobedience exacts.

A demanding attitude toward God is the third peril of prosperity (vv. 16–19). Prosperity too often causes us to take control of our own lives. But when adversity strikes, we look for someone else to blame. Moses challenges Israel not to *"tempt the Lord your God as you tempted Him in Massah"* (v. 16). To *"tempt the Lord"* is to impose on Him conditions making the people's obedience contingent upon His meeting their demands. This is exactly what happened at Massah (Exod. 17:1–7). When the Israelites needed water in the wilderness, they proposed that Moses prove God's presence by producing water himself. By doubting God's sovereignty and care during the hour of crisis, they sought to compel God to prove Himself by spectacular deeds which they themselves suggested. This attitude was also prevalent in the events referred to in Deuteronomy 1:19–46. In His day Jesus refused to offer signs to the scribes and Pharisees (Matt. 12:38–39; 16:1–4; Mark 8:11–12; Luke 11:16, 29–30).

Since the tendency of the Israelites is to attempt to manipulate God for their own interests and on their own conditions, Moses declares, *"You shall diligently keep the commandments. . . . you shall do what is right and good in the sight of the Lord"* (vv. 17, 18). This strong exhortation to live right is characteristic of Moses throughout Deuteronomy. The law has already been given; their obedience to it, not their knowledge of it, will determine their continual success.

EXPLAIN THE LAW HISTORICALLY

6:20 "When your son asks you in time to come, saying, 'What *is the meaning of* the testimonies, the statutes, and the judgments which the LORD our God has commanded you?'

21 "then you shall say to your son: 'We were slaves of Pharaoh in Egypt, and the LORD brought us out of Egypt with a mighty hand;

22 'and the LORD showed signs and wonders before our eyes, great and severe, against Egypt, Pharaoh, and all his household.

23 'Then He brought us out from there, that He might bring us in, to give us the land of which He swore to our fathers.

24 'And the LORD commanded us to observe all these statutes, to fear the LORD our God, for our good always, that He might preserve us alive, as *it is* this day.

25 'Then it will be righteousness for us, if we are careful to observe all these commandments before the LORD our God, as He has commanded us.'"

Deut. 6:20–25

Moses again reminds his people of the crucial need to pass on the covenant values to their children. The covenant was not intended for one generation only. Moses knew that the children were bound to inquire sooner or later why their parents lived a kind of life that was in contrast to the lives of those around them. Anticipating the question, Moses urged the parents to have their answer ready when the children asked why they kept the covenant stipulations (*"testimonies"*), *"statutes,"* and *"judgments"* which God had given to Israel. This passage gives excellent insight into parental responsibilities in educating their children.

The Educational Responsibilities of Parents to Their Children

Encourage your children to ask questions (v. 20). Moses' knowledge of child psychology is evident when he says, *"When your son asks you in time to come . . ."* He recognizes that it is the nature of children to be inquisitive. Wise parents will encourage this questioning spirit, thus helping their children establish their own faith. Parents who are afraid of questions and discourage the child's asking will stifle the growth of his faith. Sadly, many parents are like the one in the following story.

One day a small boy was walking with his father. When they passed an unusual looking truck, he asked, "What's that, Daddy?"

"I don't know," his father said.

Then they came to a large, old-fashioned warehouse. "What's in there, Daddy?" the little boy asked.

"I don't know," his father replied.

Then they saw a man with a pneumatic drill breaking up the pavement. "What's that man doing, Daddy?" the boy asked.

"I don't know," was again the father's answer.

After they had walked on a short way in silence, the little boy turned to his father and said, "Daddy, do you mind my asking you so many questions?"

"Of course not," replied the father. "How else are you going to learn anything?"

This type of "teaching" by parents is perhaps what caused a frustrated boy to grumble to his little friend, "First they teach you to talk, then they teach you to walk, and soon as you do it, they say, 'Sit down and shut up!'"

Explain your answers thoroughly (vv. 21–23). Moses instructs the parents to tell the story of God's redemptive activity, to explain to the children how He delivered their forefathers from Egypt and led them to the land of promise. He wants the children to see that their parents' faith is a result of God's dynamic activity in their lives; it is not some abstract formulation. The outline of the story to be told is simple, easily understood by a child: Slavery in Egypt (v. 21a), God's liberating Israel from Pharaoh and the Egyptians (vv. 21b–22), and the safe journey and arrival in the land of promise (v. 23). This confession is continually repeated in the Old Testament. Gerhard von Rad points to a similar confession made by the worshiper when he would bring a basket of his firstfruits to the tabernacle (Deut. 26:5–9). He also refers to Joshua's standing before the people exhorting them to choose between Yahweh and other gods (Josh. 24). Before presenting this choice, however, he reviews the great acts of God in the history of the people, from the time their fathers left Mesopotamia to the conclusion of their conquest.[3]

Emphasize God's intent for our good (vv. 21–25). Children should be taught that every command and action of God is *"for our good always"* (v. 24). God's loftiest goal is not to demonstrate His power as an end in itself; He uses His attributes to draw us to Him that we might have the very best of God's plan for our lives. Notice the phrases in this passage that illustrate God's desire *"for our good always."* *"The Lord brought us out of Egypt"* (v. 21). *"The Lord showed signs and wonders before our eyes"* (v. 23). *"He brought us out . . . that He might bring us in"* (v. 23). *"The Lord commanded us . . . for our good always, that He might preserve us alive"* (v. 24). *"Then it will be righteousness for us . . ."* (v. 25).

Moses realized that the recital of God's deliverance of the people of Israel from Egypt must continually be given so that the children would not only know but also obey Him. The recital of the benefits of following God becomes the motivation for following Him. This is a continuing theme throughout Deuteronomy.

Exhort your children to righteous living (v. 25). The result of observing the commands of the Lord is stated clearly by Moses: *"Then it will be righteousness for us."* Commenting on this phrase, Adam Clarke said, *"*Moses does not say that this righteousness could be wrought without the influence of God's mercy, nor does he say that they should purchase heaven by it; but God required them to be conformed to His will in all things, that they might be holy in heart, and righteous in every part of their moral conduct."[4]

Teaching without application aborts the educational process. The person who acquires knowledge but never uses it is like the farmer who plows but never sows. Obedience to God's commands will result in righteousness. Near the beginning of Deuteronomy 6, Moses stressed the need for parents to love God with their total beings. Now as the chapter closes, Moses indicates that one aspect of loving and obeying God is to pass that same love for Him on to their children.

NOTES

1. E. W. Nicholson, *Deuteronomy and Tradition* (Oxford: Basil Blackwell, 1967), p. 46.

2. A. R. G. Deasley and Jack Ford, *Beacon Bible Commentary* (Kansas City, MO: Beacon Hill Press, 1969), pp. 510–621.

3. G. Ernest Wright, *God Who Acts* (London: SCM Press, Ltd., 1952), pp. 71–72.

4. Adam Clarke, *The Holy Bible with a Commentary and Critical Notes*, vol. 1 (London: William Tegg & Co., 1854), p. 769.

CHAPTER NINE

A Chosen People

Deuteronomy 7:1–26

SEPARATED TO GOD

7:1 "When the LORD your God brings you into the land which you go to possess, and has cast out many nations before you, the Hittites and the Girgashites and the Amorites and the Canaanites and the Perizzites and the Hivites and the Jebusites, seven nations greater and mightier than you,

2 "and when the LORD your God delivers them over to you, you shall conquer them *and* utterly destroy them. You shall make no covenant with them nor show mercy to them.

3 "Nor shall you make marriages with them. You shall not give your daughter to their son, nor take their daughter for your son.

4 "For they will turn your sons away from following Me, to serve other gods; so the anger of the LORD will be aroused against you and destroy you suddenly.

5 "But thus you shall deal with them: you shall destroy their altars, and break down their *sacred* pillars, and cut down their wooden images, and burn their carved images with fire."

Deut. 7:1–5

Deuteronomy 6 stresses the importance of a proper relationship with God. Deuteronomy 7 gives instructions concerning Israel's relationship to the other nations in Canaan. Just as Israel needs to recognize the presence of the Lord and the power of His word, she also needs to recognize the enemy and where she must draw the line. Moses' counsel is clear: Do not fraternize with your neighbors.[1]

The seven nations listed in verse 1 are *"greater and mightier than"* Israel. The Hittites were a powerful nation which held sway in Syria and Asia Minor from 1800 to 900 B.C. Little is known of the Girgashites, but they probably lived in Palestine as tribal people. It is assumed that they are the tribe mentioned in Egyptian texts as allies of the Hittites. The Amorites were probably located in the Judean hill country, and the Canaanites further west toward the coastland. The Perizzites lived in unwalled villages both east and west of Jordan. The Hivites were located in the north at Lebanon and Hermon, and the Jebusites inhabited the hills around Jerusalem. They were to prove to be among the most stalwart in their resistance to Israelite settlers.

The Lord's responsibility was to deliver the enemies over to Israel. The people's responsibility was to *"conquer . . . and utterly destroy them."* This command has often been thought of as unethical for a loving God. However, it must be remembered that the Canaanites constituted a moral cancer (Deut. 20:17-18; Num. 35:55; Josh. 23:12-13). Their presence represented an infectious threat to Israel's spiritual (and eventually physical) well-being.

Today we should learn from this command that we must be as ruthless with sin in our own lives as Israel was commanded to be against the Canaanites.[2] Also remember that Israel had lost an entire generation of soldiers in the wilderness because of their sin. God is no respecter of persons.

God's hatred of sin and desire to rid man of it is underscored in the teachings of Jesus. "If your hand or foot causes you to sin, cut it off and cast it from you. It is better for you to enter into life lame or maimed, rather than having two hands or two feet, to be cast into the everlasting fire. And if your eye causes you to sin, pluck it out and cast it from you. It is better for you to enter into life with one eye, rather than having two eyes, to be cast into hell fire" (Matt. 18:8-9). This type of treatment for sin is not radical to a righteous God.

Israel was not to make a covenant with these enemies of God (v. 2). The word *"covenant"* gives an idea as to the reason for the harshness of Israel's war policy. The Israelites were bound to their covenant with the Lord. If they were to break this bond, it would indicate their unfaithfulness to God.

Marriages to people of other nations were also forbidden (v. 3). This caveat against being unequally yoked with an unbeliever appears throughout the entire Bible. Paul says, "Do not be unequally yoked together with unbelievers. For what fellowship has righteousness with lawlessness? And what communion has light with darkness?" (2 Cor. 6:14). He also teaches the widow that "she is at liberty to be married to whom she wishes, only in the Lord" (1 Cor. 7:39).

Why all this precaution? Marriage to people who do not worship God *"will turn your sons away from following Me, to serve other gods"* (v. 4). God does not want any possible stumbling block to His covenant relationship with Israel to remain, whether it be nations (vv. 1–2), marriages to unbelievers (vv. 3–4), or idolatry (v. 5).

Any time the unholy is mixed with the holy, God will remove His blessing. Variances even in godly households may result in prayers being "hindered" (1 Pet. 3:7). Believers are to agree concerning the things they shall ask, so that God's work will be accomplished (Matt. 18:19).

If a child of God marries a child of the devil, the child of God is going to have trouble with the father-in-law! A letter to "Dear Abby" amplifies the truth of this.

> Dear Abby: I think you were right when you told that fifteen-year-old girl to date boys of her own faith. I had parents that tried to tell me that, but I didn't listen. I was raised a Catholic, but I fell madly in love with a Lutheran boy. (He converted to marry me.)
>
> Now twenty-two years later, I go to church alone, and our four children don't go to church at all. When they were youngsters, they went with me. Their father went occasionally, but his heart really wasn't in it, and he slowly drifted away from the church. Soon the children stopped going, too.
>
> I go to church because it is a vital part of my life. We never know when love will "hit," and when it does, it becomes the most important thing in our life. I love my husband, but there is something missing because we don't share our prayers and religious faith. Perhaps I shouldn't complain. It only hurts on Sundays.
> —THINKING OUT LOUD
>
> DEAR THINKING: Yours was a refreshing relief from the many letters stating that dating was a far cry from marrying. I still maintain that dating usually leads to marriage. And if

religion is an important part of your life, *shop only in a store you can buy from.*

SELECTED BY GOD

7:6 "For you *are* a holy people to the LORD your God; the LORD your God has chosen you to be a people for Himself, a special treasure above all the peoples on the face of the earth.

7 "The LORD did not set His love on you nor choose you because you were more in number than any other people, for you were the least of all peoples;

8 "but because the LORD loves you, and because He would keep the oath which He swore to your fathers, the LORD has brought you out with a mighty hand, and redeemed you from the house of bondage, from the hand of Pharaoh king of Egypt.

9 "Therefore know that the LORD your God, He *is* God, the faithful God who keeps covenant and mercy for a thousand generations with those who love Him and keep His commandments;

10 "and He repays those who hate Him to their face, to destroy them. He will not be slack with him who hates Him; He will repay him to his face.

11 "Therefore you shall keep the commandment, the statutes, and the judgments which I command you today, to observe them."

Deut. 7:6–11

Choice, not chance, determines destiny. One choice had already been made. God had chosen Israel. He chose them *"to be a people for Himself, a special treasure."* They were not selected because of their numbers and greatness (v. 7). The timing of God's choosing is important in understanding His love. God calls Abraham as a childless man in a heathen city and promises to bless his descendants; God hears the cry of a minority people who are slaves in Egypt and brings deliverance; God walks with people who are not settled in their own land for forty years. His choice of a seemingly insignificant people is part of His strange strategy. He does not depend on numbers to bring about victory. He counts hearts.

Too often we count heads. John Wesley understood God's methods and said, "Give me one hundred men who fear nothing but sin and love nothing but God and I will shake the gates of hell." Elisha understood God's strategy. When the Syrian army surrounded him, the grand old prophet encouraged his terrified servant by saying, "Do not fear, for those who are with us are more than those who are with them" (2 Kings 6:16). Pharaoh would agree with that statement. God wants Israel to agree also. God is consistent throughout the Old and New Testaments in His selection of people He desires to use. Perhaps the best teaching of God's selection process was written by Paul.

> For you see your calling, brethren, that not many wise according to the flesh, not many mighty, not many noble, are called. But God has chosen the foolish things of the world to put to shame the wise, and God has chosen the weak things of the world to put to shame the things which are mighty; and the base things of the world and the things which are despised God has chosen, and the things which are not, to bring to nothing the things that are, that no flesh should glory in His presence. But of Him you are in Christ Jesus, who became for us wisdom from God— and righteousness and sanctification and redemption—that, as it is written, "He who glories, let him glory in the Lord."
>
> *1 Cor. 1:26–31*

God chose this small, insignificant group of Hebrews *"because the Lord loves you, and because He would keep the oath which He swore to your fathers"* (Deut. 7:8). God's love and faithfulness to Israel was a historical fact. Israel, an oppressed minority group in Egypt, was miraculously delivered, led through a bleak, inhospitable wilderness, and given land in which to dwell. Moses was a remarkable leader, but it was Yahweh who had chosen him and given him courage. To the Israelite it was nothing short of a miracle that a great divine Lord should take pity on them and engage in a fateful struggle with Pharaoh, the greatest temporal power of his day, and emerge the victor for their cause. The psalmist sang in awe, in praise, and in thanksgiving of the great deliverance. Prophets appealed to the conscience of the people and warned of the results of ingratitude and unfaithfulness. Who was Yahweh? Nearly all of Israel's theological confessions identified God as their Redeemer: "He is the God who brought us out of the land of Egypt, out of the house of bondage." When Israel claimed to be a chosen people, she was giving the only explanation possible to her for this historical event.[3]

The purpose of being a chosen people is given in verse 6. They were to be His and therefore holy, but these special characteristics must be clothed in humility (vv. 7–8).

The privilege of being a chosen people was to know from history and experience that God is faithful to keep His promises. His faithfulness is also for the future—even a thousand generations down the line.

The price of being a chosen people was terrible. Often God's choosing Israel brings questions about favoritism from students of the Old Testament. However, we need to remember that the privileges given Israel are balanced by the responsibilities. Jesus comments in Luke 12:48, "To whom much is given, from him much will be required; and to whom much has been committed, of him they will ask the more." Because of their privileged status, when Israel disobeyed God, they were placed in the fires of tribulation. The story of Israel as told by its own writers indicates the terrible burden that their election carried: "You only have I known of all the families of the earth; / Therefore, I will punish you for all your iniquities" (Amos 3:2). William Robertson Smith said, "If Israel would not learn to know Jehovah in the good land of Canaan, it must once more pass through the desert and enter the door of hope through the valley of tribulation."[4] Rebellious individuals within Israel will be judged for their sin just as His enemies in other nations are to be judged (v. 10). Therefore, each individual Israelite must be careful *"to observe"* God's commands.

SUCCESSFUL IN GOD

7:12 "Then it shall come to pass, because you listen to these judgments, and keep and do them, that the LORD your God will keep with you the covenant and the mercy which He swore to your fathers.

13 "And He will love you and bless you and multiply you; He will also bless the fruit of your womb and the fruit of your land, your grain and your new wine and your oil, the increase of your cattle and the offspring of your flock, in the land of which He swore to your fathers to give you.

14 "You shall be blessed above all peoples; there shall not be a male or female barren among you or among your livestock.

15 "And the LORD will take away from you all sickness, and will afflict you with none of the terrible diseases of Egypt which you have known, but will lay *them* on all those who hate you.

16 "Also you shall destroy all the peoples whom the LORD your God delivers over to you; your eye shall have no pity on them; nor shall you serve their gods, for that *will be* a snare to you.

17 "If you should say in your heart, 'These nations are greater than I; how can I dispossess them?'—

18 "you shall not be afraid of them, *but* you shall remember well what the LORD your God did to Pharaoh and to all Egypt:

19 "the great trials which your eyes saw, the signs and the wonders, the mighty hand and the outstretched arm, by which the LORD your God brought you out. So shall the LORD your God do to all the peoples of whom you are afraid.

20 "Moreover the LORD your God will send the hornet among them until those who are left, who hide themselves from you, are destroyed.

21 "You shall not be terrified of them; for the LORD your God, the great and awesome God, *is* among you.

22 "And the LORD your God will drive out those nations before you little by little; you will be unable to destroy them at once, lest the beasts of the field become *too* numerous for you.

23 "But the LORD your God will deliver them over to you, and will inflict defeat upon them until they are destroyed.

24 "And He will deliver their kings into your hand, and you will destroy their name from under heaven;

no one shall be able to stand against you until you have destroyed them.

25 "You shall burn the carved images of their gods with fire; you shall not covet the silver or gold *that is* on them, nor take *it* for yourselves, lest you be snared by it; for it *is* an abomination to the LORD your God.

26 "Nor shall you bring an abomination into your house, lest you be doomed to destruction like it. You shall utterly detest it and utterly abhor it, for it *is* an accursed thing."

Deut. 7:12-26

This is a victorious section of Scripture. The steps to pleasing God are given in verse 12. (1) *"Listen"* to His judgments; (2)*"keep"* them; and (3) *"do"* them. Israel's future will be determined by their response to their covenant obligations. This does not mean that obedience merited divine blessing, but rather that obedience maintained the proper covenant relationship with God. Obedience to God cannot be used as leverage to receive His blessing; it is what is expected if His children are to properly fulfill the covenant demands. God is the initiator, not man. He says, "Obey, and I will bless." Man ought not to say, "I will obey, if You bless me."

God's response to Israel's obedience is overwhelming. God will love them (v. 13), and bless them (with multiplication of human, animal, and plant life) (vv. 13-14). God will heal them (of present diseases) (v. 15), and protect them (from future disease) (v. 15). Egypt was noted for unhealthy conditions. Pliny, in describing Egypt, said it was "the mother of worst diseases." And God will give them victory.

The rest of this chapter deals with Israel's battles and God's ability to give them victory. His strategy for the children of Israel is applicable to us today, engaged in our daily battles.

God's Strategy for Victory

Moses, a wise leader who has entered many battles, realizes the likelihood of fear in the hearts of his people. He knows that the first battle men fight is in the mind, not on the field. He wisely admits that many of them will be fearful about entering a new land and facing other nations. But, like all great leaders, Moses had a plan that would lift his people out of their fears and prepare them for battle. It was a plan that can stand us in good stead today.

1. *Concentrate on the greatness of God, not on the strength of the enemy (v. 21).*

One way this can be done is by remembering past victories. Again Moses repeats the story of Israel's deliverance so that the people would *"remember well."* No doubt he remembered the time God spoke to him in Egypt, just before the tenth plague. After instructing His chosen leader concerning the passover God said, "So this day shall be to you a memorial; and you shall keep it as a feast to the Lord throughout your generations. You shall keep it as a feast by an everlasting ordinance" (Exod. 12:14). This miraculous deliverance of God was never to be forgotten! It was a story that magnified God's power and greatness. It was a sign that Israel was a "chosen people." It was a rallying point for God's children. If He gave deliverance yesterday, He could do it again today. We also should listen to Moses and look back at the times where God intervened and showed Himself to be greater than our own situations. The more victory experiences in our past, the greater our confidence for the future.

Claiming future promises is another way of focusing on God's greatness rather than the enemy's strength. *"So shall the Lord your God do to all the peoples of whom you are afraid."* God's ability to give Israel victory is both complete (*"all the peoples"*) and comforting (*"of whom you are afraid"*). The people's big question as they enter into Canaan will be, "Is God still able?" Moses says yes, the God of the past is also the God of the present and the future. He is more than a God of history; He is the God of eternity.

Moses wants his people to concentrate on God in the midst of their problems by sensing God's presence. In the heat of the battle the people are to remember that *"God, is among you."* If they have made God's cause theirs, He will make their cause His. Moses knows that God "will keep in perfect peace all those who trust in Him, whose thoughts turn often to the Lord" (Isa. 26:3).

2. *Face your problems (v. 22a).*

God is going to *"drive out those nations before"* Israel. He wants His people to face their enemies. Confrontation is essential. Notice the phrases that unequivocally state that God will place Israel's enemies in her hands. *"You shall destroy all the peoples whom the Lord your God delivers over to you"* (v. 16). *"The Lord your God will deliver them over* to you" (v. 23). No doubt about it—God wants His people to face their challenges head on. For a period of time there will be battle in Canaan. Israel will continually be confronted with enemies. Moses prepares and encourages them, saying, "Don't grow weary. As God brings the enemy to you, face them and destroy them."

Like the Israelites, we are not exempt from the barrage of problems that life brings. I've heard it said that problems are like cows—the hardest thing about milking cows is that they never stay milked. And, like the children of Israel, we too must be prepared to face our challenges. I love the story of the college kid who was flunking all his courses. Finally, the inevitable happened—he was kicked out of school. With some trepidation he sent a telegram to his mother, saying, "I've been kicked out of school, prepare Pop." Mom's reply was prompt and to the point, "Pop prepared, prepare yourself."

3. *Realize God will give you only what you can handle (v. 22).*

The Lord will bring the enemy to Israel *"little by little."* Why? *"You will be unable to destroy them at once, lest the beasts of the field become too numerous for you."* The conquest would not happen overnight. Israel would fight, then settle; fight, then settle. It would take time for them to grow and mature as a people. Moses does not want the people to become impatient while waiting for victory. He knows that a good general attacks only one front at a time, for it's in the winning of the small skirmishes that victory becomes possible.

Life is similar to Israel's conquest of Canaan. It is a series of peaks and valleys, each designed for our growth. The good news is that "No temptation has overtaken you except such as is common to man; but God is faithful, who will not allow you to be tempted beyond what you are able, but with the temptation will also make the way of escape, that you may be able to bear it" (1 Cor. 10:13).

4. *Recognize the power of the attitude (v. 17).*

Moses knows that the attitude of the people will determine their success against their enemies (v. 17). He tells the people that *"God will deliver them over to you, and will inflict defeat upon them until they are destroyed"* (v. 23). In other words, God will give the enemies of Israel a spirit of defeat even before they are defeated! The *"hornet"* that God will send among the enemies (v. 20) is the insidious emotion of fear. Fear will bring with it some devastating companions: panic, depression, and discouragement. God has made use of this *"hornet"* in the past. "And Moab was exceedingly afraid of the people because they were many, and Moab was sick with dread because of the children of Israel" (Num. 22:3). Moses prophesied that this would happen in his song of praise after their deliverance from Egypt.

> The people will hear and be afraid;
> Sorrow will take hold of the inhabitants of Philistia.
> Then the chiefs of Edom will be dismayed;
> The mighty men of Moab,
> Trembling will take hold of them;
> All the inhabitants of Canaan will melt away.
> Fear and dread will fall on them;
> By the greatness of Your arm
> They will be as still as a stone,
> Till Your people pass over, O Lord,
> Till the people pass over
> Whom You have purchased.
>
> *Exod. 15:14–16*

This happened again when the two men sent by Joshua to spy out Jericho faced Rahab. She said, "I know that the Lord has given you the land, that the terror of you has fallen on us, and that all the inhabitants of the land are fainthearted because of you. . . . our hearts melted; neither did there remain any more courage in anyone because of you, for the Lord your God, He is God in heaven above and on earth beneath" (Josh. 2:9, 11).

Is it not true that the battle is often won before it is begun? Moses prepares his people to think positively and feel good about their upcoming battles by reminding them of God's greatness. God prepares the enemy for battle by giving them a spirit of fear and dread. The panic instigated by their fear would spread like wildfire and would actually bring about their own destruction (1 Sam. 7:10). This is why the number of warriors engaged in the battle was irrelevant; God could save with many or with few (Judg. 7; 1 Sam. 14:1–23).

5. *Expect total victory (vv. 23–24).*

God will bring the enemy before Israel and He will inflict them with a spirit of discouragement. But—He will not destroy them. His work is to deliver the enemy to Israel. It is Israel's job to destroy them; they cannot be kept alive. Notice that God *"will deliver their kings"* into the hands of Israel. Their victory will not be over just the common people of the land; they will conquer the leaders and break the morale of the nations. Those men who were capable of instigating attack against Israel will be destroyed.

This same thing happens in our own lives. When we triumph over our "Goliaths," the "Philistines" will scatter. If we can defeat the leader, the followers will disappear. Is this not the spirit of Paul, who exclaimed, "We are more than conquerors through Him who loved us" (Rom. 8:37)?

6. *Remove all temptations that would cause you to be defeated* (*vv. 25–26*).

It is essential that Israel put away everything, whether man or inanimate object, that would turn her away from the total allegiance to God. Twice Moses warns the people that their neglecting to destroy the enemy or the images of their gods will *"snare"* them (vv. 16, 25), resulting in their own downfall. Israel is to *"utterly detest . . . and utterly abhor"* that which is *"an abomination"* to the Lord, *"for it is an accursed thing"* (v. 26). This is strong language which must be taken seriously. The defeat of Israel at Ai provides an example of what would happen if the forbidden things were kept in a person's possession (Josh. 7). As we examine our own lives looking for "snares," may our prayer be that of Charles A. Tindley in his song entitled "Nothing Between."

> Nothing between my soul and the Savior,
> Naught of this world's delusive dream;
> I have renounced all sinful pleasure,
> Jesus is mine; there's nothing between.
>
> Nothing between my soul and the Savior,
> So that His blessed face may be seen;
> Nothing preventing the least of His favor,
> Keep the way clear! Let nothing between.
>
> Nothing between, like worldly pleasure,
> Habits of life, though harmless they seem,
> Must not my heart from Him e'er sever,
> He is my all; there's nothing between.
>
> Nothing between, like pride or station,
> Self or friends shall not intervene,

Tho' it may cost me much tribulation,
I am resolved; there's nothing between.

Nothing between, e'en many hard trials,
Tho' the whole world against me convene;
Watching with prayer and much self-denial,
I'll triumph at last, with nothing between.

NOTES

1. Victor P. Hamilton, *Handbook on the Pentateuch* (Grand Rapids: Baker Book House, 1982), p. 409.

2. John F. Walvoord and Roy B. Zuck, *The Bible Knowledge Commentary*, O.T. (Wheaton, IL: Victor Books, 1978), pp. 275–76.

3. G. Ernest Wright, *The Old Testament against Its Environment* (London: SCM Press, Ltd., 1950), pp. 49–50.

4. William R. Smith, *The Prophets of Israel*, 2nd ed. (London: Adam and Charles Black, 1897), p. 69.

CHAPTER TEN

Remember the Lord's Provision

Deuteronomy 8:1–20

REMEMBER THE LORD'S BLESSINGS WHEN THINGS ARE BAD

8:1 "Every commandment which I command you today you must be careful to observe, that you may live and multiply, and go in and possess the land of which the LORD swore to your fathers.

2 "And you shall remember that the LORD your God led you all the way these forty years in the wilderness, to humble you *and* test you, to know what *was* in your heart, whether you would keep His commandments or not.

3 "So He humbled you, allowed you to hunger, and fed you with manna which you did not know nor did your fathers know, that He might make you know that man shall not live by bread alone; but man lives by every *word* that proceeds from the mouth of the LORD.

4 "Your garments did not wear out on you, nor did your foot swell these forty years.

5 "You should know in your heart that as a man chastens his son, *so* the LORD your God chastens you.

6 "Therefore you shall keep the commandments of the LORD your God, to walk in His ways and to fear Him.

7 "For the LORD your God is bringing you into a good land, a land of brooks of water, of fountains and springs, that flow out of valleys and hills;

8 "a land of wheat and barley, of vines and fig trees and pomegranates, a land of olive oil and honey;

9 "a land in which you will eat bread without
scarcity, in which you will lack nothing; a land
whose stones *are* iron and out of whose hills you can
dig copper.
10 "When you have eaten and are full, then you
shall bless the LORD your God for the good land
which He has given you."

Deut. 8:1–10

The words of Moses in Deuteronomy 8 impress upon Israel the
need to learn a significant lesson from their past: Their experience of
God's care in the wilderness period, when they were unable to help
themselves, was to teach them humility through the Lord's providential discipline. The memory of that experience should keep them
from pride in their own achievements when entering the secure and
prosperous land of Canaan.

The Value of the Wilderness Experience

Every difficult situation carries with it the possibility of an equal
or greater benefit. Our willingness to learn from our trials will determine whether or not we attain those benefits. George Mathison
prayed, "My God, I have never thanked Thee for my thorns. I have
thanked Thee a thousand times for my roses, but not once for my
thorns. I have been looking forward to a world where I shall get
compensation for my cross; but I never thought of my cross itself as
a present glory. Teach me the glory of my cross; teach me the value
of my thorn, show me that I have climbed to Thee by the path of
pain. Show me that my tears have made my rainbow."

This was the attitude Moses wanted for his people. He wanted
them to *"remember"* their wilderness experience. "Remembering" is a
common theme throughout Deuteronomy. Thirteen times in this book
Moses asks the people to *"remember."* Usually they are reminded of
their deliverance from Egypt, but here the emphasis is on their
wilderness journey. Many valuable lessons are to be learned from
this experience.

1. *They learned to trust only in God (v. 2).* To make sure this happened, the Lord led them into a place where they had no other alternative but to trust Him. They could not produce their own food or

make their own clothes. Certainly they were unable to win their battles by themselves. They had no law or foundation to establish a nation. In this setting, God taught Israel that He alone was sufficient.

2. *They learned that God's method was not theirs (v. 2).* They discovered that God would not lead them in the shortest way, but in the surest way. There would be many and sometimes massive roadblocks in God's path. It has been said, "The path that has no obstacles leads to nowhere." They were definitely going somewhere—to Canaan. But before their arrival, God had several lessons to teach them.

They learned His method of sending supplies. When God provided manna for them it was on a daily basis. Their natural inclination was to store up the food and save it for their own security. But when they tried this, worms quickly moved in and ate their bread and fouled the air. The only exception was on the sixth day when the people gathered up two days' worth of supplies. On the Sabbath, their day of rest, no manna was supplied, but the manna gathered the day before remained fresh (Exod. 16:16–30).

3. *They learned humility (v. 3).* Humility is the gift given upon graduation from the school of affliction. The testing that God gave Israel helped them to define humility as "everything from God, nothing from ourselves." The experiences that they underwent were ones that they *"did not know nor did your fathers know"* (v. 3).

On the desk of the late President Kennedy in the White House stood a small plaque bearing this inscription: "O God, Thy sea is so great and my boat is so small." As president of this great nation, he realized his own inadequacy. As God gives us greater and greater responsibilities, we should realize more and more our dependence on Him. This is humility.

William Beebe, the naturalist, used to tell this story about Teddy Roosevelt. In the evenings at Sagamore Hill, the two would go out on the lawn and search the skies for a certain spot of starlike light beyond the lower left-hand corner of the great square of Pegasus. Then Roosevelt would recite: "That is the spiral galaxy in Andromeda. It is as large as our Milky Way. It consists of a hundred billion suns. It is one of a hundred billion galaxies." Then he would grin and say, "Now I think we are small enough! Let's go to bed."

Moses wants Israel to sense their smallness without God. When that happens, then they can go into Canaan.

4. They learned that God could sustain as well as create (v. 4).

5. They learned that God's discipline reflected His love (v. 5). God knew that they could not conquer Canaan until He conquered them. For hundreds of years Israel belonged to Pharaoh. Now they were free—but free for what? They were free to enter into the land of milk and honey and reflect to all nations the care of God in their lives.

Perhaps Sir Rabindranath Tagore expressed the intent of God's heavy hand on Israel when he said, "I have on my table a violin string. It is free. I twist one end of it and it responds. It is free. But it is not free to do what a violin string is supposed to do—to produce music. So I take it, fix it in my violin, and tighten it until it is taut. Only then is it free to be a violin string."

Elisabeth Elliot said, "As a child in a Christian home I did not start out with an understanding of the word *discipline*. I simply knew that I belonged to people who loved me and cared for me. That is dependence. They spoke to me and I answered. That is responsibility. They gave me things to do and I did them. That is obedience. It all adds up to discipline."

6. God wanted to test Israel (v. 3). The most important value of the wilderness experience is the development of our character in relation to God. Nothing reveals the true self like the difficulties of life. Every new day in the wilderness brought forth another challenge. The children of Israel were forced into situations that would not leave them the same. Obey or disobey? Praise God or murmur against Him? Go forward or return to Egypt? Their decisions would reveal their readiness for entrance into Canaan.

A little boy watched an emperor butterfly emerge from its cocoon. Now, this process is painful to observe. The cocoon has a little opening at the end and the butterfly has to squeeze out of it. It is a terrible struggle. It pushes and squeezes so hard that one can actually see its body pulsating and quivering from exhaustion. And the progress is so slow—the butterfly pushes and rests, pushes and rests. Finally, it pulls itself together for one last momentous push and it's out—drained and sapped of energy, but ready to fly. As this little boy watched the emperor butterfly struggle, he felt sorry for it and decided to do it a favor. He very carefully took his pocket knife and slit the opening in the cocoon just a little bit wider to make it easy for the poor little creature to emerge. He thought he was sparing the butterfly trial and suffering. What he did, however, kept the butterfly from ever reaching its potential. He ruined the butterfly! That squeezing and pushing is necessary and vital because the pressure serves to push blood and body fluids into the wings. Because the butterfly did not go through the struggle, its wings were useless. It could never fly!

The wilderness was God's cocoon for His people. For forty years they struggled to get out. God's love guided them but it did not take away their freedom of choice. They must choose to obey. Their struggling years were their preparation years. Notice in verses 7–10 what a contrast Canaan is from the wilderness.

REMEMBER THE LORD'S BLESSINGS WHEN THINGS ARE GOOD

8:11 "Beware that you do not forget the LORD your God by not keeping His commandments, His judgments, and His statutes which I command you today,

12 "lest—*when* you have eaten and are full, and have built beautiful houses and dwell *in them;*

13 "and *when* your herds and your flocks multiply, and your silver and your gold are multiplied, and all that you have is multiplied;

14 "when your heart is lifted up, and you forget the LORD your God who brought you out of the land of Egypt, from the house of bondage;

15 "who led you through that great and terrible wilderness, *in which were* fiery serpents and scorpions and thirsty land where there was no water; who brought water for you out of the flinty rock;

16 "who fed you in the wilderness with manna, which your fathers did not know, that He might humble you and that He might test you, to do you good in the end—

17 "then you say in your heart, 'My power and the might of my hand have gained me this wealth.'

18 "And you shall remember the LORD your God, for *it is* He who gives you power to get wealth, that He may establish His covenant which He swore to your fathers, as *it is* this day.

19 "Then it shall be, if you by any means forget the

LORD your God, and follow other gods, and serve
them and worship them, I testify against you this day
that you shall surely perish.
20 "As the nations which the LORD destroys before
you, so you shall perish, because you would not be
obedient to the voice of the LORD your God."

Deut. 8:11–20

Moses does not want the people to forget that God was their Lib-
erator (v. 14) and Leader (v. 15). Twice in this chapter Moses exhorts
Israel to *"remember"* the greatness of God in their past. It was extremely important for them to remember their God. The Hebrew
word for *"remember,"* zākar, appears in many forms throughout
the Old Testament. *"Remember the Lord your God"* (v. 18). Even the
cynical preacher of Ecclesiastes counsels, "Remember now your Creator in the days of your youth" (12:1). In return, the Lord remembers
His people. "I will remember My covenant with Jacob . . . Isaac
and . . . Abraham" (Lev. 26:42).

But what does it means to *"remember"*? Certainly remembering is
a mental exercise. You remember an answer to a Trivial Pursuit question. You remember someone's phone number. But remembering has
other aspects. It implies action and honor. We commemorate an event,
perhaps reenacting it in some sort of ritual or ceremony. We make a
donation in memory of someone who has died. There are many av-
enues through which we can actively remember.

The ultimate destruction of the Amalekites and other enemies of
God's people is that God "will utterly blot out the remembrance
of Amalek from under heaven" (Exod. 17:14). In some cases the word
for memory is used synonymously with "name" and "fame."

The sense of posterity was very strong among the Hebrews. The
position of historian was an honored one; Asaph was called the "re-
corder" or "rememberer" (Isa. 36:3).

Commemoration also becomes a celebration. The NIV translates
zākar as "celebrate" in Psalms 145:7; it is paired with "joyfully sing."
Zākar is used with "thank" and "praise" in 1 Chronicles 16:4. To remember a special occasion is to observe it, to do something meaningful in regard to it. We remember someone's birthday by sending a
card or gift. The Israelites were instructed to "observe the Sabbath
day" (Deut. 5:12).[1]

"Forget Not the Lord"

Three times in verses 11–20 Moses admonishes his people about the danger of forgetting *the Lord your God* (vv. 11, 14, 19). Notice that when they experience prosperity is when Israel would be susceptible to the temptation of forgetting God (vv. 12–13). "When you have eaten and are full . . ." A lethargic spirit accompanies a full stomach and a satisfied heart. The living God is not bound by time. But man, susceptible to the pleasures of the moment, is constantly tempted to limit his horizons to what he presently sees and experiences. The very thing that has been Israel's goal (Canaan) has the possibility of being her downfall.

Disturb Us, Lord

Disturb us, O Lord, when we are too well pleased with
  ourselves;
When our dreams come true only because we dreamed too
  little;
When we arrive safely only because we sailed too close to the
  shore;
When with the abundance of things we are losing our thirst
  for more of God;
When in loving time we have ceased to dream of eternity;
When in our desire to build on this earth we have lost our
  vision of a new heaven.

Author Unknown

I once heard a missionary tell how he was working with a particular tribe and found it difficult to translate the word or the concept of "pride." He finally came to the idea of using their terminology—"the ears are too far apart." In other words, he conveyed the idea of an "inflated head." That translation is hard to improve on when we think of the problem of pride. Surely an inflated head indicates a haughty spirit.

Moses warns Israel of this possibility in their lives (v. 14). He wants to make sure they understand the negative characteristics of pride. They must remember that their pride is:

(1) Untrue—God heard their cry and delivered them. They were
   in bondage, weak and insignificant.

(2) Disloyal—The worst form of idolatry is to lift themselves up before God.
(3) Ungrateful—What can be worse than to forget the Source of all good things?
(4) Offensive—Pride is one of the seven things that God hates (Prov. 6:16–17).
(5) Exactly opposite of what God intended for Israel. He desired to humble them in the wilderness (v. 16).

The thing which Moses fears the most is that they would possess a deceived heart (v. 17). The *"heart is lifted up"* (v. 14) and now the heart says, *"My power and the might of my hand have gained me this wealth"* (v. 17). Paul, centuries after Moses, said, "Command those who are rich in this present age not to be haughty, nor to trust in uncertain riches but in the living God, who gives us richly all things to enjoy" (1 Tim. 6:17). The more kindly God deals with us, the more we ought to remember and thank Him; but the depravity of our nature too many times causes us to be insolent under God's indulgence.

Moses warns the people what will happen if they *"forget the Lord"* (v. 19) and fail to *"be obedient to the voice of the Lord"* (v. 20).

The result of forgetting God is that they will fail to keep His commandments (v. 11).

This reality leads to a "which came first, the chicken or the egg" question. Did they fail to keep God's commandments and therefore forget Him; or did they forget Him and therefore fail to keep His commandments? No matter which comes first, the other will immediately follow.

A missionary translator was endeavoring to find a word for "obedience" in the native language. This was a virtue seldom practiced among the people into whose language he was translating the New Testament. As he returned home from the village one day, he whistled for his dog and it came running at full speed. An old native, seeing this, said admiringly in the native tongue, "Your dog is all ears." Immediately the missionary knew he had his translation for obedience. To obey is to be "all ears" toward God.

Just as failure to obey God would lead to forgetting Him, so forgetting Him would lead Israel to the worship of other gods. If they forgot God, they would be in danger of breaking the first commandment and they would certainly perish (vv. 19–20).

These last two verses tie the particular topics of this chapter of Deuteronomy more closely to the overall themes of the book. One of the basic themes of Deuteronomy is the demand for covenant allegiance. In emphasizing this loyalty, Moses had to expose the danger of unfaithfulness to God's covenant. The Israelites needed to learn that if as a nation they dishonored their covenant with Yahweh, they would cease to have a claim on Him. If this ever happened, Israel would be judged, the same as other nations who had disobeyed and therefore perished. Each new generation needed to grasp this fact and decide for themselves to be obedient to God. This was not a thing to be treated lightly; it was a life or death decision. Centuries later, when the young King Josiah realized the truth of this concept, he instigated national reform.

NOTE

1. J. Randall Patterson, *The Bible Newsletter* (Evangelical Ministries, Inc., 1984).

CHAPTER ELEVEN

Remember Your Provocation

Deuteronomy 9:1–10:11

GOD'S PROVISIONS IN SPITE OF OUR PROVOCATION

9:1 "Hear, O Israel: You *are* to cross over the Jordan today, and go in to dispossess nations greater and mightier than yourself, cities great and fortified up to heaven,

2 "a people great and tall, the descendants of the Anakim, whom you know, and *of whom* you heard *it said*, 'Who can stand before the descendants of Anak?'

3 "Therefore understand today that the LORD your God *is* He who goes over before you *as* a consuming fire. He will destroy them and bring them down before you; so you shall drive them out and destroy them quickly, as the LORD has said to you.

4 "Do not think in your heart, after the LORD your God has cast them out before you, saying, 'Because of my righteousness the LORD has brought me in to possess this land'; but *it is* because of the wickedness of these nations *that* the LORD is driving them out from before you.

5 "*It is* not because of your righteousness or the uprightness of your heart *that* you go in to possess their land, but because of the wickedness of these nations *that* the LORD your God drives them out from before you, and that He may fulfill the word which the LORD swore to your fathers, to Abraham, Isaac, and Jacob.

6 "Therefore understand that the LORD your God

is not giving you this good land to possess because of
your righteousness, for you *are* a stiff-necked people."
Deut. 9:1–6

In this passage Moses refers to two past lessons. In Deuteronomy
8 the address centered on Israel's need to remember God's blessings
and to not be lifted up by pride. God was the source of their blessings and without Him they were nothing. In Deuteronomy 9, Moses
continually emphasizes that any success they might enjoy in the
Canaan conquest is not to be interpreted as a mark of approval of
their own righteousness (9:1–6). In fact, in many incidents (9:7–21,
22, 23), including the golden calf episode, Israel had shown herself
to be not righteous, but stubborn and rebellious. Only after Moses
interceded was Israel saved from destruction.

Forty years earlier, fear had struck the hearts of the people upon
hearing the twelve spies' report that enemies would oppose them.
Moses reminds them that those enemies are still there. He specifically mentions the sons of Anak. The spies had made two specific
references to the Anakim. The first was an observation which was
true: "We saw the descendants of Anak there" (Num. 13:28). The
second was an interpretation which was false: "We are not able to go
up against the people, for they are stronger than we" (Num. 13:31).
For forty years these towering giants had stood as a taunting symbol
of the national unbelief. So tall and formidable were they that Israel
had coined an expression, *"Who can stand before the descendants of
Anak?"* (Deut. 9:2). But Moses assured the Israelites that God special-
izes in Anakim! He would go before His people to destroy the giants
and give Israel the land.

From time to time we each face Anakim in our personal spiritual
journey. What impossible situation stands squarely in the way of
your spiritual progress? We, like the Israelites, may back up and stall
for "forty years," but when we are ready to move forward, we want
our problems to go away or shrink. Who hasn't felt like the lion
tamer who was tired of continually putting his life on the line with
ferocious, mean animals, and finally put the following ad in the
paper: "Lion tamer wants tamer lion!"

Moses does not shrink the enemy. Instead he redirects his people's
focus from the giants of their lives to the God of their lives as in the
words of the hymn by Helen H. Lemmel:

Turn your eyes upon Jesus,
Look full in His wonderful face;
And the things of earth will grow strangely dim
In the light of His glory and grace.

The power of God is described in three ways (v. 3). He goes before Israel *"as a consuming fire," "He will destroy them,"* and He will humble the enemy *"before you."* Again, notice that Israel also has a responsibility in battle. They are to *"destroy them quickly."* God will bring our enemies before us prepared to be conquered, but we must finish the work. Moses does not want Israel to think that their "little part" brought the victory (vv. 4–5). "The horse is prepared for the day of battle, / But deliverance is of the Lord" (Prov. 21:31).

The issue of Israel's prosperity and success has continually arisen in Deuteronomy 8:1–9:6. Behind each incident is the hand of God teaching His people a lesson.

(1) God humbled Israel in the wilderness to test her to see if she would keep the commandments. Therefore, Israel's misfortunes can be explained on the basis of the *probationary* activity of God, His testing their faith.

(2) God let Israel hunger to teach her that man does not live by bread alone; He disciplined her as a father disciplines a son (Deut. 8:3, 5). Israel's misfortunes are therefore explained as a result of the *pedagogical* activity of God, His discipline and training of character.

(3) God reminds Israel that He alone bestows the power to attain wealth. Their own ability counts for nothing (Deut. 8:18). Israel's prosperity is thus attributed to the *power* of God.

(4) Israel remembers that God was motivated to dispossess the nations, not because of her righteousness, but rather because of the wickedness of other nations and the promise to her forefathers (vv. 4–6). Israel's claim to have merited the inheritance of Canaan is now entirely undercut. Later Moses points out that the Israelites actually deserved to be destroyed (9:13–14) rather than blessed with the gift of the land. They certainly should never develop a self-righteous attitude because of their victories in the conquest. These victories were won because of three things—the enemies' wickedness, God's promises, and God's grace.

ISRAEL'S PROBLEMS BECAUSE OF PROVOKING GOD

9:7 "Remember! Do not forget how you provoked the LORD your God to wrath in the wilderness. From the day that you departed from the land of Egypt until you came to this place, you have been rebellious against the LORD.

8 "Also in Horeb you provoked the LORD to wrath, so that the LORD was angry *enough* with you to have destroyed you.

9 "When I went up into the mountain to receive the tablets of stone, the tablets of the covenant which the LORD made with you, then I stayed on the mountain forty days and forty nights. I neither ate bread nor drank water.

10 "Then the LORD delivered to me two tablets of stone written with the finger of God, and on them *were* all the words which the LORD had spoken to you on the mountain from the midst of the fire in the day of the assembly.

11 "And it came to pass, at the end of forty days and forty nights, *that* the LORD gave me the two tablets of stone, the tablets of the covenant.

12 "Then the LORD said to me, 'Arise, go down quickly from here, for your people whom you brought out of Egypt have acted corruptly; they have quickly turned aside from the way which I commanded them; they have made themselves a molded image.'

13 "Furthermore the LORD spoke to me, saying, 'I have seen this people, and indeed they are a stiff-necked people.

14 'Let Me alone, that I may destroy them and blot out their name from under heaven; and I will make of you a nation mightier and greater than they.'

15 "So I turned and came down from the mountain, and the mountain burned with fire; and the two tablets of the covenant *were* in my two hands.

16 "And I looked, and behold, you had sinned against the LORD your God—had made for yourselves a molded calf! You had turned aside quickly from the way which the LORD had commanded you.

17 "Then I took the two tablets and threw them out of my two hands and broke them before your eyes.

18 "And I fell down before the LORD, as at the first, forty days and forty nights; I neither ate bread nor drank water, because of all your sin which you committed in doing wickedly in the sight of the LORD, to provoke Him to anger.

19 "For I was afraid of the anger and hot displeasure with which the LORD was angry with you, to destroy you. But the LORD listened to me at that time also.

20 "And the LORD was very angry with Aaron *and* would have destroyed him; so I prayed for Aaron also at the same time.

21 "Then I took your sin, the calf which you had made, and burned it with fire and crushed it *and* ground *it* very small, until it was as fine as dust; and I threw its dust into the brook that descended from the mountain.

22 "Also at Taberah and Massah and Kibroth Hattaavah you provoked the LORD to wrath.

23 "Likewise, when the LORD sent you from Kadesh Barnea, saying, 'Go up and possess the land which I have given you,' then you rebelled against the commandment of the LORD your God, and you did not believe Him nor obey His voice.

24 "You have been rebellious against the LORD from the day that I knew you."

Deut. 9:7–24

This section of Scripture highlights the stubbornness of Israel and the importance of Moses' contribution to Israel's well-being. The key to Israel's continued existence is neither her power (8:17) nor her righteousness (9:4). She continues to be blessed because of God's graciousness and her great leader Moses.

If Israel was ever foolish enough to think that the gift of Canaan was because of her righteousness, she would certainly be suffering from a severe case of religious amnesia. Moses begins to illustrate Israel's rebelliousness by recalling events from her past. The main incident is that of the golden calf (vv. 8–21). These narratives parallel those in Exodus 24:12–18 and Exodus 32 and 34. The account given here by Moses is a free retelling of the story in Exodus. This is characteristic of Deuteronomy.

The most blatant example of Israel's rebellion took place at Horeb soon after she had willingly accepted the terms of the covenant (Exod. 32–34). This incident became quite significant because the renewal ceremony in Moab was a renewal of the forming of the covenant at Horeb. If the people had been guilty of provoking God, even in the midst of the awe-inspiring events associated with Horeb, then the danger is no less present now on the plains of Moab.

Significant Facts at Horeb

1. *Moses fasted while the Israelites feasted (v. 9).* Throughout this story there is a stark contrast between the behavior of Israel and that of Moses. While Moses was in communion with God, the people had turned their backs on Him. Moses was receiving the covenant while his people were breaking it. Moses prayed while the people played.

2. *The children of Israel had heard the covenant spoken before it was written (v. 10);* therefore, it was not out of ignorance, but out of rebellion, that they broke the first and second commandments.

3. *God wanted to destroy the people (vv. 13–14);* they had broken the covenant. Two curses for breaking the covenant are suggested by God: destruction of the people and blotting out their names from the memory of man. God could still fulfill His purpose and promise through Moses and his descendants who were, of course, the descendants of Abraham.

4. *Israel had turned quickly away from the Lord (v. 16).* It is no wonder that Moses continually exhorted his people to remember their God. They had a history of forgetting. But they could not afford to forget God's delivering them from Egypt.

5. *Moses broke into pieces the tablet on which the commandments were written (v. 17).* His account in Deuteronomy of this action indicates his desire to give Israel a visual image of what they had done to the covenant of God. By smashing the stones, he confirmed this breach of covenant. This procedure was continued in the ancient Near East when treaties were broken.

6. *Moses interceded and God listened (vv. 18–19).* The content of Moses' prayer is given in verses 26–29.

7. The idol was totally destroyed (v. 21). This action is in keeping with the numerous admonitions throughout Deuteronomy to destroy all cult objects.

The occurrence at Horeb was not the only one of its kind. There were incidents such as the one at Taberah, where the people complained of their misfortunes, and only because of Moses' intercession were they spared God's burning anger (Num. 11:1–3). At Massah they complained because of lack of water and put God to the test (Exod. 17:1–7). At Kibroth Hattaavah the people again had complained and several perished (Num. 11:31–35). And at Kadesh Barnea gross unbelief was displayed after the spies brought back their negative report (Deut. 1:21–36; Num. 13–14). This last example is particularly relevant because the people on the plains of Moab faced a divine command similar to that given at Kadesh Barnea.

All these examples are given to establish the point of Moses' address: *"You have been rebellious against the Lord from the day that I knew you"* (v. 24). In every case, Israel questioned God's plan for her life. She neither believed His promises nor obeyed His commands. Many times when an unforeseen problem arose, Israel reacted in a negative, non-trusting way. She could not appreciate the lessons learned from testing. George Mueller said, "The stops of a good man are ordered by the Lord as well as his steps."

Adoniram Judson, a man full of enthusiasm for preaching the gospel, clearly was appointed by God to be a missionary. Having sensed the need to go to India, he reached Calcutta in the summer of 1812, only to receive peremptory orders from the British government to leave the country at once and return to America. With sad hearts his little missionary company retreated to the Ile de France, wondering why God had seemingly opened a wide and effectual door only to violently shut it. But with unconquerable determination they returned again to India, reaching Madras in the following June.

Once again their purpose was thwarted and once more they were ordered from the country. This time they fled to Rangoon, a place which Judson had regarded with the utmost aversion as a mission field. There he was permitted to stay, only to find imprisonments awaiting him.

But all is clear now. Adoniram Judson was forbidden by the Spirit to enter India because God would have him in Burma. Those "divine rejections" kept Judson in the place of God's choosing, and more than thirty thousand people came to Christ.

MOSES' PRAYER ON BEHALF OF THE PEOPLE

9:25 "Thus I prostrated myself before the LORD; forty days and forty nights I kept prostrating myself, because the LORD had said He would destroy you.

26 "Therefore I prayed to the LORD, and said: 'O Lord GOD, do not destroy Your people and Your inheritance whom You have redeemed through Your greatness, whom You have brought out of Egypt with a mighty hand.

27 'Remember Your servants, Abraham, Isaac, and Jacob; do not look on the stubbornness of this people, or on their wickedness or their sin,

28 'lest the land from which You brought us should say, "Because the LORD was not able to bring them to the land which He promised them, and because He hated them, He has brought them out to kill them in the wilderness."

29 'Yet they *are* Your people and Your inheritance, whom You brought out by Your mighty power and by Your outstretched arm.'

10:1 "At that time the LORD said to me, 'Hew for yourself two tablets of stone like the first, and come up to Me on the mountain and make yourself an ark of wood.

2 'And I will write on the tablets the words that were on the first tablets, which you broke; and you shall put them in the ark.'

3 "So I made an ark of acacia wood, hewed two tablets of stone like the first, and went up the mountain, having the two tablets in my hand.

4 "And He wrote on the tablets according to the first writing, the Ten Commandments, which the LORD had spoken to you in the mountain from the midst of the fire in the day of the assembly; and the LORD gave them to me.

5 "Then I turned and came down from the mountain, and put the tablets in the ark which I had

made; and there they are, just as the LORD commanded me."

6 (Now the children of Israel journeyed from the
wells of Bene Jaakan to Moserah, where Aaron died,
and where he was buried; and Eleazar his son ministered as priest in his stead.

7 From there they journeyed to Gudgodah, and
from Gudgodah to Jotbathah, a land of rivers of water.

8 At that time the LORD separated the tribe of
Levi to bear the ark of the covenant of the LORD, to
stand before the LORD to minister to Him and to bless
in His name, to this day.

9 Therefore Levi has no portion nor inheritance
with his brethren; the LORD *is* his inheritance, just as
the LORD your God promised him.)

10 "As at the first time, I stayed in the mountain
forty days and forty nights; the LORD also heard me
at that time, *and* the LORD chose not to destroy you.

11 "Then the LORD said to me, 'Arise, begin *your*
journey before the people, that they may go in and
possess the land which I swore to their fathers to
give them.'"

Deut. 9:25–10:11

Moses stands tall in the field of leadership. Perhaps his greatest
contribution to Israel was in the area of intercessory prayer. Deuteronomy 9:18, 25 highlight the depth of sincerity in his prayer. Certainly this great leader illustrates the promise given to us by James:
"The effective, fervent prayer of a righteous man avails much" (5:16).
Here, Moses stands between God and the people, interceding for
them.

Moses appeals to God to spare the children of Israel on the grounds
that *they are His children* (vv. 26, 29). Notice the unusual number of
personal pronouns: *"Do not destroy **Your** people and **Your** inheritance
whom **You** have redeemed through **Your** greatness, whom **You** have
brought out of Egypt. . . . Yet they are **Your** people and **Your** inheritance, whom **You** brought out by **Your** mighty power and by **Your** outstretched arm."* Moses clearly attaches no personal claim to God's
people. He continually reminds God of His unique relationship with
Israel. He did not plead for Israel on the basis of any merit, either
theirs or his. He simply reminds God that Israel is His inheritance.

Moses reminds God of His covenant with *"Your servants, Abraham, Isaac, and Jacob"* (v. 27). It is interesting to compare Moses' use of recollected history in this prayer with his use of it in his address to the people. In addressing the people, Moses reminds them of their past unfaithfulness. On that basis he calls them to obedience and faithfulness. In his intercessory prayer, Moses recalls the long history of God's covenant faithfulness; he seeks God's forgiveness on the basis of His nature, not the people's worthiness.[1] Just as Israel has a checkered history of unfaithfulness, God's history is spotless, reflecting His faithfulness to mankind.

Moses implored God to consider His own name among the nations and to not destroy the people. If He now destroyed Israel, even though such action would be justified because of their breaking the covenant, His action would be misunderstood. The Egyptians would mock and say that God took the Israelites out of Egypt but was unable to lead them into the land of promise. If He spared their lives but didn't bring His people to Canaan, men would lose their fear of Him, thinking that His powers were limited. God's word would be held in contempt if He did not fulfill His covenant with Israel.

Moses' heartfelt appeal influenced the Lord to reconsider His intent to destroy the people. This great man joins the other great intercessors of the faith—Abraham (Gen. 18:23–32), Elijah (1 Kings 18:36–39), Daniel (Dan. 6:10), and some of the early Christians (Acts 4:23–31). Tennyson showed an awareness of the power of prayer when he said, "More things are wrought by prayer than this world dreams of." Surely God's merciful forbearance toward sinful man is closely linked with timely intercession.

Throughout history, men who have been greatly used of God were intercessors in prayer. It is reported that John Welch kept his coat by his bedside at night. In the middle of the night, he would fall to his knees, wrap the coat around his shoulders, and begin to weep and pray. His wife would say to him, "Honey, you had better get your rest. You have work to do tomorrow." Old John Welch would answer, "Woman, I have many souls at my charge and I know not how it is with their souls."

David Brainard, a missionary to the American Indians, said, "I love to be alone in my cottage where I can spend much time in prayer."

John Fletcher prayed so frequently that the walls of his room were stained by his breath. He knelt so often and stayed so long that his knees left indentations on the floor.

Eight times a day Adoniram Judson would get on his knees and spend time with God. He talked to God every day at 3:00, 6:00, 9:00, and 12:00—around the clock.

When God wanted to send a revival to America, He used Francis Asbury. For forty-five years this circuit-riding preacher took the good news to people. He rode 175,000 miles by horse, 25,000 miles by carriage, and preached 20,000 sermons. When he arrived in America in 1771 there were fewer than 80 preachers and 14,000 members of Methodism. When he died forty-five years later, there were 2,000 preachers and 200,000 members. America at that time had five million people and it is estimated that the Methodists were reaching half of them. The secret to Francis Asbury's life? He arose at 4:00 A.M. every day for prayer. Such is the commitment of men who do great things for God!

God hears Moses' fervent prayer and renews the covenant (10:1–5). Exodus 34 gives the account in detail. Here Moses condenses the incident in Deuteronomic fashion, omitting details that presumably are already well known. He also adds information about the making of the ark which would contain the commandments. The purpose of this summarizing section is to make known that God in His mercy has renewed the covenant with His rebellious people. The covenant's placement in the ark will make it secure, inaccessible, permanent, and available only as Moses teaches from it and about it.[2] The writing on the second set of tablets is the same as the first; the covenant does not change.

The writings were given to Moses and placed in the ark, *"and there they are"* (v. 5). References to the ark are rare in Deuteronomy. It is only referred to here and in 31:26. This is a little surprising when one considers the ark's important role in the life of Israel. This may be because Deuteronomy is more concerned with the covenant itself than with details about the construction of the ark or with the rituals associated with the central sanctuary.

Not only did God restore the covenant but He also restored the priesthood of Aaron, and, despite Aaron's sin at Sinai, invested his son with the same high office at his death. While the duty of high priest at the central sanctuary was confined to Aaron's family, the task of guarding the law and the ark where the covenant documents were housed was given to the tribe of Levi as a whole.

Three principal functions of the Levites are outlined (v. 8). (1) They were to carry the ark. (2) The Levites were to *stand before the Lord to minister to Him.*" In the Old Testament, this phrase is used to indicate several different kinds of service—such as that of a servant to his master, or a prophet to God, or a priest to God (Deut. 17:12; Judg. 20:28; 1 Kings 10:8; 12:8; 17:1; 18:15; Ezek. 44:15). (3) Finally, they were to *bless in His name.*" We will discuss the Levites more fully when we reach Deuteronomy 18:1–8.

The results of Moses' interceding on behalf of Israel are summed up in verses 10–11. Again, his unique ministry as mediator for the people is highlighted. The covenant relationship between God and His people was intact because of the intercession of Moses and the grace of God.

NOTES

1. P. C. Craigie, *Commentary on the Book of Deuteronomy,* New International Commentary on the Old Testament (Grand Rapids: Wm. B. Eerdmans Publishing Co., 1976), p. 197.

2. B. Peckham, "The Composition of Deuteronomy 9:1–10:11," *Word and Spirit* (Willowdale, Ontario: Regis College Press, 1975), p. 51.

CHAPTER TWELVE

Respond with Total Obedience

Deuteronomy 10:12–11:32

ISRAEL MUST OBEY GOD BECAUSE OF
HIS GREATNESS

10:12 "And now, Israel, what does the LORD your God require of you, but to fear the LORD your God, to walk in all His ways and to love Him, to serve the LORD your God with all your heart and with all your soul,

13 "*and* to keep the commandments of the LORD and His statutes which I command you today for your good?

14 "Indeed heaven and the highest heavens belong to the LORD your God, *also* the earth with all that *is* in it.

15 "The LORD delighted only in your fathers, to love them; and He chose their descendants after them, you above all peoples, as *it is* this day.

16 "Therefore circumcise the foreskin of your heart, and be stiff-necked no longer.

17 "For the LORD your God *is* God of gods and Lord of lords, the great God, mighty and awesome, who shows no partiality nor takes a bribe.

18 "He administers justice for the fatherless and the widow, and loves the stranger, giving him food and clothing.

19 "Therefore love the stranger, for you were strangers in the land of Egypt.

20 "You shall fear the LORD your God; you shall serve Him, and to Him you shall hold fast, and take oaths in His name.

21 "He *is* your praise, and He *is* your God, who has

done for you these great and awesome things which
your eyes have seen.

22 "Your fathers went down to Egypt with seventy
persons, and now the LORD your God has made you
as the stars of heaven in multitude."

Deut. 10:12–22

It is essential in the establishment of an effective relationship that
both parties understand the requirements. For a marriage to succeed,
both the husband and the wife need to have not only an understanding of expectations but also a commitment to meeting them. For
a business venture to be successful, the partners need to abide by a
contract which is clear to each of them. In this passage, Moses lays
out before the people what God requires of them.

They are *"to fear the Lord"* (v. 12). This does not mean that they
are to be frightened or afraid of Him. It does mean that they are to
possess an attitude of deep respect for Him—respect in response
to His faithfulness to them over the years. This fear or respect
begins inwardly but eventually will manifest itself outwardly. Israel's constant disobedience was outward evidence of a wrong inward attitude.

Israel is *"to walk in all His ways"* (v. 12). Our inward respect for
God will reveal itself in our walk with Him. "If we say that we have
fellowship with Him, and walk in darkness, we lie and do not practice the truth. But if we walk in the light as He is in the light, we
have fellowship with one another, and the blood of Jesus Christ His
Son cleanses us from all sin" (1 John 1:6–7). Both Moses and John
understood that our talk and our walk must be consistent.

The people are *"to love Him"* (v. 12). To love God with our total
being is the fulfillment of the great commandment. Love is giving a
person your full attention. And this is what God requires from His
people; anything less is unacceptable.

This degree of love will motivate Israel *"to serve . . . God with all
your heart and . . . soul"* (v. 12). The keeping of God's commandments and statutes demonstrates that we accept God's right to
provide rules for our conduct (v. 13). To challenge Israel to fulfill
God's requirements, Moses wisely points to the greatness and love of
God in the remaining verses. Three truths about God's greatness
stand out in verses 14–22.

First, God is *supreme, yet He stoops down to Israel* (vv. 14–15). The Lord's love for Israel is obvious: He *"delighted only in your fathers"* and *"chose their descendants."* In exhorting Israel to love God, Moses points out that her present position can be attributed directly to God's love for her in the past. The only appropriate response for Israel is to *"circumcise the foreskin of your heart, and be stiff-necked no longer"* (v. 16). An uncircumcised heart is one which is closed to acceptance of God, just as an uncircumcised ear (Jer. 6:10) is one which hears muffled sounds, and uncircumcised lips (Exod. 6:12, 30) cannot open fully to speak coherently. If the heart is circumcised, then that which hinders is cut away, and it becomes open and free from obstructions. The result of such a circumcision will be submission to the will of God and the end of stubbornness.

Second, God is *"mighty and awesome, who shows no partiality nor takes a bribe,"* yet He is sympathetic toward the weak and undefended (vv. 17–19). The combination of judicial sternness with humane consideration is unusual. It is these two qualities, which spell disaster for evildoers, that become a shield around *"the fatherless,"* *"the widow,"* and *"the stranger."* David knew God to be *"a father of the fatherless, a defender of widows"* (Ps. 68:5). Israel was to follow the example of God and *"love the stranger"* (v. 19) for a twofold reason: (1) The love of God extended beyond Israel to include aliens; (2) they were to remember that in Egypt they, too, were once aliens who lacked respect and love.

Third, God is powerful, yet also personal (vv. 20–22). This God, whom Israel is to *"fear," "serve,"* and *"hold fast,"* enabled Israel's fathers, who only numbered seventy, to bring about Egypt's downfall. One evidence of God's blessing upon them was the procreation of seven hundred thousand men from the original seventy in less than two hundred and fifty years. His greatness to His children demands a response of total obedience.

ISRAEL MUST OBEY GOD BECAUSE OF WHAT THEY HAVE SEEN

11:1 *Therefore you shall love the LORD your God, and keep His charge, His statutes, His judgments, and His commandments always.*

2 "Know today that *I do* not *speak* with your children, who have not known and who have not seen the chastening of the LORD your God, His greatness and His mighty hand and His outstretched arm—

3 "His signs and His acts which He did in the midst of Egypt, to Pharaoh king of Egypt, and to all his land;

4 "what He did to the army of Egypt, to their horses and their chariots: how He made the waters of the Red Sea overflow them as they pursued you, and *how* the LORD has destroyed them to this day;

5 "what He did for you in the wilderness until you came to this place;

6 "and what He did to Dathan and Abiram the sons of Eliab, the son of Reuben: how the earth opened its mouth and swallowed them up, their households, their tents, and all the substance that *was* in their possession, in the midst of all Israel—

7 "but your eyes have seen every great act of the LORD which He did."

Deut. 11:1–7

Once again, Moses places special emphasis on the inseparability of love and obedience (see also 6:5–6; 7:9; 10:12–13; 11:13, 22; 19:9; 30:16, 20). The ultimate test of an Israelite's love for God was his obedience to God (John 14:15).

All of Israel's history had been guided by the Lord for the purpose of motivating them to love Him totally. *"The chastening of the Lord"* (v. 2) refers to God's moral education of His people. Israel's natural bent was toward waywardness. God's response to this condition was to send Israel "to school" in Egypt so she might learn of His power. Notice in verses 3 and 4 that God is doing all the work; no credit at all is given to Israel.

After the Egyptian experience, the Lord sent His children "to school" in the wilderness for forty years. Here their education was further refined as they had to depend upon Him totally for all their needs. In the Exodus experience the people learned about God's grace and power; in the desert they learned of His providential care. Then in the rebellion of Dathan and Abiram (detailed in Num. 16), Israel learned about God's holiness. Had it not been for Moses' intercession, the Lord would have put an end to an entire nation for their grumbling and unbelief (Num. 16:41–50). The contrast between the results of the exodus and the rebellion is striking. The exodus had meant new life for the children of Israel; the rebellion had led to the death of many.

Moses exhorted the people to learn from their past, for God had constructed their history with a didactic purpose. *"Your children . . . have not known and . . . have not seen. . . . but your eyes have seen"* (vv. 2, 7) hints at the parents' responsibility to model obedient living and pass on to their children the truths learned from past experiences.

ISRAEL MUST OBEY GOD BECAUSE OF WHAT THEY WILL RECEIVE

11:8 "Therefore you shall keep every commandment which I command you today, that you may be strong, and go in and possess the land which you cross over to possess,

9 "and that you may prolong *your* days in the land which the LORD swore to give your fathers, to them and their descendants, 'a land flowing with milk and honey.'

10 "For the land which you go to possess *is* not like the land of Egypt from which you have come, where you sowed your seed and watered *it* by foot, as a vegetable garden;

11 "but the land which you cross over to possess *is* a land of hills and valleys, which drinks water from the rain of heaven,

12 "a land for which the LORD your God cares; the eyes of the LORD your God *are* always on it, from the beginning of the year to the very end of the year.

13 'And it shall be that if you earnestly obey My commandments which I command you today, to love the LORD your God and serve Him with all your heart and with all your soul,

14 'then I will give *you* the rain for your land in its season, the early rain and the latter rain, that you may gather in your grain, your new wine, and your oil.

15 'And I will send grass in your fields for your
livestock, that you may eat and be filled.'
16 "Take heed to yourselves, lest your heart be deceived, and you turn aside and serve other gods and
worship them,
17 "lest the LORD's anger be aroused against you,
and He shut up the heavens so that there be no rain,
and the land yield no produce, and you perish quickly
from the good land which the LORD is giving you."

Deut. 11:8-17

Moses wanted Israel to draw an important conclusion from his
brief review of their history. Whether they experienced God's grace
or His judgment depended on their moral behavior. Therefore, their
ability to *"be strong, and go in and . . . prolong your days in the land"*
(vv. 8-9), was ultimately a question of their obedience to God, not of
their military skill. In verse 10 Moses begins to contrast Egypt with
Canaan. There is good news and bad news for Israel as they approach the promised land. The good news is that God has made
Canaan have a greater potential for agriculture than Egypt. It *"drinks
water from the rain of heaven"* (v. 11). It enjoys the constant care of
God, for His *"eyes . . . are always on it"* (v. 12). The "bad news" is
that contrary to the situation in Egypt, where they irrigated and depended upon human ingenuity or skill to provide water for the crops
(v. 10), here they must be obedient to God and depend upon Him to
bring the rains (vv. 13-15). This is bad news when Israel's past
record of disobedience and of turning to other gods is taken into
account. If they do this, God will *"shut up the heavens so that there be
no rain, and the land yield no produce, and you perish quickly"* (v. 17).

ISRAEL MUST OBEY GOD BECAUSE OF HIS BLESSINGS ON THEIR FAMILY

11:18 "Therefore you shall lay up these words of mine
in your heart and in your soul, and bind them as a
sign on your hand, and they shall be as frontlets between your eyes.
19 "You shall teach them to your children, speaking of them when you sit in your house, when you

walk by the way, when you lie down, and when you rise up.

20 "And you shall write them on the doorposts of your house and on your gates,

21 "that your days and the days of your children may be multiplied in the land of which the LORD swore to your fathers to give them, like the days of the heavens above the earth."

Deut. 11:18–21

With slight variations, these verses are a repetition of Deuteronomy 6:6–9 (see comments previously given). Moses again stresses the importance of visual symbols of God's commands.

Experts in the field of communications say that our learning is 89 percent visual, 10 percent auditory, and 1 percent through the other senses. Moses wanted to make sure that family members continually had the law *"in your heart and in your soul."* The continual reading, teaching, and discussion of God's word would bring God's blessings.

This same principle applies to Christians today. Recently, my wife Margaret and I went out to dinner with some friends that we had not seen for eight months. Right away, we both noticed a positive change in the wife. During our conversation we both commented on this wonderful change in her attitude. She enthusiastically responded, "Lately I've spent more time alone with God. Through prayer and Bible reading I am experiencing a change of attitude toward myself and others." We all rejoiced at what God was doing in her life. Paul exhorts all Christians to "let the word of Christ dwell in you richly" (Col. 3:16).

ISRAEL MUST OBEY GOD BECAUSE OF THE VICTORIES THEY WILL ACCOMPLISH

11:22 "For if you carefully keep all these commandments which I command you to do—to love the LORD your God, to walk in all His ways, and to hold fast to Him—

23 "then the LORD will drive out all these nations from before you, and you will dispossess greater and mightier nations than yourselves.

24 "Every place on which the sole of your foot treads shall be yours: from the wilderness and Lebanon, from the river, the River Euphrates, even to the Western Sea, shall be your territory.

25 "No man shall be able to stand against you; the LORD your God will put the dread of you and the fear of you upon all the land where you tread, just as He has said to you."

Deut. 11:22–25

At this point in his speech, Moses turns from the theme of longevity in the land to the theme of successful conquest of the land. If Israel is obedient, the Lord will grant her supernatural success against superior enemies. The promise to enlarge Israel's boundaries to *"every place on which the sole of your foot treads"* was repeated to Joshua right before Israel crossed the Jordan (Josh. 1:3). But only in the days of King David did Israel ever control anything like the area promised to Abraham in Genesis 15:18–21.

ISRAEL MUST OBEY GOD BECAUSE OF THE CONSEQUENCE OF THEIR CHOICES

11:26 "Behold, I set before you today a blessing and a curse:

27 "the blessing, if you obey the commandments of the LORD your God which I command you today;

28 "and the curse, if you do not obey the commandments of the LORD your God, but turn aside from the way which I command you today, to go after other gods which you have not known.

29 "Now it shall be, when the LORD your God has brought you into the land which you go to possess, that you shall put the blessing on Mount Gerizim and the curse on Mount Ebal.

30 "*Are* they not on the other side of the Jordan, toward the setting sun, in the land of the Canaanites who dwell in the plain opposite Gilgal, beside the terebinth trees of Moreh?

31 "For you will cross over the Jordan and go in to possess the land which the LORD your God is giving you, and you will possess it and dwell in it.

32 "And you shall be careful to observe all the
statutes and judgments which I set before you today."

Deut. 11:26–32

This passage serves as a transition between the preaching of
chapters 5–11 of Deuteronomy and the list of laws that begins
in chapter 12. As W. L. Moran has observed, the subjects listed here
are in reverse order of their actual treatment in the subsequent chapters: blessing and curse (11:26–28; 28); the ceremony at Shechem
between Ebal and Gerizim (11:29–31; 27); and the laws of the Lord
(11:32; 12–26).[1]

It is clear that the commandments were not just a body of legislation that was to be obeyed simply for the sake of obedience. But
these commands reflected a right way to live. To obey brought prosperity and close relationship to God. To disobey resulted in disaster
and separation from God. Therefore, in his exposition of the details
of the law that followed, Moses' role was not that of a great legalist
or jurist, but of a leader deeply concerned that the people under his
charge should enter into the fullness of life that was their potential if
they upheld the covenant relationship with God.[2]

"Behold I set before you today a blessing and a curse" (v. 26). Israel
must make a major decision. Their choice will determine whether
they receive the blessing or the curse. What we do at the major
crossroads of life not only reveals who we are but has a great deal to
do with who we will become. William James said that every person
is in "life's living option." By this he meant four things. (1) Every
person has a choice to make. (2) Every person has the ability to
make that choice. (3) Every choice has a consequence. (4) While the
person is choosing, he or she is in one of the choices.

It is always difficult to make a decision when there is insufficient
information available. Israel, however, will not have this problem.
Their leader Moses has repeatedly reminded them of God's ability.
They lack neither illustrations of God's power nor motivation to do
what is right. Their challenge will not be knowing the right decision
but doing it. Choices may be made in a moment, but the fruit of
those choices can be endless.

In decision-making, timing and location are crucially important.
Moses, realizing that the right time and the right location have

178

coincided, calls upon Israel to make her decision. In my book, *Your Attitude: Key to Success,* I discuss the importance of decision-making at the appropriate time.

> The wrong decision at the wrong time = disaster.
> The wrong decision at the right time = mistake.
> The right decision at the wrong time = unacceptance.
> The right decision at the right time = success.[3]

NOTES

1. R. C. Fuller, ed., "Deuteronomy," *A New Catholic Commentary on Holy Scripture* (Camden, NJ: Thomas Nelson Publishers, 1969), p. 267.

2. P. C. Craigie, *Commentary on the Book of Deuteronomy,* New International Commentary on the Old Testament (Grand Rapids: Wm. B. Eerdmans Publishing Co., 1976), pp. 212–13.

3. John C. Maxwell, *Your Attitude: Key to Success,* (San Bernardino, CA: Here's Life Publication, 1984), p. 66.

CHAPTER THIRTEEN

Regulations Concerning Worship

Deuteronomy 12:1–32

12:1 "These *are* the statutes and judgments which you shall be careful to observe in the land which the Lord God of your fathers is giving you to possess, all the days that you live on the earth.

2 "You shall utterly destroy all the places where the nations which you shall dispossess served their gods, on the high mountains and on the hills and under every green tree.

3 "And you shall destroy their altars, break their *sacred* pillars, and burn their wooden images with fire; you shall cut down the carved images of their gods and destroy their names from that place.

4 "You shall not worship the Lord your God *with* such *things*.

5 "But you shall seek the place where the Lord your God chooses, out of all your tribes, to put His name for His dwelling place; and there you shall go.

6 "There you shall take your burnt offerings, your sacrifices, your tithes, the heave offerings of your hand, your vowed offerings, your freewill offerings, and the firstborn of your herds and flocks.

7 "And there you shall eat before the Lord your God, and you shall rejoice in all to which you have put your hand, you and your households, in which the Lord your God has blessed you.

8 "You shall not at all do as we are doing here to-day—every man doing whatever *is* right in his own eyes—

9 "for as yet you have not come to the rest and the inheritance which the Lord your God is giving you.

10 "But *when* you cross over the Jordan and dwell in the land which the LORD your God is giving you to inherit, and He gives you rest from all your enemies round about, so that you dwell in safety,

11 "then there will be the place where the LORD your God chooses to make His name abide. There you shall bring all that I command you: your burnt offerings, your sacrifices, your tithes, the heave offerings of your hand, and all your choice offerings which you vow to the LORD.

12 "And you shall rejoice before the LORD your God, you and your sons and your daughters, your male and female servants and the Levite who *is* within your gates, since he has no portion nor inheritance with you.

13 "Take heed to yourself that you do not offer your burnt offerings in every place that you see;

14 "but in the place which the LORD chooses, in one of your tribes, there you shall offer your burnt offerings, and there you shall do all that I command you.

15 "However, you may slaughter and eat meat within all your gates, whatever your heart desires, according to the blessing of the LORD your God which He has given you; the unclean and the clean may eat of it, of the gazelle and the deer alike.

16 "Only you shall not eat the blood; you shall pour it on the earth like water.

17 "You may not eat within your gates the tithe of your grain or your new wine or your oil, of the first-born of your herd or your flock, of any of your offerings which you vow, of your freewill offerings, or of the heave offering of your hand.

18 "But you must eat them before the LORD your God in the place which the LORD your God chooses, you and your son and your daughter, your male servant and your female servant, and the Levite who *is* within your gates; and you shall rejoice before the LORD your God in all to which you put your hands.

19 "Take heed to yourself that you do not forsake the Levite as long as you live in your land.

20 "When the LORD your God enlarges your border

as He has promised you, and you say, 'Let me eat
meat,' because you long to eat meat, you may eat as
much meat as your heart desires.

21 "If the place where the LORD your God chooses
to put His name is too far from you, then you may
slaughter from your herd and from your flock which
the LORD has given you, just as I have commanded
you, and you may eat within your gates as much
as your heart desires.

22 "Just as the gazelle and the deer are eaten, so
you may eat them; the unclean and the clean alike
may eat them.

23 "Only be sure that you do not eat the blood, for
the blood *is* the life; you may not eat the life with the
meat.

24 "You shall not eat it; you shall pour it on the
earth like water.

25 "You shall not eat it, that it may go well with
you and your children after you, when you do *what is*
right in the sight of the LORD.

26 "Only the holy things which you have, and your
vowed offerings, you shall take and go to the place
which the LORD chooses.

27 "And you shall offer your burnt offerings, the
meat and the blood, on the altar of the LORD your
God; and the blood of your sacrifices shall be poured
out on the altar of the LORD your God, and you shall
eat the meat.

28 "Observe and obey all these words which I
command you, that it may go well with you and your
children after you forever, when you do *what is* good
and right in the sight of the LORD your God.

29 "When the LORD your God cuts off from before
you the nations which you go to dispossess, and you
displace them and dwell in their land,

30 "take heed to yourself that you are not ensnared
to follow them, after they are destroyed from before
you, and that you do not inquire after their gods, saying, 'How did these nations serve their gods? I also
will do likewise.'

31 "You shall not worship the LORD your God in that
way; for every abomination to the LORD which He

hates they have done to their gods; for they burn even
their sons and daughters in the fire to their gods.
32 "Whatever I command you, be careful to observe
it; you shall not add to it nor take away from it."

Deut. 12:1–32

Deuteronomy 12–26 is a long series of laws. Some passages are
duplicates of other legal sections of the Pentateuch; others are adop-
tions of additional laws; and still others are new. In 1:5 we read,
"Moses began to explain this law." However, what immediately followed that is not what we would think of as law, but rather four
chapters of historical review accented by exhortation.

A phrase similar to that used in 1:5 is repeated in 4:44: "Now this is
the law which Moses set before the children of Israel." So the style we
saw in Deuteronomy 11 was not unusual for Moses; he again enumer-
ated a series of historical reminiscences and appealed for obedience.
This narrative had a purpose, though—it provided a foundation
upon which to superimpose the laws themselves. The God who
speaks a word of law (12–26) does so only after He has spoken a
word of grace (1–11). The divine standards are not set in a vacuum
but are set against the bountiful resources of a gracious God.

Israel is to obey these laws not in order to become holy; rather, she
is to obey them because she is holy. The observance of law is a by-
product of holiness, not a means of attaining holiness.[1]

That this first section of law should be connected with worship is,
no doubt, deliberate. Unless Israel is properly related to Yahweh, the
divine Ruler of the nation, she will never realize her full nation-
hood. A true understanding and practice of worship will ensure
Israel's place in Canaan, whereas a corruption of worship will bring
ill effects throughout the land.

Chapter 12 raises two cardinal issues. One concerns Israel's attitude toward non-Yahweh sanctuaries; the other relates to the importance of the place God chooses for the people's worship. The really
critical question about this chapter is whether it deals primarily
with centralization of worship or with purity of worship and proper
recognition of God's sovereignty. Certainly the number of sanctuaries was to be limited and not like the numerous cult centers scattered through the land. Yet, there were allowances made for those
who lived a long way from the sanctuary. Most of Deuteronomy is

concerned with ordinances which neither require nor mention a demand for centralization. It is my opinion that Deuteronomy 12 commands a central sanctuary but not necessarily a sole sanctuary. The ultimate fulfillment of the command for a central sanctuary wouldn't come until centuries later when God allowed David to move the tabernacle to Jerusalem, where his son Solomon later built the temple. The central sanctuary emphasized (1) the unity of God; (2) the purity of the Israelites' worship of the Lord; and (3) the political and spiritual unity of the people.

In dealing homiletically with this chapter, we must take it as a whole. To sever it into paragraphs in chronological order would take away from the unity of its message. The repetition in this chapter can become a bit tedious. But remember that Deuteronomy was presented to Israel in sermonic form. Normally, repetition is important in the learning process, but it is doubly important in oral presentation, as the audience does not have the privilege of rereading something missed the first time.

One of the major themes of Deuteronomy—centralization of worship—is most clearly articulated in this chapter. The phrase *"the place . . . the Lord your God chooses"* appears six times in this chapter (12:5, 11, 14, 18, 21, 26). It can also be found three times in chapter 14, one time in chapter 15, six times in chapter 16, three times in chapter 17, one time in chapters 18 and 26, for a total of twenty-one times.

This place God chooses for His people will be a place where God is present (vv. 5, 11, 21). Verses 5 and 21 say, *"the place where the Lord your God chooses to put His name."* Verse 11 reads, *"Then there will be the place where the Lord your God chooses to make His name abide."* The phrase "to put one's name," or a variation of it, is not unique to Scripture. G. J. Wenham observes that in cuneiform literature this expression has at least three nuances. The phrase is used as an affirmation of ownership, the equivalent of taking possession. It is used in texts describing conquests and is associated with the erection of victory monuments. The phrase may be used in inscribing a name on the foundation stones of sanctuaries.[2]

All three of these variations are applicable to Deuteronomy. God possesses not only the place where He is worshiped but also the people who worship Him. True worship recognizes the lordship of Jesus, the sovereignty of God. The fact that Israel would worship

God where *"He gives you rest from all your enemies round about"* (v. 10) is definitely a result of the victories God has given them over their enemies. And what could be more appropriate than for God to put His own signature on the place of worship? For He is "a chief cornerstone, elect, precious, / And he who believes on Him will by no means be put to shame" (1 Pet. 2:6).

Throughout Deuteronomy, God establishes the fact that He will walk among His people (16:16; 23:14, 16; 26:10). The children of Israel can rest assured that God will be with them as they enter the land of great challenges and opportunities. God's assurance to Joshua, "Every place that the sole of your foot will tread upon I have given you," is underscored by His presence.

One night a man had a dream. He dreamed he was walking along the beach with the Lord. Across the sky flashed scenes from his life. In each scene he noticed two sets of footprints in the sand—one belonging to him and the other belonging to the Lord. When the last scene had flashed before him, he looked back at the footprints and realized that many times along the path there was actually only one set of footprints in the sand. He also noted that this happened at the lowest and saddest times in his life. This really bothered him and he questioned the Lord, "Lord, you said that once I decided to follow You, You would walk with me all the way. But I have noticed during the most troublesome times in my life, there is only one set of footprints. I don't understand why when I needed You the most You would leave me."

The Lord replied, "My precious, precious child, I love you and would never leave you. During your times of trial and suffering, when you see only one set of footprints, it was then that I carried you."

The people will gather at the place God chooses. Notice the phrases *"there you shall go"* (v. 5); *"there you shall bring all that I command you"* (v. 11); *"there you shall offer"* (v. 14); *"there you shall do"* (v. 14). When they come to that place of worship there are several things they are to do.

They are to bring offerings to the Lord (vv. 6, 11, 13, 14, 17, 26, 27). There were seven types of offerings (v. 6). (1) *"Burnt offerings"* were to be completely burned on the altar. They were to be given at various times to achieve atonement for the offerer. (2) *"Sacrifices"* were offerings of thanksgiving to God which brought fellowship between man and God. There were three kinds of sacrifices: praise, thanksgiving, and devotional. (3) *"Tithes"* were to be comprised of grain, wine, oil, and the firstborn of the herds and flocks (see 14:22–29). (4) *"Heave offerings"* represented a portion that was lifted up from the larger mass and set aside for the use of the priests. (5) *"Vowed offerings"* represented promises made to God in time of crisis. The (6) *"freewill offerings"* and (7) *"firstborn of your herds and flocks"* have already been discussed.

They are to rejoice before the Lord (vv. 7, 12, 18). An Israelite worship service will be characterized by joy. They will rejoice in God's blessings with their families. Eating and rejoicing in the Lord's presence occurs several times in Deuteronomy (vv. 7, 11–12, 18; 14:26; 16:10–11, 14–15).

They are to obey the Lord (vv. 28, 32). Obedience to God's commands is the principal prerequisite for obtaining His blessing. This exhortation to obey is very common in Deuteronomy. The result of obedience is that it will *"go well with"* Israel and her descendants (v. 28).

The Israelites are to worship the one God in the place He chooses in a different manner than that in which *"the nations which you shall dispossess served their gods"* (v. 2). Deuteronomy 12 both begins and ends with a strong warning not to emulate the other nations' style of worship. *"Take heed to yourself that you are not ensnared to follow them . . . and that you do not inquire . . . 'How did these nations serve their gods? I also will do likewise.' You shall not worship the Lord your God in that way; for every abomination to the Lord which He hates they have done to their gods"* (vv. 30–31). This warning and the explicitness of the directions for meat sacrifices (vv. 15–27) seem to suggest that the real issue is not one sanctuary versus many sanctuaries but true worship versus false worship.

The sanctity of God's place is seen in verses 1–4. Israel was commanded to destroy *"all the places"* where the foreign gods were worshiped. The custom of placing shrines on *"mountains"* and *"hills"* and *"under every green tree"* is referred to elsewhere in the Old Testament as a practice of the Canaanites. It was copied by Israel in times of apostasy (1 Kings 14:23; 2 Kings 16:4; 17:10; 2 Chron. 28:4; Isa. 57:5; Jer. 2:20; 3:6, 13), making reform necessary. When the Israelites stood with Moses on the western side of the Jordan, they could see the promised land studded with shrines. God wanted the remnants of idolatry blotted out because He understood the temptation these would become to His people.

But it was not until a later day that God's desire that Israel rule the entire promised land would become a possibility. When the possibility arose, however, Israel lacked fortitude and did, in fact, tolerate shrines to other gods. Attempts were made at reform by Asa (1 Kings 15:11–14), Hezekiah (2 Kings 18:3–4), and Josiah (2 Kings 23:4–25; 2 Chron. 34:3–7). Only Josiah achieved a great measure of success, but on his death, pagan worship reappeared. Israel was to be different. Turning to idols would cause them to be driven out of Canaan, just as God allowed them to drive out the former inhabitants.

The place God chooses is to be a place of ministry. Deuteronomy gives much attention to the Levites, through whom God ministers to the people. The Israelites were to include the Levites in family festivals (v. 12) and to provide for their needs (v. 19). Who were these Levites to whom Moses so often refers? Originally they were members of the tribe of Levi. In early times different special duties in connection with the tabernacle were allotted to sub-branches of the tribe, although only members of one family (Aaron's) actually officiated at the altar. They may have fulfilled a teaching function within the villages (33:10). More detail on the Levites is provided in 18:1–8. Of interest in Deuteronomy 12 is the provision made for these people who ministered.

The four characteristics of a place to worship God carry over from the Old Testament to the New. Our place of worship, too, should be: (1) a place where God is present (1 Cor. 1:2; Col. 1:24); (2) a place where God's people gather (Acts 2:46–47; Heb. 10:25); (3) a place that is different from the world (John 17:14–16); (4) a place of ministry (Eph. 4:11–12; Heb. 10:24).

NOTES

1. Victor P. Hamilton, *Handbook on the Pentateuch* (Grand Rapids: Baker Book House, 1982), p. 415.
2. Gordon J. Wenham, "Deuteronomy and the Central Sanctuary," *TB* 22 (1971): 103–18.

CHAPTER FOURTEEN

Potential Influences to Idolatry

Deuteronomy 13:1–18

Moses is still dealing with the subject of purity in worship. In Deuteronomy 12 the emphasis was on idolatry. Here in Deuteronomy 13, the emphasis is on the idolater. The previous chapter dealt with places that might tempt Israel to serve other gods; here, Moses deals with people who might tempt them. These people will not be Canaanites or enemies. They will be people that Israel respects, people who have a definite influence upon them.

Helmut Thielicke, in his sermon series on the Lord's Prayer, says that the petition "lead us not into temptation" should more accurately be phrased "let nothing become a temptation to me."

A temptation is anything that might draw us away from the Father. The Evil One will use anything at any time to achieve this purpose. His goal is simple and clear; it's his strategy that is complex.

Thielicke points out that in Martin Luther's hymn, "A Mighty Fortress Is Our God," the most dangerous competitors for the kingdom of God are not "this world, with devils filled," for "the Prince of Darkness grim, / We tremble not for him." But the closing command is, "Let goods and kindred go, / This mortal life also." By this reasoning our most dangerous enemies may be not only our material possessions and our loved ones, but also intangibles, such as security, reputation, and relationships.

Moses, understanding that the temptation of idolatry may be attractive and appealing to the people, spells out for Israel three possible sources of temptation.

RELIGIOUS LEADERS

13:1 "If there arises among you a prophet or a dreamer of dreams, and he gives you a sign or a wonder,

2 "and the sign or the wonder comes to pass, of which he spoke to you, saying, 'Let us go after other gods,' which you have not known—'and let us serve them,'

3 "you shall not listen to the words of that prophet or that dreamer of dreams, for the LORD your God is testing you to know whether you love the LORD your God with all your heart and with all your soul.

4 "You shall walk after the LORD your God and fear Him, and keep His commandments and obey His voice; you shall serve Him and hold fast to Him.

5 "But that prophet or that dreamer of dreams shall be put to death, because he has spoken in order to turn *you* away from the LORD your God, who brought you out of the land of Egypt and redeemed you from the house of bondage, to entice you from the way in which the LORD your God commanded you to walk. So you shall put away the evil in your midst."

Deut. 13:1-5

The first source of temptation might be *"a prophet or a dreamer of dreams"* (v. 1). After all, both prophecy and dreams were legitimate means of revelation in Israel; prophets were highly esteemed among the people. Moses promised Israel that God would raise up another prophet after his death for the people to follow. To better understand the relationship between prophecy and the gift of a vision in a dream, see Numbers 12:6. In the eyes of Israel, a prophet's credibility would be increased when he gave them *"the sign or the wonder"* and it *"comes to pass."* Miraculous signs alone were never meant to be a proof of truth. So Moses warned the people that the standard for truth must not be a *"sign"* or *"wonder"* or any other area of human experience. The standard of truth is God's word.

If a prophet or a dreamer's prediction came true but his message contradicted God's commands, the people were to trust God and His word rather than the *"sign."* No true prophet would encourage the people to break the first commandment (5:7) or the greatest commandment, to love God wholeheartedly (6:5). The gods that Israel would be tempted to follow were ones that *"you have not known"* (v. 2). The word used here for *"known"* implies experience of something rather than intellectual knowledge. Israel *"knew"* God because of His many interactions with them: He had proved Himself faithful to the people. They had no such knowledge of other gods.

Three steps of action were to be taken by Israel when a false prophet attempted to turn their heads toward other gods. First, they were to *"not listen to the words of that prophet or that dreamer of dreams"* (v. 3). Second, they were to view each enticement to idolatry as a test *"to know whether you love the Lord your God with all your heart and with all your soul"* (v. 3). Though there was always a danger that they might yield to temptation, each time they resisted their faith and love for God would grow stronger (James 1:2–4). The most effective way to overcome this testing is to *"walk . . . fear . . . keep . . . obey . . . serve . . . hold fast to Him"* (v. 4). (Note similar comments in Deut. 10:20; 11:22; 30:20.) Here again Moses uses repetition to get the point across. Third, Israel was to kill the false prophet. Why such severe punishment? *"Because he has spoken in order to turn you away from the Lord your God"* (v. 5). This prophet has been encouraging a people redeemed by God's faithfulness to be unfaithful. He has been calling for ingratitude from a people who had every reason to be grateful. Therefore, Moses instructs them to *"put away the evil in your midst"* (v. 5). Throughout Deuteronomy, he continually admonished the people to maintain spiritual purity (13:5; 17:7, 12; 19:19; 21:21; 22:21, 22, 24; 24:7). The consequence of not obeying this command was punishment for the evildoer and destruction of the community.

FAMILY AND CLOSE FRIENDS

13:6 "If your brother, the son of your mother, your son or your daughter, the wife of your bosom, or your friend who is as your own soul, secretly entices you, saying, 'Let us go and serve other gods,' which you have not known, neither you nor your fathers,

7 "of the gods of the people which *are* all around you, near to you or far off from you, from *one* end of the earth to the *other* end of the earth,

8 "you shall not consent to him or listen to him, nor shall your eye pity him, nor shall you spare him or conceal him;

9 "but you shall surely kill him; your hand shall be first against him to put him to death, and afterward the hand of all the people.

10 "And you shall stone him with stones until he dies, because he sought to entice you away from the LORD your God, who brought you out of the land of Egypt, from the house of bondage.

11 "So all Israel shall hear and fear, and not again do such wickedness as this among you."

Deut. 13:6-11

Moses now addresses the most painful of all temptations he can envision, the temptation to idolatry by a loved one. Notice the endearing terminology Moses uses to describe family members: *". . . the wife of your bosom, or your friend who is as your own soul . . ."* (v. 6). The temptation of the false prophet or dreamer would be made openly, based on a sign or a wonder. Now Moses points out the possibility of being tempted by a trusted friend or a relative who *"secretly entices you, saying, 'Let us go and serve other gods.'"*

We do not need to live in Moses' day to understand the influence of friends and relatives. The following statistics underline the fact that loved ones have a tremendous influence on our lives. In a survey ten thousand people were asked the question, "What was responsible for your coming to the church?" The results:

Special Need	2%
Walk-In	3%
Pastor	6%
Visitation	1%
Sunday School	5%
Evangelistic Crusade	1%
Program	3%
Friend/Relative	79%

The response of the person being tempted is to be fivefold. *"You shall* (1) *not consent to him* (2) *or listen to him,* (3) *nor shall your eye pity him,* (4) *nor shall you spare him or conceal him;* (5) *but you shall surely kill him"* (vv. 8–9). It would be easy for a family member to rationalize the behavior of the evildoer or at least try to "sweep it under the rug." The tempter placed his family under enormous pressure. To yield was to lose God's blessing. Not to yield was to lose human affection and to deal with the tempter according to the law. Here we see that God's commands were designed to overrule human feelings and experiences. The tempted person was to throw the first stone at the tempter, thereby testifying to the truth of the testimony against the tempter. The participation of the rest of the community showed their allegiance to the Lord and their resolute hostility toward anything that might endanger that allegiance and *"entice [them] away from the Lord"* (v. 10).

The result of such drastic action would be that *"all Israel shall hear and fear, and not again do such wickedness as this among you"* (v. 11). This extreme measure of discipline will bring fear to the people and stop the slide into idolatry. A graphic illustration of this is given in the story about Ananias's and Sapphira's lying to God about the selling of one of their possessions. After Peter exposed their deceitfulness, they fell dead (Acts 5:1–10). The result? "Great fear came upon all the church and upon all who heard these things" (Acts 5:11).

COMMUNITY LEADERS

13:12 "If you hear someone in one of your cities, which the LORD your God gives you to dwell in, saying,

13 'Corrupt men have gone out from among you and enticed the inhabitants of their city, saying, "Let us go and serve other gods"'—which you have not known—

14 "then you shall inquire, search out, and ask diligently. And *if it is* indeed true *and* certain *that* such an abomination was committed among you,

15 "you shall surely strike the inhabitants of that city with the edge of the sword, utterly destroying it,

all that is in it and its livestock—with the edge of the sword.

16 "And you shall gather all its plunder into the middle of the street, and completely burn with fire the city and all its plunder, for the LORD your God. It shall be a heap forever; it shall not be built again.

17 "So none of the accursed things shall remain in your hand, that the LORD may turn from the fierceness of His anger and show you mercy, have compassion on you and multiply you, just as He swore to your fathers,

18 "because you have listened to the voice of the LORD your God, to keep all His commandments which I command you today, to do *what is* right in the eyes of the LORD your God."

Deut. 13:12–18

In the situation Moses envisions here the crime of idolatry has already been committed on a large scale and measures are given to deal with large-scale apostasy.

The punishment of this sin was to be so drastic that before any action was taken the truth of the report must be confirmed by a thorough investigation. If the report was confirmed, then they were to treat the city like a Canaanite city—*"utterly destroying it, all that is in it and its livestock—with the edge of the sword"* (v. 15). The fact that *"all its plunder"* was to be destroyed, and that *"it shall not be built again"* eliminated greedy or illegitimate motivations on the part of those who were to carry out the punishment. The phrase *"it shall be a heap forever"* (v. 16) signifies that the town was to be an eternal hill. Every time outsiders saw the hill they would be reminded of God's judgment on idolatry. This is what happened to Achan and his family (Josh. 7:24–26) when he kept some of the spoil of Jericho. Only this drastic action will turn the Lord from His anger and bring back His mercy, compassion, and blessings upon the people (v. 17).

For the most part, Israel failed to obey the commands of Deuteronomy 13. The result of this failure was that eventually both the Northern and Southern Kingdoms fell and the people were carried into exile. Although these commands are not directly for today's Christians since we do not live under a theocracy, the principal lesson should be followed. Anything within our lives that turns us away from serving God must be dealt with quickly and severely (Matt. 18:8–9).

In each of these three paragraphs in Deuteronomy 13, Moses gives a different reason for the enticement to idolatry. In verses 1–5 he talks about temptation that results from a sign or wonder. Might Jesus have had this passage in mind when He spoke of false christs and prophets who would "show great signs and wonders" that appear so authentic as to fool even the elect (Matt. 24:24)?

In the second paragraph (vv. 6–11) it is the family that influences others to yield to temptation. Deuteronomy 12 highlights the home as a place of worship, rejoicing, and festivity. Deuteronomy 13 presents the other side of the home. It may be a place of temptation, a stumbling block rather than a stepping stone.

The third temptation to idolatry is peer pressure (vv. 12–18). *"[All] the inhabitants"* of a city have adopted the heretical teachings of others. Can "everyone" be wrong? Can a whole community be swayed? Can there be mass apostasy? Yes. But mass sinning also leads to mass repercussions.[1]

NOTE

1. Victor P. Hamilton, *Handbook on the Pentateuch* (Grand Rapids: Baker Book House, 1982), p. 422.

CHAPTER FIFTEEN

Regulations Concerning Mourning and Eating

Deuteronomy 14:1-21

IMPROPER MOURNING

14:1 "You *are* the children of the LORD your God; you shall not cut yourselves nor shave the front of your head for the dead.

2 "For you *are* a holy people to the LORD your God, and the LORD has chosen you to be a people for Himself, a special treasure above all the peoples who *are* on the face of the earth."

Deut. 14:1-2

In Deuteronomy 14, Moses is still concerned with the idea that Israel is to be distinctive from other nations. He not only desires that God's people shun the wicked things (Deut. 12–13), but also the more innocent things. Here, their leader turns his attention to the everyday affairs of life and calls for a distinctive lifestyle that would reflect Israel's unique position among all the nations.

The phrases *"you are the children of the Lord your God"* (v. 1) and *"for you are a holy people to the Lord your God"* (v. 2) are strongly emphasized in the Hebrew text by their position at the beginning of their respective sentences. Israelites' recognition of their identity as God's people should prepare them for the regulations that follow. Earlier in Deuteronomy Moses used the concept of a father/son relationship to illustrate the relationship between God and Israel (1:31) and to explain God's provision and care for His people (8:5). In this context, the emphasis is on the responsibility that rested upon the Israelites because of their intimate relation to God as "sons."[1]

God wanted His people's actions to reflect a different attitude toward death. Other nations symbolized their mourning the loss of loved ones by cutting themselves, drawing their own blood (cf. Jer. 16:6; 41:5; 47:5; 48:37). Even today mutilation of the body persists in some cultures. In New Guinea, a mourner, especially a woman, will remove a tip of a finger up to the first joint, and in extreme cases, more than one finger joint. Such practices were forbidden in Israel because they hinted at conformity to pagan practices.

John Milton said, "Death is the golden key that opens the palace of eternity." The Christian's approach to the death of a loved one should be outstandingly different from the world's approach. Paul wrote to the church of Thessalonica giving them timely words about the Christian's reaction to death. "But I do not want you to be ignorant, brethren, concerning those who have fallen asleep, lest you sorrow as others who have no hope. For if we believe that Jesus died and rose again, even so God will bring with Him those who sleep in Jesus. . . . Therefore, comfort one another with these words" (1 Thess. 4:13–14, 18). E. Stanley Jones declared, "Death is the anesthetic God uses while His children pass from one life to another."

And D. L. Moody, in discussing his own death with a friend, said, "One day you'll see in the paper: 'Moody is dead!' Don't you believe it! I'll be more alive than ever."

C. H. Spurgeon tells of a child who once found some beautiful eggs in a nest. A week later he visited the nest again, only to return home crying, "Mother, I had some beautiful eggs in this nest and now they're destroyed! There's nothing left but a few pieces of broken shell!" His mother's reply was comforting, "The eggs weren't destroyed. There were little birds inside those eggs and they've flown away and are singing in the branches of the trees."

"And," said Spurgeon, "so it is that when we look at our departed loved ones we are apt to say, 'Is this all you have left us, ruthless spoiler?' But faith whispers, 'No, the shell is broken, but among the birds of paradise, singing amid unwithering bowers, you shall find the spirits of your beloved ones; their true manhood is not here, but has ascended to its Father God.' You see it's not a loss to die; it is a gain, a lasting, a perpetual and unlimited gain!"

When Richard Baxter lay dying, racked with pain and disease, a friend asked him, "Dear Mr. Baxter, how are you?"

"Almost well!" replied Baxter—and he was right.

EATING

14:3 "You shall not eat any detestable thing.

4 "These *are* the animals which you may eat: the ox, the sheep, the goat,

5 "the deer, the gazelle, the roe deer, the wild goat, the mountain goat, the antelope, and the mountain sheep.

6 "And you may eat every animal with cloven hooves, having the hoof split into two parts, *and that* chews the cud, among the animals.

7 "Nevertheless, of those that chew the cud or have cloven hooves, you shall not eat, *such as* these: the camel, the hare, and the rock hyrax; for they chew the cud but do not have cloven hooves; they *are* unclean for you.

8 "Also the swine is unclean for you, because it has cloven hooves, yet *does* not *chew* the cud; you shall not eat their flesh or touch their dead carcasses.

9 "These you may eat of all that *are* in the waters: you may eat all that have fins and scales.

10 "And whatever does not have fins and scales you shall not eat; it *is* unclean for you.

11 "All clean birds you may eat.

12 "But these you shall not eat: the eagle, the vulture, the buzzard,

13 "the red kite, the falcon, and the kite after their kinds;

14 "every raven after its kind;

15 "the ostrich, the short-eared owl, the seagull, and the hawk after their kinds;

16 "the little owl, the screech owl, the white owl,

17 "the jackdaw, the carrion vulture, the fisher owl,

18 "the stork, the heron after its kind, and the hoopoe and the bat.

19 "Also every creeping thing that flies is unclean for you; they shall not be eaten.

20 "You may eat all clean birds.

21 "You shall not eat anything that dies *of itself;* you may give it to the alien who *is* within your gates, that he may eat it, or you may sell it to a foreigner;

for you *are* a holy people to the LORD your God. You
shall not boil a young goat in its mother's milk."

Deut. 14:3-21

Verses 13–21 will be treated as a whole rather than individually,
since the principle of clean and unclean food is more important than
the particular foods that are declared clean or unclean. In the New
Testament God abolished the food laws of the Old Testament (Mark
7:14–23; Acts 10:9–16). However, Christians should just as clearly
demonstrate their unique relationship with God by the purity of
their lives.

Scholars over many centuries have debated over the reasons underlying the regulations on permitted and prohibited food. Students
of these laws support a number of explanations for the distinction
between clean and unclean animals.

Perhaps the most popular modern explanation of the laws is that
certain animals were prohibited for sanitary purposes. An American
doctor conducted a series of experiments to determine the levels of
toxicity in the unrefrigerated meat of the animals, aquatic creatures,
and birds mentioned in Deuteronomy 14. He discovered that the
various types of prohibited meats contained a higher percentage of
toxic substances than those which were permitted.[2]

However, if this is the only explanation acceptable to the reader,
problems arise. (1) Why would God protect only the health of the
Jews? Verse 21 says, *"You shall not eat anything that dies of itself; you
may give it to the alien who is within your gates, that he may eat it, or
you may sell it to a foreigner; for you are a holy people to the Lord your
God."* If the unclean food would harm the health of the Israelite,
why does God authorize the giving or selling of it to an alien and
foreigner? (2) Jesus declared that all foods should be considered
clean (Mark 7:14–23). This was confirmed in a heavenly vision given
to Peter (Acts 10:9–16). It is difficult to believe that God was concerned about the health of His people in the Old Testament but
abandoned that concern in the New Testament. (3) Eating some of
the clean animals may represent a greater danger to health than eating some of the unclean ones. (4) No hygienic reasons are given in
Old Testament texts as motives for observing the law of the clean
and unclean; nowhere does the Old Testament state that the Israelites considered the unclean animals dangerous to their health.

God's people were to be separate. It was imperative that broad distinctions between Israel and the nations round about be maintained, and the food laws helped fulfill this purpose. The Canaanites lived a coarser, more animal-like life. Animal passions were fostered by the glutting of the appetites. The food laws brought discipline into the Jewish eating habits. The gluttonous habits of others were not to be the standards by which God's people should measure their own conduct. This was a visible means of their desire and effort to "not be conformed to this world." What is acceptable for others was not permitted for God's people. This would explain why Israel could give or sell meat that they personally were forbidden to eat. All the food laws reminded Israel of her unique status before God. No Israelite could eat without realizing that in every area of his life he was to be consecrated to God. Likewise, in the presence of Gentiles, an Israelite's diet served as a testimony of his special relationship to the Lord.

A friend of mine keeps a small cross in his pocket. He realizes that this cross does not act as a "good luck" charm; it is not placed there for superstitious reasons. But every time he reaches into his pocket for some change, it reminds him of who he is as a child of God and causes him to rejoice in his relationship with God. Perhaps the reason for the food regulations for God's people was similar. He made the distinctions so that Israel might have a way of expressing her unique relationship to Him, a relationship that was reflected even in what they ate.

Some unclean animals were used in pagan cultic rites. Evidence for this is that unclean animals are said to be *"detestable"* (v. 3). The Hebrew word used here is used also in 7:25 and 12:31, where it has been translated "abomination." In both those passages the word indicates an association with foreign religions. In 7:25, for example, silver and gold were to be discarded because of their association with the images of foreign gods. However, this explanation does not hold true when considering all the animals given in Deuteronomy 14. There are examples which contradict this explanation. For instance, the bull was a common symbol in the religions of the ancient Near East; yet it was permitted as food for the Israelites. Certainly this explanation cannot stand by itself in regard to this passage of Scripture.

Clean and unclean animals were symbolic of good and evil in the human realm. This explanation became extremely subjective and perhaps bordered on the ridiculous among earlier interpreters of the Old Testament. For instance, some held that chewing the cud (14:6–8) represented the faithful believer who meditated on the law. Others taught that the sheep was clean because it served as a reminder that the Lord is His people's shepherd. This symbolic interpretation should be rejected since it is impossible to validate.

The animals are divided into three classes: those that live on land, those that live in the water, and those that live in the air. It has been suggested that certain animals in each class provide the standard for that class and any deviation from that standard renders the animal unclean. For example, the unclean birds are birds of prey that eat the flesh without draining the blood, whereas the clean birds are presumably those that eat grain. Some suggest that this symbolizes the two classes of people: Gentiles who eat animal blood and animal flesh that they find dead already (v. 21), and Israelites who refrain from both. However, if such a standard exists, it is sometimes difficult to discern. *If* the clean and unclean animals symbolize the human realm, then the food laws serve the following function: They were pedagogical illustrations to Israel of her relationship to God and the nations.[3]

It was essential that the faith of Israel be maintained and displayed and *the food laws provided an opportunity to exercise faith and obedience*. Very clearly, God has assured them that this is His will concerning their dietary habits, and whether the regulations seemed reasonable or not, they were to obey. Such a test is quite similar to the one given to Adam and Eve concerning the forbidden fruit. Apart from God's command to the contrary, both they and Israel could have chosen to eat or not eat without any violation of conscience. From a human standpoint, God's rules made no sense. Therefore, according to this explanation, this was a higher test of obedience. To obey this command meant no sacrifice or hunger since many good meats were allowed. Here then was a true test of whether Israel would simply obey God's word. It was not the observance of the food laws per se that distinguished Israel as holy, but an attitude of total and willing allegiance to God in love and obedience. This obedience transcended human reasoning; it relied not upon outward conditions.

D. L. Moody said, "Our faith must be tested. God builds no ships but what He sends them to sea." Part of the training of a soldier is in the area of obedience. Each man must learn to unquestioningly obey orders without first having to understand the purpose behind them.

NOTES

1. P. C. Craigie, *Commentary on the Book of Deuteronomy*, New International Commentary on the Old Testament (Grand Rapids: Wm. B. Eerdmans Publishing Co., 1976), p. 229.

2. D. I. Macht, "An Experimental Pharmacological Appreciation of Leviticus 11 and Deuteronomy 14," *Bulletin of the History of Medicine* 27 (1953): 444–50.

3. John F. Walvoord and Roy B. Zuck, *The Bible Knowledge Commentary*, *O.T.* (Wheaton, IL: Victor Books, 1978), p. 288.

CHAPTER SIXTEEN

Regulations Concerning Giving

Deuteronomy 14:22–15:23

GIVING SUPPORT TO GOD'S WORK

14:22 "You shall truly tithe all the increase of your grain that the field produces year by year.

23 "And you shall eat before the LORD your God, in the place where He chooses to make His name abide, the tithe of your grain and your new wine and your oil, of the firstborn of your herds and your flocks, that you may learn to fear the LORD your God always.

24 "But if the journey is too long for you, so that you are not able to carry *the tithe, or* if the place where the LORD your God chooses to put His name is too far from you, when the LORD your God has blessed you,

25 "then you shall exchange *it* for money, take the money in your hand, and go to the place which the LORD your God chooses.

26 "And you shall spend that money for whatever your heart desires: for oxen or sheep, for wine or similar drink, for whatever your heart desires; you shall eat there before the LORD your God, and you shall rejoice, you and your household.

27 "You shall not forsake the Levite who *is* within your gates, for he has no part nor inheritance with you.

28 "At the end of *every* third year you shall bring out the tithe of your produce of that year and store *it* up within your gates.

29 "And the Levite, because he has no portion nor

> inheritance with you, and the stranger and the fa-
> therless and the widow who *are* within your gates,
> may come and eat and be satisfied, that the LORD
> your God may bless you in all the work of your
> hand which you do."
>
> *Deut. 14:22-29*

No subject grabs the attention of the congregation more than that of money. Recently I saw a humorous cartoon that showed a pastor standing in the pulpit saying, "I take my text this morning from line 34b of Form 1040, which deals with charitable contributions." Every year in January, I preach a series of messages concerning steward-ship. The entire congregation is again reminded of their responsibility concerning the management of the resources that God has given them. For many, January has been a life-changing month.

Here Moses gives Israel a stewardship sermon. He gives seven truths about tithing which are still valid today.

Tithing is to be a regular exercise (v. 22). The tithe specified in these verses deals only with the agricultural produce which the land would provide. Most of this chapter has dealt with what the Israelites could eat. Now they are given instructions on how much food they can keep and on when they should tithe it to the Lord. They are taught to *"tithe all the increase of your grain"* and to do so *"year by year."* By returning a tithe to God regularly, the people would know that their prosperity did not depend on irrigation or advanced agricultural techniques, but on the provision of their God. Deuteronomy 11:10-15 describes how God will bless the land so that it will yield crops for Israel.

Tithing is a spiritual exercise (v. 23). Israel is instructed to take the tithe and *"eat before the Lord your God."* Tithing is more than club dues! It is more of a spiritual matter than a financial one. Hundreds of years later, God spoke to Israel on the issue of tithing,

> 7   "Yet from the days of your fathers
>   You have gone away from My ordinances
>   And have not kept them.
>   Return to Me, and I will return to you,"
>   Says the LORD of hosts.
>   "But you said,
>   'In what way shall we return?'

8 Will a man rob God?
    Yet you have robbed Me!
    But you say
    'In what way have we robbed You?'
    In tithes and offerings."

Mal. 3:7–8

Israel's unwillingness to tithe was the indication of and the result of a deeper problem: They had left God! To rectify the matter they must first return to the Lord, then bring Him their tithes. God wants us before He wants the tithe. And we are to personally bring the tithe, not send it. By doing so, we recognize the place that God occupies within our lives and the blessings He has given us.

When I was pastoring a church in Ohio several years ago, a member of the congregation was displeased with the direction the church was headed. One Sunday morning he approached me holding up his tithe envelope and said, "I have decided to withhold this until a few things are straightened out."

I replied that he should tell God, not me. I said, "Repeat after me: 'Dear God, I've decided to rob You!'"

Immediately he pulled back and responded, "Pastor, I didn't mean it like that!" It finally dawned on him—the withholding of the tithe was not an affront to me but to God. In humbly placing our tithes before God, we honor Him with a portion of that with which He has blessed us. Only in that context will tithing be a spiritual exercise.

Tithing is a learning exercise (v. 23). By bringing their *"grain . . . new wine . . . oil . . . the firstborn of your herds,"* they would *"learn to fear the Lord your God always."* Tithing would teach the Israelites dependence upon God. God must supply the rain for the crops to grow. Tithing would teach them the place God should occupy in their lives. God represented the "firstlings" of the flocks and herds, not the "lastlings."

Tithing is a flexible exercise (vv. 24–26). God is tenderly considerate of the circumstances of His people. Where laws could not be kept to the letter, practical modifications were introduced which kept obedience from being a hardship. Some of the people would be living too far away from the future sanctuary for it to be practical to take quantities of produce and animals there. Therefore, they could sell their tithe of produce and livestock for silver and then travel to the central sanctuary and buy whatever they wished to *"eat there before the Lord"* (v. 26). This practice was the reason for the money-changers' presence in the temple during the time of Jesus (John 2:14–16). God was more interested in the *attitude* of giving than in the act itself, although the festival in Jerusalem remained a requirement. His flexibility regarding the form of the tithe removed the excuse most likely to be used by those whose hearts might not yearn for His rightful place in their lives.

Tithing is to be a joyful exercise (v. 26). Israel was to bring the tithe before the Lord and *"rejoice, you and your household."* Their giving was to be distinctively marked with joy. Paul understood this principle and exhorted the church at Corinth, "So let each one give as he purposes in his heart, not grudgingly or of necessity; for God loves a cheerful giver" (2 Cor. 9:7). Just as the tithe is an indication of the place God has within our hearts, the joy with which we give reflects our attitude toward Him.

Tithing is a beneficent exercise (vv. 27–29). Every third year the tithe was used to feed the Levites and other less fortunate members of society. The tithe was not to be taken to the sanctuary but to be kept within the tither's home community. It was to be stored and distributed to *"the stranger and the fatherless and the widow"* (see also Deut. 10:18). It is a strong concern of Deuteronomy that the unfortunate be properly cared for and protected. By providing care for these people in need, the Israelites were remembering that at one time they too lived in a strange land and were unfortunate (10:19).

Today the church should follow the instruction given to Israel and be more willing and better prepared to respond to the many needs within our society. A few years ago Billy Graham stated that "if every church in America would take care of eight welfare families the problem would be eliminated immediately." The church should seize the opportunity to fill the void created by the cutting of several federal programs that assisted the needy.

Tithing is a blessed exercise (v. 29). If the Israelites obeyed this command to share, then they could continue to be generous, knowing that God would bless them and *"all the work of your hand which you do."* Again we see Paul picking up on this principle: "He who sows sparingly will also reap sparingly, and he who sows bountifully will also reap bountifully" (2 Cor. 9:6).

Dr. Charles Allen, former Senior Pastor of First Methodist Church in Houston, tells of receiving the following letter from one of his members during a stewardship drive:

Dear Dr. Allen: In reply to your request to send a check, I wish to inform you that the present condition of my bank account makes it almost impossible.

My shattered financial condition is due to the federal laws, state laws, county laws, corporation laws, mother-in-law, sisters-in-law, and outlaws.

Through these laws, I am compelled to pay a business tax, amusement tax, head tax, school tax, gas tax, light tax, water tax, and sales tax. Even my brains are taxed.

I am required to get a business license, dog license, not to mention a marriage license. I am also required to contribute to every organization or society which the genius of man is capable of bringing to life; women's relief, unemployment relief, every hospital and charitable institution in the city, including the Red Cross, the black cross, the purple cross, and the double cross.

For my own safety, I am required to carry life insurance, property insurance, liability insurance, burglary insurance, accident insurance, business insurance, earthquake insurance, tornado insurance, unemployment insurance, old age insurance, and fire insurance.

I am inspected, expected, disrespected, rejected, dejected, examined, re-examined, informed, reformed, summoned, fined, commanded, and compelled, until I find an inexhaustible supply of money for every known need, desire, or hope of the human race. Simply because I refuse to donate something or the other, I am boycotted, talked about, lied about, held up, held down, and robbed until I am ruined.

I can tell you honestly that had not the unexpected happened, I could not enclose this check. The wolf that comes to so many doors nowadays just had pups in the kitchen. I sold them and HERE IS THE MONEY.

GIVING RELEASE TO DEBTORS

15:1 "At the end of *every* seven years you shall grant a release of *debts*.

2 "And this *is* the form of the release: Every creditor who has lent *anything* to his neighbor shall release

it; he shall not require *it* of his neighbor or his brother, because it is called the LORD's release.

3 "Of a foreigner you may require *it;* but you shall give up your claim to what is owed by your brother,

4 "except when there may be no poor among you; for the LORD will greatly bless you in the land which the LORD your God is giving you to possess *as* an inheritance—

5 "only if you carefully obey the voice of the LORD your God, to observe with care all these commandments which I command you today.

6 "For the LORD your God will bless you just as He promised you; you shall lend to many nations, but you shall not borrow; you shall reign over many nations, but they shall not reign over you."

Deut. 15:1-6

Deuteronomy 15 is mainly an exposition of laws relating to the year of release. The situation prompting this section is the existence of various classes of needy people. Here, the details of the release are vague in comparison with other legislation on the subject (Exod. 23:10–11; Lev. 25). A humanitarian concern for the needy becomes the center of attention.[1]

Deuteronomy 14:22 instructs Israel to tithe her possessions "year by year." The same chapter mentions what she is to do with her possessions "every third year" (v. 28). This emphasis on time is continued in Deuteronomy 15: *"At the end of every seven years . . . "* (v. 1).

This particular year was initially described in Exodus 23:10–11. There the emphasis was on allowing the land to lie fallow for the sake of the poor and the animals. A second emphasis is found in Leviticus 25:1–7. The land, or rotating portions thereof, is to lie fallow every seventh year. The purpose is to allow the land to have a rest from continual production. Deuteronomy 15 adds yet another factor. In the sabbatical year there is to be a remission of debts.

Here Moses gives direction concerning the year of *"release."* Israelites were not to be pressed to pay their debts during this year. The phrase *"at the end"* (v. 1) is included because money debts were not paid until the crops were gathered or the farmer had been paid.

Then he could pay his debts. However, the seventh year was different. There is much debate over whether a debt was to be terminated permanently or suspended for one year, meaning the repayment could not be demanded during the course of the seventh year. The latter alternative seems probable. At the end of seven years all debts that had been contracted were again extended for another year. The total debts were forgiven in the year of jubilee (every fiftieth year).

Ideally, if this command were obeyed, there would eventually be *"no poor among you"* (v. 4). But Moses' past experience causes him to doubt whether this could be a reality and verse 11 states: "For the poor will never cease from the land." Nevertheless, the promise of God's financial blessing is given in verse 6. There have been partial fulfillments of this promise, notably in the reigns of David and Solomon.

GIVING GENEROUSLY TO THE POOR

15:7 "If there is among you a poor man of your brethren, within any of the gates in your land which the LORD your God is giving you, you shall not harden your heart nor shut your hand from your poor brother,

8 "but you shall open your hand wide to him and willingly lend him sufficient for his need, whatever he needs.

9 "Beware lest there be a wicked thought in your heart, saying, 'The seventh year, the year of release, is at hand,' and your eye be evil against your poor brother and you give him nothing, and he cry out to the LORD against you, and it become sin among you.

10 "You shall surely give to him, and your heart should not be grieved when you give to him, because for this thing the LORD your God will bless you in all your works and in all to which you put your hand.

11 "For the poor will never cease from the land; therefore I command you, saying, 'You shall open your hand wide to your brother, to your poor and your needy, in your land.'"

Deut. 15:7–11

In this paragraph, Moses teaches that helping the poor is a heart issue because it is a financial one. Three times he speaks of an open heart's resulting in an open hand (vv. 7–8, 10, 11). Matthew Henry said, "If the hand is shut it is a sign that the heart is hardened."[2]

The heart or attitude is a steady theme throughout Deuteronomy. It is interesting that a book known for its treatment of law should continually emphasize the heart. Moses warns the children of Israel about the dangers of a proud heart that lifts self above God (Deut. 8:11–20). In 9:4 he says, "Do not think in your heart, after the Lord your God has cast them out before you, saying, 'Because of my righteousness the Lord has brought me in to possess this land.'"

Although this section deals with loaning to the poor rather than giving, the attitude plays a prominent place because of the year of release. A potential creditor might be unwilling to make a loan to a poor person if the year of release were coming very soon. If a loan were requested in the latter part of Israel's sixth year, the loan could not be recalled during the seventh and, in essence, the loan would be a gift. Because the poor always had needs, it would be inevitable that some would need financial assistance just before the year of release. Therefore, a loan to the poor during the sixth year meant the creditor would not be able to collect it. To avoid an unwillingness by the wealthy to lend money at that time, Moses appeals for a generous attitude. By acting generously, the people will experience God's blessing and will prosper (v. 10).

The main points of this paragraph are: (1) The poor will continually be needing help from the wealthy (v. 11). (2) These needs are to be generously and gladly met (v. 10). (3) The desire to evade any obligation is a wicked violation of the spirit of the law (v. 9). (4) The cry of the neglected and oppressed will rise up to God and be heard (v. 9). The Lord will bless those whose hearts and hands are open to the needy (v. 10).

The treatment of the less fortunate is also dealt with in the New Testament. Matthew 25:31–46 gives us the strong words of Jesus on this subject. Our Lord assures us that "inasmuch as you did it to one of the least of these My brethren, you did it to Me" (v. 40). Paul applies this truth when he says, "Bear one another's burdens, and so fulfill the law of Christ. . . . Therefore, as we have opportunity, let us do good to all, especially to those who are of the household of faith" (Gal. 6:2, 10).

The neglect of the poor is dealt with in the New Testament. If a man knowingly neglects the poor, the love of God is not in his heart (1 John 3:17). The apostle James declares that to neglect or despise the poor is a sin against God (James 2:5–9; 5:1–4). Jesus tells us that our judgment will be based on our kindness to the needy (Matt. 25:31–46).

Dr. Karl Menninger was once asked what a person should do if he or she felt on the verge of a nervous breakdown. The famous psychiatrist said, "Lock up your house, go across the railroad tracks, find someone in need and do something for him."

Each year at Christmas, our family reaches out to someone in an unfortunate position and makes their needs our Christmas project. It is the most rewarding thing that we experience during that season. We bake cookies for the family, prepare a Christmas meal, buy them clothes, and send them Christmas gifts. Since we prefer to do this anonymously, we have another pastor take all the "goodies" to them. Our only request is that a picture be taken of the family. On Christmas day, Margaret and I place the picture on the table where our children will see it often. Many times during that special day, they will pick up the picture and be reminded that it is more blessed to give than to receive.

Giving Freedom to the Bondservant

15:12 "If your brother, a Hebrew man, or a Hebrew woman, is sold to you and serves you six years, then in the seventh year you shall let him go free from you.

13 "And when you send him away free from you, you shall not let him go away empty-handed;

14 "you shall supply him liberally from your flock, from your threshing floor, and from your winepress. *From what* the LORD has blessed you with, you shall give to him.

15 "You shall remember that you were a slave in the land of Egypt, and the LORD your God redeemed you; therefore I command you this thing today.

16 "And if it happens that he says to you, 'I will not go away from you,' because he loves you and your house, since he prospers with you,

17 "then you shall take an awl and thrust *it* through his ear to the door, and he shall be your servant forever. Also to your female servant you shall do likewise.

18 "It shall not seem hard to you when you send him away free from you; for he has been worth a double hired servant in serving you six years. Then the LORD your God will bless you in all that you do."

Deut. 15:12–18

This law is concerned with when the Israelite who has reached the bottom rung on the poverty scale is sold as a servant to a fellow Israelite. The servant is not to automatically become the wealthier person's permanent possession. In seven years the servant is to be freed and provided for liberally. This law regarding bondservants enhances the theme of this chapter—generosity toward those within the covenant community who are unfortunate. They must not be abused or abandoned; they must be helped.

In studying the bondservant law in this chapter, one could ask why it was that Moses, a divinely commissioned leader, tolerated a form of slavery. The answer is to be found in these Scriptures and on examining Moses' provisions elsewhere concerning this issue. We can see that he was slowly educating his people away from this form of servitude. Notice the following regulations:

1. The Hebrew servant was held for six years only; in the seventh year he or she was freed (v. 12).

2. Rigorous demands and harshness were forbidden (Lev. 25:43).

3. If a master inflicted serious bodily injury on a servant, that servant was to have his freedom (Exod. 21:26–27).

4. A servant could acquire assets and might even save enough money to buy his or her own freedom (Lev. 25:47–49).

5. Two special privileges were given to the servants: They were to be free from work on the Sabbath, and they were to participate in the great national feast times (Exod. 23:12; Deut. 16:11, 14).

6. Upon the seventh year, a servant was to be freed and supplied "*liberally*" with food and other provisions (vv. 13–14).

7. As the nation matured, its laws toward slavery became more progressive. During Moses' lifetime, provisions which were at first intended only for male servants were extended to female servants (Exod. 21:7; Deut. 15:17).

8. The idea of freedom (through seventh-year release) was continually kept before the master and his servant.

9. When a slave escaped from his master, the moment he touched Hebrew soil, he was free (Deut. 23:15–16).

The master is given a threefold reason for treating his servant well: (1) He himself has been generously treated by the Lord (v. 14); (2) his forefathers were slaves *"in the land of Egypt, and the Lord your God redeemed you"* (v. 15); (3) he has already received more than his money's worth—now, God will bless him because of his generosity toward his servant (v. 18).

Provision was made for a servant to stay if he or she wished to do so (vv. 16–17). In such a case, on confession of love for the master and his household, the servant received a mark of lifelong servanthood at the door of the master's house (v. 17).

Three things mark this servant for life (v. 16): his determination, *"I will not go away from you"*; his motive, *"because he loves you and your house"*; and his reason, *"since he prospers with you."*

As the master obeys God's command to free Hebrew servants, there is the promise of blessing (v. 18). The obedience/blessing principle so often found in Deuteronomy appears three times in this chapter alone (vv. 4–6, 10, 18).

SACRIFICE OF FIRSTBORN ANIMALS

15:19 "All the firstborn males that come from your herd and your flock you shall sanctify to the LORD your God; you shall do no work with the firstborn of your herd, nor shear the firstborn of your flock.

20 "You and your household shall eat *it* before the LORD your God year by year in the place which the LORD chooses.

21 "But if there is a defect in it, *if it is* lame or blind *or has* any serious defect, you shall not sacrifice it to the LORD your God.

22 "You may eat it within your gates; the unclean and the clean *person* alike *may eat it,* as *if it were* a gazelle or a deer.

23 "Only you shall not eat its blood; you shall pour it on the ground like water."

Deut. 15:19–23

God is supreme, therefore His claim to recognition and obedience must have consideration above all other claims. He claims and sanctifies the first day of the week; the first fruits of the soil are His for a religious offering; He demands the first place in our affections; the firstborn males of the herd, He marks for His own. This is His due.

The sacrificing of firstborn animals reminded the Israelites of their redemption from Egypt when all the firstborn Egyptian sons died. It provided another occasion for the Israelites to teach their children about God's redemption of their nation.

Notice the conditions placed on the sacrifice of firstborn animals: (1) These animals were to be set aside as special, and there was to be no dilution of this sanctification by shearing or working them the same as if they were common animals from which the owner might receive some benefit himself (v. 19). (2) Annually, the young firstborn animals were to be taken to the sanctuary to be sacrificed and eaten (v. 20). (3) An imperfect firstborn animal was not acceptable as a sacrifice, so it was to be treated like a game animal—eaten at home but not sacrificed (vv. 21–22). (4) The blood of the animals was not to be eaten (v. 23).

God was asking Israel to consecrate only the best to Him—and to do it wholly and often. He asks the same of us today.

NOTES

1. C. M. Weinfeld, *Deuteronomy and the Deuteronomic School* (Oxford: Clarendon Press, 1972), pp. 282–84.

2. Matthew Henry, *An Exposition of the Old and New Testaments* (London: James Nisbet and Co., 1857), p. 787.

CHAPTER SEVENTEEN

Regulations Concerning Feasts

Deuteronomy 16:1–17

This chapter reviews the three major festivals to be observed throughout the year: Passover (vv. 1–8), the Feast of Weeks (vv. 9–12), and the Feast of Tabernacles (vv. 13–15).[1]

THE PASSOVER

16:1 "Observe the month of Abib, and keep the Passover to the LORD your God, for in the month of Abib the LORD your God brought you out of Egypt by night.

2 "Therefore you shall sacrifice the Passover to the LORD your God, from the flock and the herd, in the place where the LORD chooses to put His name.

3 "You shall eat no leavened bread with it; seven days you shall eat unleavened bread with it, *that is,* the bread of affliction (for you came out of the land of Egypt in haste), that you may remember the day in which you came out of the land of Egypt all the days of your life.

4 "And no leaven shall be seen among you in all your territory for seven days, nor shall *any* of the meat which you sacrifice the first day at twilight remain overnight until morning.

5 "You may not sacrifice the Passover within any of your gates which the LORD your God gives you;

6 "but at the place where the LORD your God chooses to make His name abide, there you shall

sacrifice the Passover at twilight, at the going down
of the sun, at the time you came out of Egypt.
7 "And you shall roast and eat *it* in the place
which the LORD your God chooses, and in the morning you shall turn and go to your tents.
8 "Six days you shall eat unleavened bread, and
on the seventh day there *shall be* a sacred assembly
to the LORD your God. You shall do no work *on it.*"

Deut. 16:1–8

The detailed legislation regarding the Passover is contained
in other places in the Pentateuch (Exod. 12:43–13:10; Lev. 23:5–8;
Num. 28:16–25). In this address, Moses provides only a summarizing statement. Remember, Deuteronomy is a collection of widely
different sermons about old sacral ordinances; it is not a legal code.

Deuteronomy is not a literary unity, as is obvious from the repeated superscriptions (1:1; 4:44–5:1a; 10:6–9; 27:1a, 9a, 11; 29:1–
2a, 16–17; 31:1, 9, 14–16, 22–25, 30; 32:44–45, 48; 33:1; 34:1–12) or
from the numerous shifts between the singular and the plural.
Deuteronomy grew as the generations of Israel grew. It was not
stored away in a museum after its first appearance; Israel lived with
this book and recognized it as God's living word. It did not speak to
Israel in just one historical situation. Deuteronomy stands in the
middle between promise and fulfillment.[2] Moses speaks of this
Passover feast from both a past and future perspective. The exodus
from Egypt is a period from Israel's past which is remembered in the
feasts (vv. 1, 3, 6). The future is anticipated in the reference to
"the place where the Lord chooses to put His name" (v. 2).

The Passover was to be celebrated in the month of *"Abib,"* which
means "green ears." Passover was a celebration and commemoration
of the event on which the covenant community was established. Because of the liberation from servitude which God had granted His
people in the exodus, the new commitment of the Israelites to God in
the Sinai covenant had become possible. Thus the Passover was
a celebration of freedom, but at the same time it was a reminder that
the freedom from Egypt and worldly domination had been ex-
changed almost immediately for a new commitment. The new commitment was made evident in this celebration of the Israelites as the
covenant people of God.[3]

215

The first Passover, in Egypt, was celebrated by the families in their homes (Exod. 12:21–28). Now that Israel had been delivered from Egypt and the covenant had been formed at Sinai, the tribes of Israel were a single nation—they were the family of God. Therefore, the Passover became a symbolic act of one large family of God celebrating in the place that God chose.

They were to eat *"no leavened bread"* (v. 3) for the following reasons: The leavening process was considered to be impure and therefore not suitable for the festive occasion. It commemorated the *"haste"* of their flight from Egypt, for unlike leavened bread, it could be made quickly. As a *"bread of affliction"* it also symbolized the Israelites' slavery in Egypt.

The prohibition of leaven and the complete consumption of meat during each night of the festival (v. 4) symbolized purity in the celebration. Leaven, as well as old meat, would begin to decay in the heat of the day following its preparation.

The sacrifice could not be offered randomly; it was to be cooked in the vicinity of the sanctuary (vv. 5–6). After the sacrifice and night vigil, the people would return to their tents in the morning (v. 7). On the seventh day of unleavened bread, there was to be a closing *"sacred assembly"* (v. 8).

THE FEAST OF WEEKS

16:9 "You shall count seven weeks for yourself; begin to count the seven weeks from *the time* you begin *to put* the sickle to the grain.

10 "Then you shall keep the Feast of Weeks to the LORD your God with the tribute of a freewill offering from your hand, which you shall give as the LORD your God blesses you.

11 "You shall rejoice before the LORD your God, you and your son and your daughter, your male servant and your female servant, the Levite who *is* within your gates, the stranger and the fatherless and the widow who *are* among you, at the place where the LORD your God chooses to make His name abide.

12 "And you shall remember that you were a slave
in Egypt, and you shall be careful to observe these
statutes."

Deut. 16:9-12

The Feast of Weeks was also known as the "Feast of Harvest"
(Exod. 23:16) and the "day of firstfruits" (Num. 28:26). Later it was
given the title "Pentecost" based on the translation of "fifty days"
(Lev. 23:16) in the Septuagint. The Feast of Weeks was a celebration
of God's gracious provision of the harvest. Moses emphasized only
certain points of this feast. Four phrases, each at the beginning of its
respective verse, highlight this section.

"You shall count . . ." (v. 9). The people are to count off seven
weeks from the time they begin to harvest the grain in March or
April. This would mean the Feast of Weeks was in late May or early
June. Perhaps the children of Israel were to count the days up to this
feast because of their tendency to forget. This feast was the least
attended of the three mentioned in this chapter. How many times do
we take God's blessing for granted?

"You shall keep . . ." (v. 10). The observance of this feast was kept
by giving freely *"as the Lord your God blesses you."* The apostle Paul
may have had this standard of giving in mind when he directed the
Corinthian Christians to give as each one prospered (1 Cor. 16:2).
We are reminded that our gifts are worthless unless they are the
expression of a willing heart, and that they are to be proportionate
to our prosperity.

"You shall rejoice . . ." (v. 11). This joy is to be expressed *"before
the Lord your God"* and other people. All three festivals mentioned in
this chapter require a journey to a central place of worship (v. 16).
These pilgrimages were to be a regular reminder to the people
of their nature as a community. The solidarity of the covenant community would thus be expressed and strengthened each year, even
when the population became scattered. Charles Spurgeon said,
"When we bless God for mercies we prolong them, and when we
bless Him for miseries we usually end them. Praise is the honey of
life, which a devout heart sucks from every bloom of providence and
grace. We may as well be dead as be without praise; it is the crown
of life."

"You shall remember . . ." (v. 12). God wanted Israel to remember their obligation to Him (deliverance from Egypt) and to others. Since the Lord had been generous with the Israelites, they were to be generous with others—especially the less fortunate (v. 11). God's goodness to us should open our hearts to compassion for others. It was during this feast, known also as the Feast of Pentecost, that God gave the gift of the Holy Spirit to the early church (Acts 2). This generous and needed gift demonstrated once again the generosity of God.

THE FEAST OF TABERNACLES

16:13 "You shall observe the Feast of Tabernacles seven days, when you have gathered from your threshing floor and from your winepress.

14 "And you shall rejoice in your feast, you and your son and your daughter, your male servant and your female servant and the Levite, the stranger and the fatherless and the widow, who *are* within your gates.

15 "Seven days you shall keep a sacred feast to the LORD your God in the place which the LORD chooses, because the LORD your God will bless you in all your produce and in all the work of your hands, so that you surely rejoice.

16 "Three times a year all your males shall appear before the LORD your God in the place which He chooses: at the Feast of Unleavened Bread, at the Feast of Weeks, and at the Feast of Tabernacles; and they shall not appear before the LORD empty-handed.

17 "Every man *shall give* as he is able, according to the blessing of the LORD your God which He has given you."

Deut. 16:13–17

The Feast of the Tabernacles was so called because after the fall harvest (Lev. 23:39), the Israelites were to live for one week in tabernacles or "booths" (Lev. 23:42) constructed of tree branches and foliage (Lev. 23:40). Also called the "Feast of Ingathering" (Exod. 23:16; 34:22), it began on the fifteenth day of Tishri (September-October).

Joy, which was to mark the celebration of the Feast of Weeks, was also to characterize this festival (v. 15). The people were to rejoice in God's provision, but also (as Lev. 23:42–43 indicates) they were to rejoice in their deliverance from Egypt. The week of living in booths was to commemorate the journey through the desert after the nation had come out of Egypt. The events of John 7 occurred during this feast.

Joyfulness in worship is an important motif in Deuteronomy, as in other Old Testament Scriptures. Expressions of joy were the core of the psalms that were sung in worship at the temple (Ps. 16:11; 27:6; 63:5; 66:1; 81:1). When the worshiper becomes aware of God's past mercies, His present forgiveness and the prospect of His future blessing, the expression of deep joy in His presence is natural and spontaneous.

NOTES

1. Victor P. Hamilton, *Handbook on the Pentateuch* (Grand Rapids: Baker Book House, 1982), p. 428.

2. Gerhard von Rad, "Ancient Word and Living Word," *Interpretation* (1961): 5–6.

3. P. C. Craigie, *Commentary on the Book of Deuteronomy*, New International Commentary on the Old Testament (Grand Rapids: Wm. B. Eerdmans Publishing Co., 1976), p. 241.

219

CHAPTER EIGHTEEN

Regulations Concerning Society

Deuteronomy 16:18-19:21

The preceding sections (12:1–16:17) are mainly concerned with laws that relate to the worship of the Lord by His people. This section deals with the responsibilities of the officials to maintain pure worship within the promised land and to administer justice impartially.

ADMINISTRATION OF JUSTICE

16:18 "You shall appoint judges and officers in all your gates, which the LORD your God gives you, according to your tribes, and they shall judge the people with just judgment.

19 "You shall not pervert justice; you shall not show partiality, nor take a bribe, for a bribe blinds the eyes of the wise and twists the words of the righteous.

20 "You shall follow what is altogether just, that you may live and inherit the land which the LORD your God is giving you.

21 "You shall not plant for yourself any tree, as a wooden image, near the altar which you build for yourself to the LORD your God.

22 "You shall not set up a sacred pillar, which the LORD your God hates.

17:1 "You shall not sacrifice to the LORD your God a bull or sheep which has any blemish *or* defect, for that *is* an abomination to the LORD your God.

2 "If there is found among you, within any of your gates which the LORD your God gives you, a man or a

woman who has been wicked in the sight of the LORD your God, in transgressing His covenant,

3 "who has gone and served other gods and worshiped them, either the sun or moon or any of the host of heaven, which I have not commanded,

4 "and it is told you, and you hear *of it,* then you shall inquire diligently. And if *it is* indeed true *and* certain that such an abomination has been committed in Israel,

5 "then you shall bring out to your gates that man or woman who has committed that wicked thing, and shall stone to death that man or woman with stones.

6 "Whoever is deserving of death shall be put to death on the testimony of two or three witnesses; he shall not be put to death on the testimony of one witness.

7 "The hands of the witnesses shall be the first against him to put him to death, and afterward the hands of all the people. So you shall put away the evil from among you.

8 "If a matter arises which is too hard for you to judge, between degrees of guilt for bloodshed, between one judgment or another, or between one punishment or another, matters of controversy within your gates, then you shall arise and go up to the place which the LORD your God chooses.

9 "And you shall come to the priests, the Levites, and to the judge *there* in those days, and inquire *of them;* they shall pronounce upon you the sentence of judgment.

10 "You shall do according to the sentence which they pronounce upon you in that place which the LORD chooses. And you shall be careful to do according to all that they order you.

11 "According to the sentence of the law in which they instruct you, according to the judgment which they tell you, you shall do; you shall not turn aside *to* the right hand or *to* the left from the sentence which they pronounce upon you.

12 "Now the man who acts presumptuously and will not heed the priest who stands to minister there

before the LORD your God, or the judge, that man
shall die. So you shall put away the evil from Israel.
13 "And all the people shall hear and fear, and no
longer act presumptuously."

Deut. 16:18–17:13

The appointed *"judges and officers"* were to *"judge the people with
just judgment"* (v. 18). To succeed in this, they must do four things.

They *"shall not pervert justice"* (v. 19). This implies that God had
given them a pattern to follow. Their actions were to conform to this
pattern.

They *"shall not show partiality"* (v. 19). Literally, this reads, "You
shall not recognize faces." In other words, they were to treat each
person as though they had no prior knowledge of him or her.

They *"shall not . . . take a bribe"* (v. 19). Accepting a bribe was
obviously wrong, for it distorted the ability of judges to act in fair-
ness to the parties in dispute.

They *"shall follow what is altogether just"* (v. 20). Moffatt translates
this phrase "justice, justice you must aim at." Dale Patrick says some
insightful things about this passage. He states that the codes and
laws were not an exhaustive, comprehensive revelation of God's will
for the people. The most sensitive task of Israelite judges was to hear
the disputants in a case and decide who was in the right and who was
guilty of wrongdoing. It is noteworthy that none of the admonitions
to judges (Lev. 19:15–16; Deut. 16:19–20) have a command to consult
the lawbooks or to adhere to the letter of the law. But if judgments
were not rendered on the basis of a set code of law, how were they
decided? How could righteousness be protected? It is obvious that the
Scriptures are concerned with preventing the corruptions of judicial
proceedings. The judges and participants are warned to avoid any
action that would interfere with the dispensing of justice.

In Exodus 18:13–26 and Deuteronomy 1:9–18, Moses delegates
judicial authority to men who conform to high ethical standards,
"able men, such as fear God, men of truth, hating covetousness"
(Exod. 18:21). Their quality of character makes these men fit for deliberating on judicial cases. It is noteworthy that legal training is not
stated as a requirement for judges. Integrity of character takes prece-
dence over technical skill as a qualification for judicial office.[1]

Leadership may be defined in terms of what we are (character) and what we do (action). A leader's action will reflect his or her character. Therefore, it is of great importance that the leader *be* right (with God) so he or she can *do* right. When right action is rooted in right character the fruit will be right results. This is the message of Deuteronomy in the selection of judges.

The first matter brought to the judges' attention is prevention of idolatrous worship practices in the land (16:21–17:1). Anything that facilitates adapting worship of the Lord to pagan systems of worship is prohibited.

Just as the use of a pagan Asherah pole or a *"sacred pillar"* would be incompatible with the worship of God (16:22), so too would the bringing of a defective sacrifice be foreign to genuine worship (17:1). Such a sacrifice would be *"an abomination to the Lord."* To offer less than the best to God is to *"despise"* His name (Mal. 1:6–8). Offering a less than perfect sacrifice would be failing to acknowledge Him as the ultimate Provider of all that is best in life.

The priests were normally responsible for maintaining purity of worship at the sanctuary, but if they failed to do so it was necessary for the judges to intervene.

The second responsibility of the judges was to see that false worshipers were executed. A person who *"served other gods and worshiped them"* (v. 3) deserved capital punishment because his act threatened the nation's very existence (17:2–5). The crime, though religious in form, was political in significance. It could be compared to the modern crime of espionage or treason in a time of war, resulting as it would in weakening the security of a nation.

Obviously, the seriousness of the crime demanded a thorough and exacting procedure before the wrongdoer could be convicted. Notice the order of expression in verses 4–5: (1) *"It is told you,"* (2) *"and you hear of it,"* (3) *"then you shall inquire diligently,"* (4) *"and if it is indeed true and certain . . . then [and only then] you shall bring out to your gates that man or woman . . . ."*

Observe that everyone was held to be innocent unless proved otherwise. No one's character was put at the mercy of any one uncorroborated witness (v. 6). Those who reported with the tongue were responsible for following words with action (v. 7). The people were to cooperate in *"putting away evil"* whenever it had been proved to exist (v. 7).

It is important for us to realize our responsibility to keep the church

223

pure today. Several New Testament Scriptures deal with the discipline process and give us biblical procedures to follow. The procedure for church discipline involves four steps (Matt. 18:15–17).

The first step is for the witness, in the spirit of love, to approach the person who has sinned. "Moreover if your brother sins against you, go and tell him his fault between you and him alone. If he hears you, you have gained your brother" (Matt. 18:15). Paul tells us that only spiritually mature people with the right attitude should approach those who have erred. "Brethren, if a man is overtaken in any trespass, you who are spiritual restore such a one in a spirit of gentleness, considering yourself lest you also be tempted" (Gal. 6:1).

Usually the first step is sufficient to cause the one in error *to want to repent.* However, if the person who has sinned does not respond in a positive manner, the next step is for two or three witnesses to approach him or her. "But if he will not hear, take with you one or two more, that 'by the mouth of two or three witnesses every word may be established'" (Matt. 18:16).

If this fails, the next step is to tell the church. "And if he refuses to hear them, tell it to the church" (Matt. 18:17). The church should not be told until everything possible has been done to restore the individual to a right relationship with God and with his or her fellow Christians. If the accused does not respond after the first two steps, then the matter should go before the church in order to enlist the help of the entire congregation in convincing the person to reconcile with the person he or she has sinned against.

If the person still does not listen, he or she must be turned out of the church. "But if he refuses even to hear the church, let him be to you like a heathen and a tax collector" (Matt. 18:17).

There is an example of biblical discipline in 1 Corinthians 5. A man in the church fell into a serious sin; he was guilty of incest. Paul insisted that they should withdraw fellowship from him (1 Cor. 5:1–13). In this case the man repented and Paul wrote to the same church asking them to forgive the man and take him into their fellowship again (2 Cor. 2:6–7).

Moses provides a way for local judges to receive assistance when they have a difficult case before them. They are to *"come to the priests, the Levites, and to the judge there in those days, and inquire of them"* (v. 9). This procedure was to be followed in cases *"too hard for you to judge, . . . matters of controversy"* (v. 8). Moses repeatedly exhorts the people to completely obey the decisions of the higher court (vv. 10–11). Refusal to obey brought the harsh penalty of death. The purpose of the penalty, as in the previous section (17:7), was to completely *put away the evil from Israel"* (v. 12). When godly discipline is enforced, whether in Moses' time or ours, *"all the people shall hear and fear, and no longer act presumptuously"* (v. 13).

PRINCIPLES FOR ISRAEL'S KINGS

17:14 "When you come to the land which the LORD your God is giving you, and possess it and dwell in it, and say, 'I will set a king over me like all the nations that *are* around me,'

15 "you shall surely set a king over you whom the LORD your God chooses; *one* from among your brethren you shall set as king over you; you may not set a foreigner over you, who *is* not your brother.

16 "But he shall not multiply horses for himself, nor cause the people to return to Egypt to multiply horses, for the LORD has said to you, 'You shall not return that way again.'

17 "Neither shall he multiply wives for himself, lest his heart turn away; nor shall he greatly multiply silver and gold for himself.

18 "Also it shall be, when he sits on the throne of his kingdom, that he shall write for himself a copy of this law in a book, from *the one* before the priests, the Levites.

19 "And it shall be with him, and he shall read it all the days of his life, that he may learn to fear the LORD his God and be careful to observe all the words of this law and these statutes,

20 "that his heart may not be lifted above his brethren, that he may not turn aside from the commandment *to* the right hand or *to* the left, and that he may prolong *his* days in his kingdom, he and his children in the midst of Israel."

Deut. 17:14–20

This passage, containing laws relating to kingship, is the only one of its kind in the Pentateuch. It anticipates a time when Israel might institute a monarchy. This legislation does not expound in detail the character of the kingly office; rather, it specifies the attitudes and characteristics that would be required of a king in a state that was primarily a theocracy.

Israel's king was to be *divinely appointed,* one *"whom the Lord your God chooses"* (v. 15). Later history records that prophets speaking on God's behalf would declare His choice (1 Sam. 9–12; 1 Sam. 16; 1 Kings 1). God's choosing the king assured the people that their ruler was qualified. If a king failed, it would not be due to a lack of ability, but to a failure *"to fear the Lord his God and . . . to observe all the words of this law and these statutes"* (v. 19).

Israel's king was to be *one of their own* (v. 15). The Bible implies that Israel had at times had "outsiders" either ruling or attempting to oversee Israel. In the time of the judges there are two references to Shamgar (Judg. 3:31; 5:6), whose father was named after a Canaanite goddess—which would seem to indicate that he was not of Israel. Also during this period before Saul's kingship, Abimelech reigned for a short time. Abimelech's mother was a Shechemite and her relatives made him king, after financing his takeover with money from the temple of Baal-Berith (Judg. 8:30–9:6).[2]

The king of Israel was to *depend upon God for victory.* He was not to *"multiply horses for himself"* (v. 16). Horses represented the cavalry, used by the enemies of Israel. The obedient Israelite king was not to build his own military strength, but to depend on God alone. God had already demonstrated His ability to crush a large, superior army (Exod. 14–15), and He would continue to defend Israel in the future (Judg. 4–5). God wanted His people to rely completely upon Him, thereby demonstrating His power to all nations.

The king was to be *faithful to God and His covenant.* If a king would *"multiply wives for himself"* (v. 17), his affections would be divided between God and others. The forbidding of many wives was given because kings often married foreign women to form political alliances. If the king was in partnership with God, however, he would not need political alliances. A political marriage alliance would be a deviation from the one and only true treaty of the Israelite state, namely, their covenant with the Lord.

Israel's king was to *stay close to his people.* The prohibition against the king's acquiring *"silver and gold"* (v. 17) was intended to keep him from developing a sense of independence and a lust for material wealth (Prov. 30:8, 9). The commands against multiplying possessions were designed to reduce the king to the status of a servant totally dependent upon his Master—in this case, the Lord. The resulting tragedy of ignoring these commands is seen in the life of Solomon, who broke all three prohibitions (1 Kings 10:14–15, 23, 26–28; 11:1–6).[3]

The king of Israel was to be *a diligent student of God's word* (vv. 18–20). He was to write out with his own hand a copy of Deuteronomy. Then he was to *"read it all the days of his life"* (v. 19). This kind of perseverance would give the king a reverential obedience to God; it would keep him humble and assure him a long dynastic succession.

Von Rad observes correctly, "Deuteronomy sees in kingship not an office which Yahweh could use for the welfare of the people, but only an institution in which the holder must live in a sphere of extreme peril because he is tempted by his harem or his wealth either to turn away from Yahweh or 'to lift up his heart above his brethren.'"[4]

A heart turned away from God is often a heart turned away from people. Earlier Israel as a nation had been warned about saying in her heart: My own power made me wealthy (8:17). Not just Israel, but her leadership as well is potentially vulnerable to this downfall. The leader must be reminded that he is not autonomous. He is not God; he is an instrument of God. And as God's instrument, he must touch the lives of his people.

PROVISION FOR THE PRIESTS AND LEVITES

18:1 "The priests, the Levites—all the tribe of Levi—shall have no part nor inheritance with Israel; they shall eat the offerings of the LORD made by fire, and His portion.

2 "Therefore they shall have no inheritance among their brethren; the LORD is their inheritance, as He said to them.

3 "And this shall be the priest's due from the people, from those who offer a sacrifice, whether *it is* bull or sheep: they shall give to the priest the shoulder, the cheeks, and the stomach.

4 "The firstfruits of your grain and your new wine and your oil, and the first of the fleece of your sheep, you shall give him.

5 "For the LORD your God has chosen him out of all your tribes to stand to minister in the name of the LORD, him and his sons forever.

6 "So if a Levite comes from any of your gates, from where he dwells among all Israel, and comes with all the desire of his mind to the place which the LORD chooses,

7 "then he may serve in the name of the LORD his God as all his brethren the Levites *do*, who stand there before the LORD.

8 "They shall have equal portions to eat, besides what comes from the sale of his inheritance."

Deut. 18:1-8

From the offices of judge and king, Deuteronomy now turns to a discussion of the office of priest. Unlike Deuteronomy 16 and 17 which emphasized the necessary qualities for those holding the position of judge or king, Deuteronomy 18 says nothing about the quality of the life of a priest or Levite. The emphasis of this section is on providing for these religious workers.

Unlike the other eleven tribes, the tribe of Levi was not given an allotment of land to settle and cultivate. *"The priests, the Levites —all the tribe of Levi"* were to be sustained by offerings the people made to the Lord (vv. 1–2). Levites who did not assist at the central sanctuary were not to be excluded from this support (Deut. 14:28–29; 16:10–11). Verses 6–8 add that any Levite who *"comes with all the desire of his mind"* may serve in the Lord's temple.

It is significant that early in the history of God's people, provision was made for the support of His ministers. The apostle Paul appealed to the law to sustain his rights in this connection, even though he declined to exercise them (1 Cor. 9:1, 6–15).

PROHIBITION OF WICKED CUSTOMS

18:9 "When you come into the land which the LORD your God is giving you, you shall not learn to follow the abominations of those nations.

10 "There shall not be found among you *anyone* who makes his son or his daughter pass through the fire, *or one* who practices witchcraft, *or* a soothsayer, or one who interprets omens, or a sorcerer,

11 "or one who conjures spells, or a medium, or a spiritist, or one who calls up the dead.

12 "For all who do these things *are* an abomination to the LORD, and because of these abominations the LORD your God drives them out from before you.

13 "You shall be blameless before the LORD your God.

14 "For these nations which you will dispossess listened to soothsayers and diviners; but as for you, the LORD your God has not appointed such for you."

Deut. 18:9-14

A crucial question throughout the religious history has been, how may the will of God be known? Each summer I preach a series of sermons entitled "You Asked for It." The topics for these sermons are the ones most frequently requested by the congregation. Each year the question of God's will for our lives ranks high on the list. This also was uppermost in the minds of the people in Moses' day.

It was particularly important that it be answered for the Israelites *before* they entered Canaan, because after they arrived they would be exposed to the many evil methods that the Canaanite people used in attempting to discern the future. This passage lists various techniques the pagans employed to obtain these answers.[5]

Children were sometimes made to *"pass through the fire"* in an attempt to determine the course of events. The use of children in this way is "an abomination to the Lord which He hates" (Deut. 12:31).

Seventeen times the Bible mentions the word *"witchcraft,"* usually in a negative sense. These references can be grouped into four basic teachings. (1) Witchcraft is rebellion against God (1 Sam. 15:23). (2) Witchcraft is a work of the flesh (Gal. 5:19-21). (3) Witches' powers are strong but limited (Acts 13:6-11). (4) Witches are to be dealt with harshly (Deut. 18:10).

Soothsayers attempted to control circumstances or people through power given by evil spirits.

Omen interpretation was the telling of the future based on signs such as fire, rain, or the movement of birds.

229

Sorcerers practiced magic by incantations. One who *"conjures spells"* is literally "one who ties in knots," binding other people by magical mutterings. *"A medium, or a spiritist"* is one who supposedly communicates with the dead but who actually communicates with demons.[6]

Such detestable practices were one of the reasons God used Israel to destroy the Canaanites (vv. 12, 14). By avoiding these pagan customs, the Israelites would *"be blameless before the Lord your God"* (v. 13).

Why were these practices such an abomination to God? Why were they so dangerous? There are a number of reasons.

Participation in these pagan practices *will bring down God's judgment* on the offenders.

They are modes of *deception used by Satan to ensnare people.* Scripture warns against "the lust of the flesh, the lust of the eyes, and the pride of life" (1 John 2:16). This is exactly what Satan offers through the occult. He cajoles people into believing they are gaining possessions, power, and prestige by occult practices, when it is actually his power working through them. Those participating in the occult become Satan's puppets.

When God's children try to discern future events that Scripture has not revealed, they *demonstrate a lack of faith in God.* Since the Fall, God has permitted us to know good and evil. Yet He has His reasons for keeping some things secret from us. "The secret things belong to the Lord our God, but those things which are revealed belong to us and to our children forever, that we may do all the words of this law" (Deut. 29:29).

Why must some things be concealed from us? Suppose you knew that one week from today you would die. Could you function normally? Of course not! God wants His people to live each day for Him, one at a time, regardless of what tomorrow will bring (Matt. 6:34).

Does an astrologer really understand the universe better than the Lord? When we trust in stars, sorcery, or spirits to give us answers God has chosen not to reveal, we are turning our backs on our Creator.

Participants in the occult withdraw into their "innermost selves" to find ultimate peace and good. But the Bible says that nothing good dwells in men.

In Matthew 12:43–45, the Lord says that if a man empties his mind of an unclean spirit and sweeps it clean, wicked spirits may nevertheless return sevenfold if the man fails to occupy his mind with Someone stronger than himself. Our minds are not neutral ground; to remain clean, they must be God-controlled.

When we yield to the flesh, *we give Satan control.* "For we do not wrestle against flesh and blood, but against principalities, against powers, against the rulers of the darkness of this age, against spiritual hosts of wickedness in the heavenly places" (Eph. 6:12).

God warns us about evil spirits. He explains that His specially designed armor is our only defense (Eph. 6:10–18). In every instance of occult practice recorded in the Scriptures, God's power proves greater. "You are of God, little children, and have overcome them, because He who is in you is greater than he who is in the world" (1 John 4:4).

Today the occult is big business. Astrology entices millions to trust the stars for daily guidance. Mediums flourish because people want to consult the "other side" to know what lies beyond the grave. Occult literature sells fast. Movies dealing with demon possession are box-office hits. An article on satanism stated, "Today, more than forty-five identifiable groups are involved in sorcery [witchcraft, satanism, voodoo] in America."[7] Our society is searching for answers in the wrong places.

ANOTHER MOSES PROMISED

18:15 "The LORD your God will raise up for you a Prophet like me from your midst, from your brethren. Him you shall hear,

16 "according to all you desired of the LORD your God in Horeb in the day of the assembly, saying, 'Let me not hear again the voice of the LORD my God, nor let me see this great fire anymore, lest I die.'

17 "And the LORD said to me: 'What they have spoken is good.

18 'I will raise up for them a Prophet like you from among their brethren, and will put My words in His mouth, and He shall speak to them all that I command Him.

231

19 'And it shall be *that* whoever will not hear My words, which He speaks in My name, I will require *it* of him.

20 'But the prophet who presumes to speak a word in My name, which I have not commanded him to speak, or who speaks in the name of other gods, that prophet shall die.'

21 "And if you say in your heart, 'How shall we know the word which the LORD has not spoken?'—

22 "when a prophet speaks in the name of the LORD, if the thing does not happen or come to pass, that *is* the thing which the LORD has not spoken; the prophet has spoken it presumptuously; you shall not be afraid of him."

Deut. 18:15–22

In contrast with the dark magic of the Canaanite diviners, God gave Israel a prophet who would speak His words to the people. This section has two levels of significance: the continual provision of prophets after the death of Moses, and the prophecy of a future Prophet like Moses.

A continued line of prophets was instituted because of the events at Horeb (v. 16). The people were afraid to listen directly to the voice of God, so they requested that Moses act as a mediator on their behalf (5:23–27). This divinely appointed leader provided the congregation of Israel with a way of knowing and understanding the course of human events, a way that was completely different from that of their neighbors.

Here we find one of the very few instances in the legal section of Deuteronomy where Moses speaks about himself: *"The Lord your God will raise up for you a Prophet like me from your midst. . . . I will raise up for them a Prophet like you from among their brethren"* (vv. 15, 18). Moses specifies himself as the model for the office of prophet. Even Joshua could not be compared to Moses for "there has not arisen in Israel a prophet like Moses, whom the Lord knew face to face" (Deut. 34:10). Moses set the standard for every future prophet. However distinguished a future prophet's role might be in Israel, none would be like Moses until the Mediator of the New Covenant came.

232

The official leaders of Judaism in the first century were still looking for the fulfillment of Moses' prophecy. They asked John the Baptist, "'Are you the Prophet?' And he answered, 'No'" (John 1:21).

Philip, after meeting Jesus, went and found Nathanael and said to him, "We have found Him of whom Moses in the law, and also the prophets, wrote—Jesus of Nazareth, the son of Joseph" (John 1:45). One day while Jesus was conversing with the Jews He said, "For if you believed Moses, you would believe Me; for he wrote about Me. But if you do not believe his writings, how will you believe My words?" (John 5:46–47). Peter, in his message at Pentecost, declared, "For Moses truly said to the fathers, 'The Lord your God will raise up for you a Prophet like me from your brethren. Him you shall hear in all things, whatever He says to you. And it shall be that every soul who will not hear that Prophet shall be utterly destroyed from among the people'" (Acts 3:22–23). Peter was saying that the people's search, which began with the prophecy of Moses, had stopped with the Lord Jesus.

The parallel between Moses and Jesus is striking. The prophet Moses, in his role as leader of the people and spokesman for God, was instrumental in founding the first kingdom, the kingdom of Israel. Though he was followed by many genuine prophets, not one compared with him. Jesus also marked the coming of a new kingdom; it was not a political kingdom of this world, but the kingdom of God. The prophet Moses mediated the covenant which was to be the constitution of Israel, whose true king was God. The prophet Jeremiah signaled the end of this age and pointed forward to a new covenant (Jer. 31:31–34) and a new kind of kingdom. These prophetic points of the past found their fulfillment in Jesus.[8]

Since the people were to obey God's prophet without question, to prophesy falsely was to usurp the place of God. Such an act was a sentence of death to the false prophet (v. 20).

Two tests could be used to determine whether a prophet was speaking the words of God: (1) The message had to be given "in the name of the Lord," and (2) the prophecy must "come to pass" (v. 22). If the prophecy was not fulfilled the people would know that the "prophet" had "spoken . . . presumptuously," and that "the Lord has not spoken." They could also be assured that they need not fear him (v. 22), and that he would die for his arrogance (v. 20).

To summarize, God's people can know the truth by avoiding the ways of the world (occult) (vv. 9–14), by listening to and obeying God's messengers (vv. 15–19), and by testing the message of God's prophets (vv. 20–22).

THE CITIES OF REFUGE

19:1 "When the LORD your God has cut off the nations whose land the LORD your God is giving you, and you dispossess them and dwell in their cities and in their houses,

2 "you shall separate three cities for yourself in the midst of your land which the LORD your God is giving you to possess.

3 "You shall prepare roads for yourself and divide into three parts the territory of your land which the LORD your God is giving you to inherit, that any manslayer may flee there.

4 "And this *is* the case of the manslayer who flees there, that he may live: Whoever kills his neighbor unintentionally, not having hated him in time past—

5 "as when *a man* goes to the woods with his neighbor to cut timber, and his hand swings a stroke with the ax to cut down the tree, and the head slips from the handle and strikes his neighbor so that he dies—he shall flee to one of these cities and live;

6 "lest the avenger of blood, while his anger is hot, pursue the manslayer and overtake him, because the way is long, and kill him, though he *was* not deserving of death, since he had not hated the victim in time past.

7 "Therefore I command you, saying, 'You shall separate three cities for yourself.'

8 "Now if the LORD your God enlarges your territory, as He swore to your fathers, and gives you the land which He promised to give to your fathers,

9 "and if you keep all these commandments and do them, which I command you today, to love the LORD your God and to walk always in His ways, then you shall add three more cities for yourself besides these three,

10 "lest innocent blood be shed in the midst of your land which the LORD your God is giving you *as* an inheritance, and *thus* guilt of bloodshed be upon you.

11 "But if anyone hates his neighbor, lies in wait for him, rises against him and strikes him mortally, so that he dies, and he flees to one of these cities,

12 "then the elders of his city shall send and bring him from there, and deliver him over to the hand of the avenger of blood, that he may die.

13 "Your eye shall not pity him, but you shall put away *the guilt of* innocent blood from Israel, that it may go well with you.

14 "You shall not remove your neighbor's landmark, which the men of old have set, in your inheritance which you will inherit in the land that the LORD your God is giving you to possess.

15 "One witness shall not rise against a man concerning any iniquity or any sin that he commits; by the mouth of two or three witnesses the matter shall be established.

16 "If a false witness rises against any man to testify against him of wrongdoing,

17 "then both men in the controversy shall stand before the LORD, before the priests and the judges who serve in those days.

18 "And the judges shall make careful inquiry, and indeed, *if* the witness *is* a false witness, who has testified falsely against his brother,

19 "then you shall do to him as he thought to have done to his brother; so you shall put away the evil from among you.

20 "And those who remain shall hear and fear, and hereafter they shall not again commit such evil among you.

21 "Your eye shall not pity: life *shall be* for life, eye for eye, tooth for tooth, hand for hand, foot for foot."

Deut. 19:1–21

With Deuteronomy 19 we leave behind Moses' orderly treatment of the laws. The next few chapters (19–26) deal with a wide variety of topics, most of which appear merely in outline form. Only the issues

235

of homicide (19:1–13) and the holy war (20:1–10) have a more extended treatment.

This entire nineteenth chapter deals with justice for the defenseless: justice for the unintentional killer (vv. 1–13), justice for the landowner (v. 14), and justice for the accused (vv. 15–21).

When Israel entered Canaan, they were to designate three cities to be places of refuge for those who had unintentionally killed another person. These cities were to be equally spaced geographically throughout the land, to be accessible to those in need of immediate sanctuary.

Moses gives special attention to the issue of blood revenge since this was a common practice in ancient nomadic societies. The cities of haven offered protection from an *"avenger of blood, while his anger is hot"* (v. 6). The avenger was essentially a family protector. Traditionally he was the nearest male relative, the one responsible for bringing a relative out of slavery (Lev. 25:48–49), for redeeming a relative's property (Lev. 25:25), for marrying a relative's widow and raising up children in the name of the deceased (Ruth 3:12–13; 4:5–10), and for avenging the death of a relative (Num. 35:19).

The manslayer is defined as one who *"kills his neighbor unintentionally"* and without previous feelings of hatred toward his neighbor (v. 4). The case of a deliberate slaying motivated by hatred is a different matter (vv. 11–13). When this happened, the elders of the murdered man's hometown were responsible for bringing the slayer from the city of refuge and handing him over to that kinsman who would exact blood revenge. The elders were in a position to decide the guilt of the man without being influenced by any sense of personal loss. The avenger of blood was the instrument designated to carry out the death penalty. A more detailed discussion of the cities of refuge is found in Numbers 35:9–34.

The following lessons can be learned from the establishment of the cities of refuge: (1) the value of human life, (2) the duty of the government to provide for the unfortunate, (3) the need to correctly identify the perpetrators of a crime, and (4) the value of a judicial system that is emotionally neutral.

From the discussion of the cities of refuge, Moses proceeds to a one-sentence law concerning the removal of a neighbor's landmark (v. 14), then follows with another law regarding the evidence of witnesses, especially malicious ones (vv. 15–21).

How do these laws fit together? Perhaps the first two laws tie together because of common vocabulary. *"You shall prepare roads for yourself, and divide into three parts the territory of your land"* (v. 3) and *"You shall not remove your neighbor's landmark, which the men of old have set"* (v. 14).

S. Kaufmann suggests the following organization of Deuteronomy 19: How to deal with homicide (vv. 1–13); how to prevent homicide (v. 14); how to deal with the accusation of homicide (vv. 15–21).[9] Obviously, the laws about both asylum and witnesses have a common concern—that innocent blood not be shed, either by the avenger of blood or, indirectly, by the witness who perjures himself against the defendant.

Verse 21 has caused great debate throughout the centuries. The law of retribution was previously given in Exodus 21:23–25 and Leviticus 24:17–22. It was given to encourage appropriate punishment of a criminal in cases where there might be a tendency to be either too lenient or too strict. The law codes of the ancient Near East made provision for the maiming of a criminal (e.g., gouging out an eye, cutting off a lip). With one exception (Deut. 25:11–12), however, Israelite law did not explicitly allow such mutilation. Only the first part of this law, *"life shall be for life,"* was applied to indicate that the punishment ought to fit the crime. For example, if a slave lost his eyes at the hands of an angry master, that slave was to be freed (Exod. 21:26). This law also served as a restraint in cases where the disciplinarian might be inclined to be excessive in administering punishment. Jesus did not deny the validity of this principle for the courtroom, but He denied its use in personal relationships (Matt. 5:38–42).[10]

NOTES

1. Dale Patrick, *Old Testament Law* (Atlanta: John Knox Press, 1985), pp. 189–92.

2. David Daube, *"One from Among Your Brethren Shall You Set King over You,"* *JBL* 90 (1971): 480ff.

3. John F. Walvoord and Roy B. Zuck, *The Bible Knowledge Commentary, O.T.* (Wheaton, IL: Victor Books, 1978), p. 295.

4. Gerhard von Rad, *Deuteronomy: A Commentary,* Old Testament Library (Philadelphia: Westminster Press, 1966), p. 120.

5. P. C. Craigie, *Commentary on the Book of Deuteronomy,* New International Commentary on the Old Testament (Grand Rapids: Wm. B. Eerdmans Publishing Co., 1976), p. 260.

6. Walvoord and Zuck, *The Bible Knowledge Commentary,* p. 296.

7. Pamela J. Koerbel, "It's Not a Game," *Moody Monthly,* January 1983.

8. Craigie, *Commentary,* pp. 263–64.

9. Stephen Kaufmann, "Structure of the Deuteronomic Law," *Maaraz* 1 (1979): 137.

10. Walvoord and Zuck, *The Bible Knowledge Commentary,* p. 298.

CHAPTER NINETEEN

Regulations Concerning War

Deuteronomy 20:1-20

The book of Deuteronomy is permeated with the atmosphere of war. Moses' pressing concern that Israel maintain her existence in the face of foreign nations gives rise to his treatment of a holy war. This holy war is marked by a number of distinctives which set it apart from other types of wars: (1) A holy war was not undertaken without consulting Yahweh (1 Sam. 28:5-6; 30:7-8; 2 Sam. 5:19, 22-23). (2) The men of Israel were consecrated to the Lord before (and during) battle (1 Sam. 21:5; 2 Sam. 11:11; Isa. 13:3). (3) Men that would offend God were removed from camp (Deut. 23:9-11). (4) Yahweh was present in the camp (Deut. 23:14), and He gave His leader special powers, although it was God Himself who was the Captain of the hosts of Israel and could alone deliver His people (Judg. 4:14-15; 7:2ff.; 1 Sam. 13:5, 15; 14:6-23). (5) At the climax of the battle God sent terror and panic into the midst of the enemy, thus bringing about their overthrow (Deut. 2:25; Josh. 2:9; 5:1; 1 Sam. 5:11; 7:10). (6) The spoils of war were under the ban of sacred consecration and were the exclusive right of God.[1]

PREPARING THE ARMY SPIRITUALLY

20:1 "When you go out to battle against your enemies, and see horses and chariots and people more numerous than you, do not be afraid of them; for the LORD your God is with you, who brought you up from the land of Egypt.

2 "So it shall be, when you are on the verge of battle, that the priest shall approach and speak to the people.

3 "And he shall say to them, 'Hear, O Israel: Today you are on the verge of battle with your enemies.
Do not let your heart faint, do not be afraid, and do
not tremble or be terrified because of them;
    4 'for the LORD your God *is* He who goes with you,
to fight for you against your enemies, to save you.'"

Deut. 20:1-4

The most significant lesson of this section is that the army of Israel
should not fear the enemy in battle—however, their tendency to be
afraid is understandable considering that their numbers were few
and their military strength minimal (v. 1).

Realizing the importance of mental preparation before battle,
Moses sends out the priests to encourage the soldiers (v. 2). He knows
that the battle is won *before* the battle is begun! These men of God say
to the fearful soldiers, *"Do not let your heart faint, do not be afraid, and
do not tremble or be terrified because of them"* (v. 3). Then verse 4 gives
three reasons why the soldiers should have a winning attitude:
(1) *"The Lord . . . goes with you"*; (2) He will *"fight for you"*; (3) He
will *"save you."* After this strong, concise message the warriors knew
without a doubt in whose strength they stood.

At this point we encounter again the two major themes running
throughout Deuteronomy that are not found in Exodus or Leviticus.
This setting seems to be an appropriate place for an overview of
these themes.

The first great theme centers on *man's utter weakness and inability
to accomplish great things on his own strength.* Obviously, their success
in battle had little to do with their own worth or actual military
ability.

"When your son asks you in time to come, saying, 'What is the
meaning of the testimonies, the statutes, and the judgments which
the Lord our God has commanded you?'" (Deut. 6:20)—in other
words, when your son asks, "Why do you go through all these cere-
monies? Why do you kill these lambs and goats and sheep? Why
do you go to the tabernacle? What is the purpose of all of this?"—
"then you shall say to your son: 'We were slaves . . . in Egypt. . . .
Then He brought us out from there, that He might bring us in, to
give us the land of which He swore to our fathers'" (Deut. 6:21, 23).

And the fathers tell their sons about their humble beginnings as slaves and how Yahweh rescued them.

And Moses continues to explain, saying:

> "For you are a holy people to the Lord your God; the Lord your God has chosen you to be a people for Himself, a special treasure above all the peoples on the face of the earth. The Lord did not set His love on you nor choose you because you were more in number than any other people, for you were the least of all peoples; but because the Lord loves you, and because He would keep the oath which He swore to your fathers, the Lord has brought you out with a mighty hand, and redeemed you from the house of bondage, from the hand of Pharaoh king of Egypt."
>
> *Deut. 7:6-8*

"It wasn't anything in you; you have nothing. It was God who did it—not man," Moses tells them.

> "Do not think in your heart, after the Lord your God has cast them out before you, saying, 'Because of my righteousness the Lord has brought me in to possess this land'; but it is because of the wickedness of these nations that the Lord is driving them out from before you. *It is not because of your righteousness or the uprightness of your heart* that you go in to possess their land, but because of the wickedness of these nations that the Lord your God drives them out from before you, and that He may fulfill the word which the Lord swore to your fathers, to Abraham, Isaac, and Jacob. Therefore understand that the Lord your God is not giving you this good land to possess because of your righteousness, for *you are a stiff-necked people.*"
>
> *Deut. 9:4-6*

After forty years of training in the wilderness Moses says, "Watch out! You never get to the place where you can stand on your own. Never."

241

You see, we never get to stand on our own strength. God never makes us so strong that we no longer need Him. Never. We will continually be dependent upon Him. Ironically, realizing our weakness and dependence is the secret to our strength and success.

Going into battle, the soldiers needed to remember this fact. They were not skilled soldiers—their roots were in slavery. Nor could they rely on horses and chariots as did many of their enemies. They must rely on God!

The second great theme in this book is *God's continual, abiding presence.* This was the secret of Israel's success in battle!

"If you should say in your heart, 'These nations are greater than I; how can I dispossess them?'—you shall not be afraid of them, but you shall remember well what the Lord your God did to Pharaoh and to all Egypt" (Deut. 7:17–18).

When you are up against problems in life—giants, difficulties, and various trials—you say to yourself, "I don't have it in myself. I can't deal with this." What should you remember? That God does it for you. God in you can meet that difficult situation. Your weakness becomes God's strength.

"So He humbled you, allowed you to hunger, and fed you with manna which you did not know nor did your fathers know, that He might make you know that man shall not live by bread alone; but man lives by every word that proceeds from the mouth of the Lord" (Deut. 8:3). Sound familiar? Those are the very words of Jesus when he explained to Satan why He would not turn the stones into bread (Matt. 4:1–4). He said, "You don't understand how I live. I don't live by doing remarkable signs to make everyone look in amazement. Man doesn't live like that. Man lives not 'by bread alone, but by every word that proceeds from the mouth of God.' God is in Me—that is what makes Me strong."

Deuteronomy 30 is a remarkable chapter. It is a marvelous explanation of the dynamic that makes obedience to the law possible for mortal men and women. In the first part of this chapter Moses reminds the people of their covenant with God. He tells the people of the blessings that will come with obedience and warns of the curses if they disobey. Then he says: "For this commandment which I command you today *is not too difficult for you*" (Deut. 30:11, NASB).

Every person who falls short says, "It's no use. The law is too hard

242

for me. I can't do that." But Moses says, "Yes you can; it's not too hard for you!"

And he continues, "Nor is it far off. It is not in heaven, that you should say, 'Who will ascend into heaven for us and bring it to us, that we may hear it and do it?' Nor is it beyond the sea, that you should say, 'Who will go over the sea for us and bring it to us, that we may hear it and do it?'" (Deut. 30:11–13).

How can we obey God's law and keep right before Him? Moses, leaving no room in our minds for doubt, says, "But the word is very near you, in your mouth and in your heart, that you may do it" (Deut. 30:14). The presence of the indwelling God enables us to successfully live the Christian life.

Notice how the themes of man's weakness and God's strength and presence are present in Deuteronomy 20. From verses 1–4, it is apparent that the soldiers are "nothing" when it comes to military tools and skill. It is equally obvious that it is God's presence that is the secret to their victories in battle.

The key to success for Israel's army then, and for our Christian life now, is in our understanding these two themes and keeping them in proper balance within our lives. Too often the tendency is to increase our own independence and decrease our dependence on God. The result is that at best we receive only what *we* can accomplish alone—which, in the end, amounts to nothing.

PREPARING THE ARMY INTERNALLY

20:5 "Then the officers shall speak to the people, saying: 'What man *is there* who has built a new house and has not dedicated it? Let him go and return to his house, lest he die in the battle and another man dedicate it.

6 'Also what man *is there* who has planted a vineyard and has not eaten of it? Let him go and return to his house, lest he die in the battle and another man eat of it.

7 'And what man *is there* who is betrothed to a woman and has not married her? Let him go and return to his house, lest he die in the battle and another man marry her.'

243

8 "The officers shall speak further to the people,
and say, 'What man *is there who is* fearful and fainthearted? Let him go and return to his house, lest the
heart of his brethren faint like his heart.'
9 "And so it shall be, when the officers have finished speaking to the people, that they shall make
captains of the armies to lead the people."

Deut. 20:5–9

The officers (v. 5) were responsible for making sure that the army
was composed of qualified men. However, those most qualified were
not necessarily those most gifted for battle. The qualified were the
committed—those whose eyes were on the Lord, those who were
not distracted by circumstances or events that might dampen their
spirits for battle.

Since God's assistance was already assured, many men were exempted from military service. Verses 5–7 show that some were
exempted because they had undertaken certain responsibilities and
had not yet enjoyed the privileges accruing from them: The man
who *"has built a new house"* (v. 5), or *"who has planted a vineyard and
has not eaten of it"* (v. 6), or the engaged man who *"has not married
her"* yet (v. 7).

These exemptions had an important bearing on the stability of
Israel's possession of Canaan. Although in later times war was
fought for defensive purposes, in the early stages of Israel's history
the purpose of war was to take possession of the land promised to
God's people so that Israel could live and prosper in it. Building
homes and planting vineyards, marrying and having children—this
was the essence of life in the promised land. Without these things,
war would be pointless. We see God leading the Hebrews in two
concurrent activities as they establish their home in Canaan: (1) in
doing battle to take the land and (2) in working at those things that
would establish it as their own.

The exemption of the *"fearful and fainthearted"* (v. 8) was given for
reasons of morale. Since the best army was the one most committed
to the Lord, anything or anyone who might affect the faith and confidence of the Israelite army was to be removed. Cowardice in this
setting was recognized as a spiritual problem. Notice that this exemption was given to the men only *after* the priests had encouraged

244

them by pointing to the might of God. To continue fearfully was to not trust God completely.

There are many examples throughout the Bible that point to the value of commitment and trust in God. One such example is the deliberate reduction of Gideon's army from thirty-two thousand men to three hundred. Why? "The Lord said to Gideon, 'The people who are with you are too many for Me to give the Midianites into their hands, lest Israel claim glory for itself against Me, saying, 'My own hand has saved me'" (Judg. 7:2). Gideon and all of Israel learned that God counts hearts, not heads, when He wants a great work accomplished.

PREPARING THE APPROACH EXTERNALLY

20:10 "When you go near a city to fight against it, then proclaim an offer of peace to it.

11 "And it shall be that if they accept your offer of peace, and open to you, then all the people *who are* found in it shall be placed under tribute to you, and serve you.

12 "Now if the city will not make peace with you, but war against you, then you shall besiege it.

13 "And when the LORD your God delivers it into your hands, you shall strike every male in it with the edge of the sword.

14 "But the women, the little ones, the livestock, and all that is in the city, all its spoil, you shall plunder for yourself; and you shall eat the enemies' plunder which the LORD your God gives you.

15 "Thus you shall do to all the cities *which are* very far from you, which *are* not of the cities of these nations.

16 "But of the cities of these peoples which the LORD your God gives you *as* an inheritance, you shall let nothing that breathes remain alive,

17 "but you shall utterly destroy them: the Hittite and the Amorite and the Canaanite and the Perizzite and the Hivite and the Jebusite, just as the LORD your God has commanded you,

18 "lest they teach you to do according to all their

abominations which they have done for their gods, and you sin against the LORD your God.

19 "When you besiege a city for a long time, while making war against it to take it, you shall not destroy its trees by wielding an ax against them; if you can eat of them, do not cut them down to use in the siege, for the tree of the field *is* man's *food.*

20 "Only the trees which you know *are* not trees for food you may destroy and cut down, to build siegeworks against the city that makes war with you, until it is subdued."

Deut. 20:10–20

This section shifts from military personnel to strategy. Cities that were outside the borders of the promised land were to be given an initial *"offer of peace"* (vv. 10–15). For the city to accept meant that they acknowledged the sovereignty of Israel's God and of Israel. They were also to become servants of God's people (v. 11). If a city refused terms of peace, the men were to be executed. But the women and children were to be spared, and they along with *"all that is in the city . . . you shall plunder for yourself"* (v. 14).

But inside Canaan absolutely nothing was to be spared: *"You shall let nothing that breathes remain alive, but you shall utterly destroy them"* (vv. 16–17). There are two reasons for this total destruction, only one of which is stated in this passage. (1) The Israelites were instruments of God's judgment. The conquest was not only the means by which God granted the people the promised land; it was also the means by which God executed His judgment on the Canaanites for their sinfulness (9:4). (2) If the people of Canaan survived, their unholy religion could turn Israel aside from serving the Lord (v. 18).

The women in the nations mentioned in 20:10–15 (the Aramean culture) were not like those from the Canaanite culture. Aramean women traditionally adopted the religions of their husbands. It was for this reason that God allowed the Aramean women and children to be spared. The influence of Jezebel, who brought her husband Ahab under the worship of Baal, demonstrates the destructive effects of marriage to a Canaanite wife.[1]

Today, as we reflect upon Deuteronomy 20, we sense a curious mixture of enlightened humanitarianism and primitive savagery.

There are some Christians who question the sanctity of war. The teaching of this section of Scripture must be seen in the total context of the progressiveness of divine revelation. Moses' writing cannot be viewed as a series of isolated or unrelated events.

In Deuteronomy 20, war is an instrument of divine policy; Israel could not have survived without it. But war does not always have the stamp of divine approval. Even in the Old Testament, David is denied the privilege of building the temple because his hands are stained with blood (1 Kings 5:3). One of the features of the coming Messianic kingdom is the abolition of war (Isa. 2:4; Mic. 4:3). That our society today still resorts to war proves nothing except that men are terribly resistant to the grace of God.

NOTE

1. Gerhard von Rad, *Studies in Deuteronomy*, trans. by D. Stalker (London: SCM Press, Ltd., 1953), pp. 45-59.

CHAPTER TWENTY

Regulations Concerning Murder, War, and Family Affairs

Deuteronomy 21:1-23

UNSOLVED MURDER

21:1 "If *anyone* is found slain, lying in the field in the land which the LORD your God is giving you to possess, *and* it is not known who killed him,

2 "then your elders and your judges shall go out and measure *the distance* from the slain man to the surrounding cities.

3 "And it shall be *that* the elders of the city nearest to the slain man will take a heifer which has not been worked *and* which has not pulled with a yoke.

4 "The elders of that city shall bring the heifer down to a valley with flowing water, which is neither plowed nor sown, and they shall break the heifer's neck there in the valley.

5 "Then the priests, the sons of Levi, shall come near, for the LORD your God has chosen them to minister to Him and to bless in the name of the LORD; by their word every controversy and every assault shall be *settled.*

6 "And all the elders of that city nearest to the slain *man* shall wash their hands over the heifer whose neck was broken in the valley.

7 "Then they shall answer and say, 'Our hands have not shed this blood, nor have our eyes seen *it.*

8 'Provide atonement, O LORD, for Your people Israel, whom You have redeemed, and do not lay

innocent blood to the charge of Your people Israel.'
And atonement shall be provided on their behalf for
the blood.
9 "So you shall put away the *guilt of* innocent
blood from among you when you do *what is* right in
the sight of the LORD."

Deut. 21:1-9

This section discusses the procedures to be followed when the
body of a murdered man is discovered in the open country and there
is no knowledge of the circumstances surrounding his death. Such a
murder involved the whole community in blood guilt. Both the people and the land were defiled, and some kind of ceremonial atonement was required to satisfy the demands of justice. The procedures
outlined underscore how extremely valuable a human life is to God.

Deliverance from guilt was granted when certain regulations were
followed.

The elders were to take a heifer, one that had never been worked,
down to a valley which had never been cultivated. By a flowing
stream they were to break the animal's neck (vv. 3–4). The cruel
killing of a heifer symbolized the tragedy of a man's having been
murdered. This dramatic exercise would deepen their sense of the
sin of murder.

The Levites supplied the liturgy which was repeated by the elders
over the dead animal (v. 5).

The elders of the city accepting responsibility for the dead man
washed their hands over the heifer (v. 6). The hand washing symbolized the community's freedom from the guilt attached to the crime;
it gave public testimony of their innocence.

The elders, on behalf of all Israel, prayed for atonement. The basis
for atonement is not Israel's merit, but the fact that God has redeemed His people from bondage (v. 8).

There is much about this ritual to raise interest and speculation.
The killing of the heifer was not an expiatory sacrifice, for blood
was not sprinkled according to standard rituals. Since the procedure
was a compromise solution, it must be assumed that if the murderer
were subsequently found, he would bear his own guilt. But if not,
inter-city strife was avoided since the avenger of blood could not
rashly demand satisfaction from men of another city.

The ritual raises the whole question of corporate guilt. There is a sense in which the whole nation is corporately responsible for some sins. Today we see examples of racial discrimination, neglect of the underprivileged, and a variety of other social evils that bring widespread tragic consequences. These are a result of national indifference or neglect or irresponsibility. Deuteronomy again declares, "We are community."

FEMALE WAR PRISONERS

21:10 "When you go out to war against your enemies, and the LORD your God delivers them into your hand, and you take them captive,

11 "and you see among the captives a beautiful woman, and desire her and would take her for your wife,

12 "then you shall bring her home to your house, and she shall shave her head and trim her nails.

13 "She shall put off the clothes of her captivity, remain in your house, and mourn her father and her mother a full month; after that you may go in to her and be her husband, and she shall be your wife.

14 "And it shall be, if you have no delight in her, then you shall set her free, but you certainly shall not sell her for money; you shall not treat her brutally, because you have humbled her."

Deut. 21:10–14

An Israelite was permitted to marry *"a beautiful woman"* from the captives if that battle was against "the cities which are very far from you, which are not of the cities of these nations" (20:15). The prospective wife could not be a Canaanite woman since there was a prohibition against marrying Canaanite people (7:1, 3–4).

If an Israelite soldier genuinely desired one of the captives, he could have her only through marriage. This helped protect the dignity of the women captives and the purity of the Israelite soldiers. Israelites were not to rape or otherwise mistreat captives as other armies of the ancient Near East did.

A soldier's marriage to a female captive could take place only after the following steps were taken:

She was brought to the man's home (v. 12). This would give her a sense of identity and security.

Her head was to be shaved and her nails trimmed (v. 12). This would be either a ritual for mourning or purification.

Her clothes of captivity were discarded (v. 13). Again there is a visual change occurring in the life of the female war captive. She is experiencing a positive change of status in her life.

She mourned for her parents (v. 13). This full month not only allowed her proper time for expression of sorrow, it also gave the prospective husband opportunity to reflect on his initial decision to marry her.

After the above requirements were met *"you may go in to her and be her husband, and she shall be your wife"* (v. 13). Verse 14 could be easily misinterpreted. It reads as though the husband can easily get rid of his wife for any trivial reason. I prefer to think that the phrase *"if you have no delight in her"* refers to the new wife's refusal to accept her husband's spiritual values. This explanation seems reasonable since her previous culture and religion have been foreign to Israel. If this was the case, the husband could dissolve the marriage by giving up all rights over her. Because her ex-husband was forbidden to treat her as a slave, the woman still retained a measure of dignity even though she was dishonored through the divorce.

THE FIRSTBORN INHERITANCE RIGHTS

21:15 "If a man has .two wives, one loved and the other unloved, and they have borne him children, *both* the loved and the unloved, and *if* the firstborn son is of her who is unloved,

16 "then it shall be, on the day he bequeaths his possessions to his sons, *that* he must not bestow firstborn status on the son of the loved wife in preference to the son of the unloved, the *true* firstborn.

17 "But he shall acknowledge the son of the unloved wife *as* the firstborn by giving him a double

portion of all that he has, for he *is* the beginning of
his strength; the right of the firstborn *is* his."

Deut. 21:15–17

The previous law was designed to protect the captive woman
against an unpredictable husband. This law protects the rights of
the eldest son of a man who has more than one wife. Monogamy
was always the divine ideal for marriage in the Old Testament
(Gen. 2:20–24). Polygamy, though practiced by some, never appears
in a positive light in the Old Testament. The Bible never describes a
truly happy polygamous marriage. One reason was that one of the
wives would always be loved more than the other. Favoritism was
an inevitable problem in a polygamous marriage. Jacob's marriage
illustrates what could happen when a man married two wives.
"Then Jacob also went in to Rachel, and he also loved Rachel more
than Leah" (Gen. 29:30).

This law states that the father's personal preference did not justify
his setting aside his eldest son in favor of a younger one. His firstborn son must be given a *"double portion"* (v. 17) of the inheritance
even though he was the son of his father's unloved wife. The same
phrase is used in 2 Kings 2:9: "And so it was, when they had crossed
over, that Elijah said to Elisha, 'Ask! What may I do for you, before I
am taken away from you?' Elisha said, 'Please let a double portion of
your spirit be upon me.'" This request is often mistakenly interpreted
to mean that Elisha desired twice as much of the spirit as Elijah
possessed. Not so. He is asking Elijah to declare him his primary
successor, his spiritual heir.

THE REBELLIOUS SON

21:18 "If a man has a stubborn and rebellious son
who will not obey the voice of his father or the voice
of his mother, and *who*, when they have chastened
him, will not heed them,
19 "then his father and his mother shall take hold
of him and bring him out to the elders of his city, to
the gate of his city.

20 "And they shall say to the elders of his city,
'This son of ours is stubborn and rebellious; he will
not obey our voice; he is a glutton and a drunkard.'
21 "Then all the men of his city shall stone him to
death with stones; so you shall put away the evil
from among you, and all Israel shall hear and fear."

Deut. 21:18-21

Deuteronomy continually points to the stability of the family as the
foundation for a strong society. An extreme violation of the fifth commandment, "Honor your father and your mother" (5:16), was to be
punished by death. This harsh penalty did not refer to an occasional
lapse into disobedience but a persistent rebellion against his father
and mother even after the son had been warned by the parents of the
consequences of his rebellious actions (v. 18). After the parents had
tried everything within their power to bring their son under parental
authority, they could bring the issue before the elders of the city. If
the elders found the son guilty, the sentence was death by stoning.

The deterrent effect of severe public discipline is once again highlighted: *"and all Israel shall hear and fear"* (v. 21). The children of
Israel were instructed to kill by stoning anyone who tried to entice
them to serve another god. Why? "So all Israel shall *hear* and *fear*,
and not again do such wickedness as this among you" (Deut. 13:11).
If witnesses have testified that a fellow Israelite has worshiped other
gods and if the accused is found guilty, then that person shall be
"put away" and "all the people shall *hear* and *fear*, and no longer act
presumptuously" (Deut. 17:12, 13).

No record in the Bible indicates that this punishment was ever
carried out. The fear of death apparently deterred Israelite children
from becoming stubborn and rebellious.

Too often in the church today, when a person is confronted with
his own disobedience to biblical commands, he or she is more likely
to "hear and sneer" than to "hear and fear." Why? The church body
lacks discipline. The greatest deterrent to sin in a society is that the
people love God and fear (reverence) Him by obeying His commands. Love without fear is mush. Fear without love is legalism.
Only the two together in proper balance will bring about the obedience required by God.

253

A Hanged Man

21:22 "If a man has committed a sin deserving of death, and he is put to death, and you hang him on a tree,
23 "his body shall not remain overnight on the tree, but you shall surely bury him that day, so that you do not defile the land which the LORD your God is giving you *as* an inheritance; for he who is hanged *is* accursed of God."

Deut. 21:22, 23

The sequence of verse 22 indicates that hanging was not a method of execution but something that was done after the death of a criminal. His already lifeless body would be hung publicly to call attention to the gravity of breaking God's law. As soon as the public had seen the effect of sin upon a man's life, the corpse was buried, always before sunset of the day of the hanging.

Paul, in Galatians 3:13, draws from this Scripture a brief analogy. "Christ has redeemed us from the curse of the law, having become a curse for us (for it is written, 'Cursed is everyone who hangs on a tree')." Just as the corpse of a condemned criminal publicly displayed the curse of God, so Christ hanging on the cross as a condemned and executed criminal publicly exhibited the judgment of God. He bore the same shame as every executed criminal and was publicly exhibited as one who was accursed of God. To free us from the curse of the law Jesus Himself had to become accursed.

CHAPTER TWENTY-ONE

Regulations Concerning Various Issues

Deuteronomy 22:1–23:25

ASSISTING YOUR NEIGHBOR

22:1 "You shall not see your brother's ox or his sheep going astray, and hide yourself from them; you shall certainly bring them back to your brother.

2 "And if your brother *is* not near you, or if you do not know him, then you shall bring it to your own house, and it shall remain with you until your brother seeks it; then you shall restore it to him.

3 "You shall do the same with his donkey, and so shall you do with his garment; with any lost thing of your brother's, which he has lost and you have found, you shall do likewise; you must not hide yourself.

4 "You shall not see your brother's donkey or his ox fall down along the road, and hide yourself from them; you shall surely help him lift *them* up again."

Deut. 22:1–4

Recently a friend of mine spotted a couple along the freeway having car trouble. The temptation to pass them by was very strong; his wife and child were expecting him to meet them soon. Yet he had a strong feeling that God wanted him to stop and offer his assistance, so he pulled over. Their continual expression of appreciation as he drove them to a garage made my friend feel good about his decision. He also had an opportunity to witness for Christ. As he was returning the couple to their disabled vehicle, they were surprised to see a

255

crowd of people gathered around the approximate spot where they had left it. They soon discovered that while they were gone another car had hit and demolished theirs. No doubt the couple would have been seriously hurt or killed if my friend had not stopped and offered his help.

Why did my friend stop to help a total stranger? It was his relationship with God and his understanding of his neighbor that motivated him to do this good deed.

This particular passage deals with our actions toward another person. If a *"brother"* has a problem, Moses declares that *"you shall not . . . hide yourself from them."* In other words, don't withhold your help from him. The parallel law in Exodus 23:4, 5 uses the word *"enemy"* in place of Deuteronomy's *"brother."* This reminds us of Jesus' exhortation in Matthew 5:44 to love our enemies and of His teaching in the parable of the Good Samaritan (Luke 10:30–37). Our *"neighbor"* is anyone in need, whether friend or foe.

Certainly the expression "finders keepers, losers weepers" has no validity in light of this teaching. The finder is to take positive action to ensure that the lost item is returned to its rightful owner. Too often, our natural tendency is to consider our time and energy more valuable than someone else's lost possession.

"What does it profit, my brethren, if someone says he has faith but does not have works? Can faith save him? If a brother or sister is naked and destitute of daily food, and one of you says to them, 'Depart in peace, be warmed and filled,' but you do not give them the things which are needed for the body, what does it profit?" (James 2:14–16).

TRANSVESTISM

> 22:5 "A woman shall not wear anything that pertains to a man, nor shall a man put on a woman's garment, for all who do so *are* an abomination to the LORD your God."
>
> *Deut. 22:5*

This short section of Scripture has caused much debate in some Christian circles. What does it mean? Here are some possible explanations:

One explanation is that this practice was associated with the religion of Canaan; therefore, it was *an abomination to the Lord.*" Apparently women appeared in male garments and men in women's clothes when they worshiped their pagan deities. Yahweh wanted His people to be unique and to do nothing that was in any way connected with foreign religions.

Another theory is that this verse could refer to war. A woman was not to put on the trappings of a soldier or dress like a man in order to try to gain admission into the army. Nor were men to attempt to avoid military obligation by dressing as women.[1]

Another explanation often given for this ban is that it obscured the distinction between the sexes and therefore violated an essential part of the created order of life (Gen. 1:27). The Hebrew phrase for *"pertains to"* is used elsewhere in referring to decorations or utensils used by the opposite sex. During the days of Moses, garments worn by men and women were very similar (robes); so this command was designed to keep a woman from appearing as a man for purposes of licentiousness. The major difference between male and female robes was their decoration or ornamentation. This passage does not teach against women's wearing slacks, hats, shoes, gloves, or other items that are now worn by both sexes, but rather against the wearing of any item specifically intended for the opposite sex. The distinctives of each sex should be maintained and protected in regard to outward appearance. The New Testament instruction in Galatians 3:28 that "there is neither male or female; for you are all one in Christ Jesus" applied to status in God's sight and not to dress. While we realize that we are one in Christ, recognition of the differences between the sexes is a principle worth safeguarding.

Still another explanation is that this verse refers to the practice of transvestism, a deviant form of sexual behavior which is often characterized by cross-dressing. The verse says women should not wear things "pertaining to" the male. This phrase includes not only clothing, but also ornaments, weapons, and other items normally associated with men. In the second clause, women's clothing is explicitly forbidden men.

Transvestism is sometimes associated with homosexuality, and in the ancient world its practice was associated with the cults of certain deities. Whatever the circumstance, the practice of transvestism was *"an abomination to the Lord."*[2]

BIRDS

22:6 "If a bird's nest happens to be before you along the way, in any tree or on the ground, with young ones or eggs, with the mother sitting on the young or on the eggs, you shall not take the mother with the young;

7 "you shall surely let the mother go, and take the young for yourself, that it may be well with you and *that* you may prolong *your* days."

Deut. 22:6–7

It has been suggested that this law taught the Israelites compassion or reverence for parental relationships by using an object lesson from the animal world. However, the fact that the people were permitted to take the young birds from the mother seems to discredit this view. More likely, Moses was teaching the Israelites to protect their food source. By letting the mother go they could anticipate the production of more young in the future. Again we see the relationship between our obedience and God's blessing, *"that it may be well with you, and that you may prolong your days."*

HOME SAFETY

22:8 "When you build a new house, then you shall make a parapet for your roof, that you may not bring guilt of bloodshed on your household if anyone falls from it."

Deut. 22:8

The roof of a house was used for many purposes, such as sleeping in the summertime, doing household chores, and entertaining. Because of this constant use, a parapet was to be built around the outside edge of the roof for safety purposes.

If an accident occurred and there was no wall or railing around the roof, the homeowner would be liable. The building of a parapet not only protected the host from guilt but was an opportunity to "love your neighbor as yourself" (Lev. 19:18) by showing concern for the safety of others.

Today we are still reminded that we are our brother's keeper. If each member of society took seriously his or her responsibility for others, we would not need laws protecting us from drunken drivers and other irresponsible and reckless people. God values human life and He expects us to do the same. That truth is the emphasis of this teaching. Deuteronomy, then and now, reminds us that we are a community. The behavior of one affects others.

PROHIBITION OF CERTAIN MIXTURES

22:9 "You shall not sow your vineyard with different kinds of seed, lest the yield of the seed which you have sown and the fruit of your vineyard be defiled.

10 "You shall not plow with an ox and a donkey together.

11 "You shall not wear a garment of different sorts, such as wool and linen mixed together."

Deut. 22:9-11

The reason for the prohibitions against planting *"different kinds of seed"* in a field, yoking together *"an ox and a donkey,"* and wearing *"a garment of different sorts"* is uncertain. They may have had a symbolic function in teaching the Israelites something about the created order of things. They may have referred to pagan cultic practices. Perhaps they were yet another way of reminding the Israelites that God wanted His people to be separate from the rest of the world.

TASSELS

22:12 "You shall make tassels on the four corners of the clothing with which you cover *yourself.*"

Deut. 22:12

The command to wear tassels on the four corners of a garment gives Israel a distinction in her dress. Numbers 15:37-41 explains this requirement: By attaching four tassels to the garment worn most frequently, an Israelite would be reminded often of God's law and of the need to obey it.

Again God is reminding His people not to forget their unique relationship to Him. In Deuteronomy 6:8–9, the Israelites are commanded to keep God's word visually in front of them so that they will have no excuse for forgetting it. In this verse of Deuteronomy, tassels are used in this way as a visual reminder. Today God still does not want His people to forget His commands and go their own way.

In a secular society, what reminders do we have that keep our minds on Christ? I know one person who keeps a small cross in his pocket. Whenever he reaches into it for his keys, he feels the cross and remembers who he is and what Jesus did for him. The celebration of the Lord's Supper is another time to reflect upon our relationship with God. We observe Communion in remembrance of Him.

Sexual Morality

22:13 "If any man takes a wife, and goes in to her, and detests her,

14 "and charges her with shameful conduct, and brings a bad name on her, and says, 'I took this woman, and when I came to her I found she *was* not a virgin,'

15 "then the father and mother of the young woman shall take and bring out *the evidence of* the young woman's virginity to the elders of the city at the gate.

16 "And the young woman's father shall say to the elders, 'I gave my daughter to this man as wife, and he detests her.

17 'Now he has charged her with shameful conduct, saying, "I found your daughter *was* not a virgin," and yet these *are the evidences of* my daughter's virginity.' And they shall spread the cloth before the elders of the city.

18 "Then the elders of that city shall take that man and punish him;

19 "and they shall fine him one hundred *shekels* of silver and give *them* to the father of the young woman, because he has brought a bad name on a virgin of Israel. And she shall be his wife; he cannot divorce her all his days.

20 "But if the thing is true, *and evidences of* virginity are not found for the young woman,

21 "then they shall bring out the young woman to the door of her father's house, and the men of her city shall stone her to death with stones, because she has done a disgraceful thing in Israel, to play the harlot in her father's house. So you shall put away the evil from among you.

22 "If a man is found lying with a woman married to a husband, then both of them shall die—the man that lay with the woman, and the woman; so you shall put away the evil from Israel.

23 "If a young woman *who is* a virgin is betrothed to a husband, and a man finds her in the city and lies with her,

24 "then you shall bring them both out to the gate of that city, and you shall stone them to death with stones, the young woman because she did not cry out in the city, and the man because he humbled his neighbor's wife; so you shall put away the evil from among you.

25 "But if a man finds a betrothed young woman in the countryside, and the man forces her and lies with her, then only the man who lay with her shall die.

26 "But you shall do nothing to the young woman; *there is* in the young woman no sin *deserving* of death, for just as when a man rises against his neighbor and kills him, even so *is* this matter.

27 "For he found her in the countryside, *and* the betrothed young woman cried out, but *there was* no one to save her.

28 "If a man finds a young woman *who is* a virgin, who is not betrothed, and he seizes her and lies with her, and they are found out,

29 "then the man who lay with her shall give to the young woman's father fifty *shekels* of silver, and she shall be his wife because he has humbled her; he shall not be permitted to divorce her all his days.

30 "A man shall not take his father's wife, nor uncover his father's bed."

Deut. 22:13-30

Perhaps the three brief laws about not mixing (vv. 9–11) serve as a prelude to the unlawful mixing at the sexual level. Six situations are discussed. The first three focus on the married woman; the last three are concerned with the unmarried woman.

A man falsely charges his wife with having engaged in premarital sex (vv. 13–19). The law allowing a man to divorce a bride who was not a virgin was intended to enforce premarital sexual purity and to encourage parents to instill within their children the value of sexual purity. Here a man and woman are married. In an attempt to get rid of her, he charges her falsely with having had premarital intercourse with another man and, therefore, not being a virgin at the time of the wedding.

The legal responsibility of defending the young woman fell on her parents. They had to produce evidence of her virginity at the time of marriage. This evidence would be a blood-stained cloth or bedsheet from the wedding night. The parents were to make this evidence public before the elders of the city (vv. 15–17), who then were to pronounce a threefold judgment upon the man.

(1) They were to *"punish him"* (v. 18). This probably meant forty stripes with the whip for lying. (2) They were to *"fine him one hundred shekels of silver,"* which he was to pay to the father of the young girl. This fine was given to the father because his name was slandered. The accusation against his daughter called into question his desire or ability to pass on to his children God's values regarding sexual purity. (3) The elders were to deprive the man of his divorce rights (v. 19).

A charge against a wife of premarital sex is substantiated (vv. 20–21). If the charges made by the husband were found to be true, then the woman would be stoned to death outside the father's house. The location of the execution points to responsibility of the family to uphold God's law. This harsh punishment was intended to be not only for the sin of premarital sex, but also for deceiving the prospective husband and, as head of the household, the father was partially responsible.

The entire community became involved in a private sin. Today, although the stigma and the punishment of premarital sex have been greatly reduced, others are still affected by one person's immorality. There is no such thing as a "casual affair." One need only read the statistics concerning abortions, sexually transmitted diseases, and government assistance for unwed mothers to realize

that private sexual sins quickly become public matters of concern.
A man commits adultery with a married woman (v. 22). Although
the death penalty was to be administered for sexual unfaithfulness
in marriage (Lev. 20:10), the precise manner in which it was to be
carried out was not specified. In Mesopotamia, an adulterous couple
was to be thrown into the water (Code of Hammurabi, Law 129).
The official leaders of Judaism in Jesus' day interpreted the penalty
to mean death by stoning (John 8:5), but later Rabbinic tradition pre-
scribed death by strangulation.

A man has sexual intercourse with an engaged virgin in the city
(vv. 23–24). An engaged woman was to be treated under the law as if
she were married. The bride-price had been paid and the marriage
was being finalized. The engaged woman, like one who was married,
was committed to a relationship with a particular man. This sexual sin
was not considered to have been rape if it occurred within the city,
since the woman could have screamed and been heard by others.

A man has sexual intercourse with an engaged virgin outside of the city
(vv. 25–27). If the assault happened in the countryside the woman
was given the benefit of the doubt. She could have screamed and no
one would have heard her. Whereas verses 23–24 imply that the engaged woman could have been a willing partner, the terminology
here suggests rape. In verse 23 the *"man finds her . . . and lies with
her,"* but here, he finds her and *"forces her and lies with her."* So, in
this kind of case, only the man was put to death.

A man has sexual intercourse with a virgin (vv. 28–29). A man who
raped a virgin who was not engaged was forced to marry her, and
he forfeited the right of divorce. To a degree, this protected the girl's
honor and assured her of permanent support. This may have been a
deterrent to rape, since the man had to marry and support the
woman the rest of his life.

Verse 30 probably refers to a man's marrying his stepmother after
his father dies. Such a marriage would have been regarded as incestuous (Lev. 18:8).

ADMISSION INTO THE LORD'S ASSEMBLY

23:1 "He who is emasculated by crushing or mutilation shall not enter the assembly of the LORD.

2 "One of illegitimate birth shall not enter the assembly of the LORD; even to the tenth generation none of his *descendants* shall enter the assembly of the LORD.

3 "An Ammonite or Moabite shall not enter the assembly of the LORD; even to the tenth generation none of his *descendants* shall enter the assembly of the LORD forever,

4 "because they did not meet you with bread and water on the road when you came out of Egypt, and because they hired against you Balaam the son of Beor from Pethor of Mesopotamia, to curse you.

5 "Nevertheless the LORD your God would not listen to Balaam, but the LORD your God turned the curse into a blessing for you, because the LORD your God loves you.

6 "You shall not seek their peace nor their prosperity all your days forever.

7 "You shall not abhor an Edomite, for he *is* your brother. You shall not abhor an Egyptian, because you were an alien in his land.

8 "The children of the third generation born to them may enter the assembly of the LORD."

Deut. 23:1–8

The elders called *"the assembly of the Lord"* together for a variety of reasons, such as war and annual feasts. In their assembly, the religious community undertook various sacred rites, particularly worship (4:10; 9:10; 10:4; 18:16). The following categories of people were either to be barred permanently from the community of the Lord or to be admitted under certain specified conditions.

Men whose reproductive organs were mutilated were not allowed in the congregation. This exclusion may have been another reminder that mutilation of the body was unacceptable to God (14:1–2). It probably was not intended for the man who had been castrated by accident. Or it may have been directed to the person who intentionally had himself castrated for pagan religious purposes.

Those *"of illegitimate birth"* were excluded. The meaning of this phrase is uncertain. Traditionally it has been thought to refer to a child born out of wedlock. However, it's possible the term refers to the child of an incestuous relationship or the child of a cult prostitute.

264

It could also mean the child of a mixed marriage (such as an Israelite married to an Ammonite). This harsh punishment would help deter Israelites from entering this kind of marriage.

The Ammonites and Moabites were not allowed to attend Israel's religious gatherings because of their treatment of Israel during the wilderness period. The Ammonites were forbidden because they had not shown hospitality to the Israelites as they left Egypt. The Moabites were punished because they had attempted in Balaam to bring down the curse of God on Israel (Num. 22–24). God turned their attempted curse into a blessing for Israel, and now the curse is having a boomerang effect on the Moabites. Also, the Moabites and Ammonites were descendants of the incestuous unions of Lot and his daughters (Gen. 19:30–38). Perhaps that would be another reason for the severe exclusion of these two groups from the congregation of Israel.

The treatment of the Edomite people (vv. 7–8) was more lenient, since they were descended from Esau (Gen. 36:43). The Egyptian people also were protected from harsh judgment, perhaps because of Israel's long stay in that country and because of the initial positive treatment given to Joseph and his family when they first entered Egypt (Gen. 37–50). The third generation of these peoples could *enter the assembly of the Lord."*

CLEANLINESS IN THE CAMP

23:9 "When the army goes out against your enemies, then keep yourself from every wicked thing.

10 "If there is any man among you who becomes unclean by some occurrence in the night, then he shall go outside the camp; he shall not come inside the camp.

11 "But it shall be, when evening comes, that he shall wash with water; and when the sun sets, he may come into the camp.

12 "Also you shall have a place outside the camp, where you may go out;

13 "and you shall have an implement among your equipment, and when you sit down outside, you shall dig with it and turn and cover your refuse.

14 "For the LORD your God walks in the midst of
your camp, to deliver you and give your enemies over
to you; therefore your camp shall be holy, that He
may see no unclean thing among you, and turn away
from you."

Deut. 23:9-14

Moses directs the people of God to be pure in the military camp.
The general principle is stated first (v. 9), followed by two specific
examples (vv. 10–11, 12–13), and then the reason behind the principle is given (v. 14). This legislation deals with matters of personal
hygiene, emphasizing the close relationship between cleanliness and
godliness, or God's presence.

The first example relates to a man who is *"unclean by some occurrence in the night"* (v. 10). This probably refers to the nocturnal emis-
sion of semen as described in Leviticus 15:16–17. It could also apply
to a man who urinates in the camp at night because he is too tired to
get up and go outside the camp. The man who became unclean at
night was required to stay outside the camp the following day. Toward evening he would wash himself and be permitted to enter the
camp after sunset (v. 11). This was to maintain ritualistic purity.

The second example deals with the provision and maintenance of
toilet facilities outside the camp. Perhaps this was the origin of public
restrooms! The men were to leave the camp and go to the designated
area, where they were to dig a hole and bury their excrement (v. 13).

Verse 14 explains the reason for such ritualistic habits of cleanliness. Yahweh walked in the midst of the camp to protect His people
and to deliver their enemies into their hands. The camp was to remain undefiled so that God would not depart. The symbol of His
presence in the camp was the ark. Before the ark had a permanent
resting place, it was the visible sign of the presence of God. When it
arrived in the Israelite camp, the enemy said, "God has come into the
camp!" (1 Sam. 4:7). In the presence of the ark no unholy thing
would be tolerated.

From this section of Scripture the following observations may be
made: (1) The presence of God is everywhere. He observes our behavior even in our most private moments. (2) Our most mundane
acts are significant and can be an honor or dishonor to God. (3) The
pressures of life (war) are not an excuse for a lower standard of

living. (4) God is concerned about cleanliness and hygiene. His laws are for our protection and if obeyed will lead to a better life.

ESCAPED SLAVES

23:15 "You shall not give back to his master the slave who has escaped from his master to you.

16 "He may dwell with you in your midst, in the place which he chooses within one of your gates, where it seems best to him; you shall not oppress him."

Deut. 23:15-16

These were slaves from other countries who sought sanctuary in Israel. The command, *"You shall not give back to his master the slave who has escaped"* was contrary to normal practice in the ancient Near East. The treaties of that day included provisions for escaped slaves and other fugitives to be returned. In the Hammurabi Code, a man who harbored a runaway slave was to be put to death. Perhaps this command of God helped the Israelites to remember that their alliance was with God, and they did not need to obey other treaties or form political alliances with other nations. Possibly this law protecting fugitive slaves was meant to remind the Israelites of their former status as slaves in Egypt.

PROSTITUTION

23:17 "There shall be no *ritual* harlot of the daughters of Israel, or a perverted one of the sons of Israel.

18 "You shall not bring the wages of a harlot or the price of a dog to the house of the LORD your God for any vowed offering, for both of these *are* an abomination to the LORD your God."

Deut. 23:17-18

Two distinct laws in this passage relate to the subject of prostitution. First, young men and women in Israel were not to become cult prostitutes. Temple prostitution was common in Near Eastern religions; this command was to prevent the practice of a foreign religion by Israel and to keep the worship of the Lord from being contaminated by temple prostitution. The history of Israel is full of examples of her failure to keep this command (1 Kings 14:24; 15:12; 22:46; 2 Kings 23:7; Hos. 4:14).

Second, the people were not to pay promised offerings with money obtained from this sinful practice. The payment of a vow allowed an Israelite to express his gratitude for God's gracious provision in his life. Therefore, to use money that had been acquired by sinful means would be hypocritical. The use here of *"dog"* (v. 18) may refer to the doglike manner in which *"a perverted one of the sons of Israel"* debased himself when he became a temple prostitute.

LENDING WITH INTEREST

> 23:19 "You shall not charge interest to your brother—
> interest on money *or* food *or* anything that is lent out
> at interest.
> 20 "To a foreigner you may charge interest, but to
> your brother you shall not charge interest, that the
> LORD your God may bless you in all to which you
> set your hand in the land which you are entering to
> possess."
>
> *Deut. 23:19–20*

While living back East, I frequently stopped at a clothing store that was owned and operated by Jewish people. Over the years one of the tailors became a good friend of mine. One day I asked Lou to explain to me why he felt God had blessed so many Jewish people financially. He cited Deuteronomy 23:19–20 and said, "We always help our people."

Here God shows how financial prosperity can be a blessing to others. The secret lies in an unselfish spirit. If a man has wealth, he has the means to help the oppressed by lending them money without interest. Charging a brother interest would ultimately increase the debt that produced his need for the loan in the first place. It would also reveal an attitude unworthy of a member of the covenant community.

An Israelite was permitted to charge interest to a foreigner since he was not a member of the covenant community. Most likely, the

foreigner would be a merchant, and the loan given to him would be
for business purposes.

MAKING A VOW

23:21 "When you make a vow to the LORD your God,
you shall not delay to pay it; for the LORD your
God will surely require it of you, and it would be sin
to you.
22 "But if you abstain from vowing, it shall not be
sin to you.
23 "That which has gone from your lips you shall
keep and perform, for you voluntarily vowed to the
LORD your God what you have promised with your
mouth."

Deut. 23:21-23

Underlying God's command concerning vows is the covenant He
made with His people. God spoke His promise audibly to the people. His words were reliable and would be fulfilled. They were not
spoken to manipulate the people; neither were they withdrawn under the heat of anger. God's people were to follow His example. For
the Israelites to make a vow and not follow through on it would be
contrary to the whole spirit of the covenant.

Several observations are made here concerning vows to the Lord.
(1) No one is forced to make a vow to God (v. 23). (2) When no vow
is made, no sin is committed (v. 22). (3) God holds us accountable for
our voluntary vows (vv. 21, 23).

In my last pastorate, a lady in my congregation spent many hours
worrying over a legalistic vow she had made to God in her youth.
This vow had been made under pressure to conform to the standards
of others. Her desire to please others as well as God was the motivation for the vow. Now, many years later, her spirit was heavy under
self-imposed bondage to a rule that had nothing to do with her relationship with God. During a counseling session she asked, "Pastor,
will I forever be bound to this foolish vow?" My reply was, "No, not
unless you have a fool for a God."

The covenant principle in this passage promotes the deepening
of the relationship between God and His people. The vow which the

269

Israelites made to God was to be an expression of sincerity that could enhance their relationship with Him. The purpose of the vow was for blessing, not binding.

EATING OTHER PEOPLE'S CROPS

23:24 "When you come into your neighbor's vineyard, you may eat your fill of grapes at your pleasure, but you shall not put *any* in your container.
25 "When you come into your neighbor's standing grain, you may pluck the heads with your hand, but you shall not use a sickle on your neighbor's standing grain."

Deut. 23:24–25

Here, a traveler was given the right to momentarily refresh himself in a neighbor's vineyard or grainfield, but he was not given the right to carry the grapes away with him or to harvest the grain. Since God had been gracious in providing for the farmer, he in turn should be gracious to a person traveling through the land. The dispute over grain plucking between the Pharisees and Jesus in Matthew 12:1–8 did not take place because the disciples plucked someone else's grain, but because they did it on the Sabbath. That distinction is important.

Three thoughts concerning our possessions arise out of Deuteronomy 23:17–25. (1) Our possessions must be gained by honorable means (vv. 17–18). (2) Our possessions are a result of God's blessings (vv. 19–23). (3) We are to use them to help those who are less fortunate (vv. 24–25).

NOTES

1. Calum M. Carmichael, "A Time for War and a Time of Peace: The Influence of the Distinction upon Some Legal and Literary Material," in *Studies in Jewish Legal History: Essays in Honor of David Daub*, ed. B. S. Jackson (London: Jewish Chron. Pub., 1974), pp. 51ff.
2. Samuel R. Driver, *Deuteronomy*, 3rd ed. (Geneva, AL: Allenson, 1902), p. 250.

CHAPTER TWENTY-TWO

Responsibilities Concerning the Weak and the Wrong

Deuteronomy 24:1–25:19

REMARRIAGE AFTER DIVORCE

24:1 "When a man takes a wife and marries her, and it happens that she finds no favor in his eyes because he has found some uncleanness in her, and he writes her a certificate of divorce, puts *it* in her hand, and sends her out of his house,

2 "when she has departed from his house, and goes and becomes another man's *wife,*

3 "*if* the latter husband detests her and writes her a certificate of divorce, puts *it* in her hand, and sends her out of his house, or if the latter husband dies who took her as his wife,

4 "*then* her former husband who divorced her must not take her back to be his wife after she has been defiled; for that *is* an abomination before the LORD, and you shall not bring sin on the land which the LORD your God is giving you *as* an inheritance."

Deut. 24:1–4

This section of Scripture does not deal with divorce in general but with the issue of remarriage after divorce. If a man·divorces his wife and she marries another man who either dies or divorces her, the first husband is forbidden to remarry her. The first three verses set the conditions that apply to the legislation in verse four.

This law concerns the case in which a husband *"has found some uncleanness in"* his wife and divorced her. The Hebrew word for

271

"uncleanness" means "shame" or "disgrace." Its application was disputed among the rabbis. It cannot refer to adultery or premarital sex, since both of these acts had already been declared punishable by death. Because its meaning was unclear, the Pharisees tempted Jesus by asking, "Is it lawful for a man to divorce his wife for just any reason?" (Matt. 19:3). This question arose from a dispute between two camps of Jewish scholars. The conservative school of Shammai believed a man could not divorce his wife unless she was unfaithful. The school of Hillel was much more liberal. They believed the uncleanness referred to *anything* displeasing to the husband—such as appearing in public with disheveled hair, spinning and exposing her arms in public, conversing indiscriminately with men, speaking disrespectfully of her husband's parents in his presence, or spoiling a dish for him.

According to the liberal school of thought, these women only got one chance. If they burned supper, spoke too loudly, or exposed their arms in public, they were given a bill of divorcement.

What does the Bible mean by *"uncleanness"*? The word comes from a verb meaning "to be bare or empty." It is used figuratively in the Old Testament in referring to disgrace or to a blemish. From the way this word is used elsewhere in the Old Testament we know that uncleanness does not refer to trivial things such as burning a dish or talking too loudly. Its use is reserved for more disgraceful activities, possibly public nudity or improper sexual conduct which falls short of adultery.

The Hebrew word for divorcement means "a cutting off," which carries with it the idea of breaking the marriage covenant. Marriage was established by a formal legal covenant, and a formal legal document was required to dissolve marriage. The custom of writing a *"certificate of divorce"* (v. 1) was probably adopted by the Israelites when they were in Egyptian bondage.

The divorce procedure was simple. The husband was to write the wife a bill of divorcement, give it to her, and send her out of the house.

The Hebrew divorce was intended to protect the wife. In ancient civilization women were second-class citizens. In the heathen cultures around Israel, women were bought, sold, and traded like animals. The bill of divorcement mentioned here actually protected the woman and released her from further domestic obligations in the man's house. She was awarded financial protection. Custom required the husband who divorced his wife to return her dowry and give her a portion of his own estate equal to that dowry. She left the marriage with twice the lands, property, or money that she brought into the marriage.

After divorce there was only one prohibition against remarriage: The wife who was divorced from her second husband could not return to her first husband. Even if her second husband died, she could not return to the first, because she had been *"defiled"* (v. 4).

Since remarriage was allowed, why was going back to the first husband considered *"an abomination before the Lord"*? Perhaps God gave this prohibition to ensure that marriage was not reduced to wife-swapping, a practice that defiled the very meaning and covenant of marriage. No one could say, "I'll go marry someone else and if that doesn't work, I'll go back to my first mate." God wanted the sanctity of marriage to be maintained.[1]

The instructions on divorce in Deuteronomy 24 in no way indicate that God commanded divorce. Rather, He condoned divorce in certain circumstances, and gave guidelines to control a problem that was evident before Deuteronomy was written.

Leviticus 21:7 gives special regulations for priests' marriages; they could not marry a divorced person or one who was defiled. Here God is teaching that those in a position of spiritual leadership must exemplify God's ideal in precept and in practice.

Although divorce stems from sin, divorce itself is not sin. Several times God threatened to divorce Israel (Isa. 50:1). In Malachi 2:16 we read that *"God . . . hates divorce."* He hates divorce; he does not hate the divorced person. God loves people, regardless of their sins.

RESPONSIBILITIES CONCERNING THE WEAK

24:5 "When a man has taken a new wife, he shall not go out to war or be charged with any business; he shall be free at home one year, and bring happiness to his wife whom he has taken.

6 "No man shall take the lower or the upper millstone in pledge, for he takes *one's* living in pledge.

7 "If a man is found kidnapping any of his brethren of the children of Israel, and mistreats him or sells

him, then that kidnapper shall die; and you shall put away the evil from among you.

8 "Take heed in an outbreak of leprosy, that you carefully observe and do according to all that the priests, the Levites, shall teach you; just as I commanded them, so you shall be careful to do.

9 "Remember what the LORD your God did to Miriam on the way when you came out of Egypt.

10 "When you lend your brother anything, you shall not go into his house to get his pledge.

11 "You shall stand outside, and the man to whom you lend shall bring the pledge out to you.

12 "And if the man is poor, you shall not keep his pledge overnight.

13 "You shall in any case return the pledge to him again when the sun goes down, that he may sleep in his own garment and bless you; and it shall be righteousness to you before the LORD your God.

14 "You shall not oppress a hired servant who is poor and needy, whether one of your brethren or one of the aliens who is in your land within your gates.

15 "Each day you shall give him his wages, and not let the sun go down on it, for he is poor and has set his heart on it; lest he cry out against you to the LORD, and it be sin to you.

16 "Fathers shall not be put to death for their children, nor shall children be put to death for their fathers; a person shall be put to death for his own sin.

17 "You shall not pervert justice due the stranger or the fatherless, nor take a widow's garment as a pledge.

18 "But you shall remember that you were a slave in Egypt, and the LORD your God redeemed you from there; therefore I command you to do this thing.

19 "When you reap your harvest in your field, and forget a sheaf in the field, you shall not go back to get it; it shall be for the stranger, the fatherless, and the widow, that the LORD your God may bless you in all the work of your hands.

20 "When you beat your olive trees, you shall not go over the boughs again; it shall be for the stranger, the fatherless, and the widow.

21 "When you gather the grapes of your vineyard, you shall not glean *it* afterward; it shall be for the stranger, the fatherless, and the widow.

22 "And you shall remember that you were a slave in the land of Egypt; therefore I command you to do this thing."

Deut. 24:5-22

Verse 5 reveals God's concern for the health of a marriage. Imagine the luxury! Newlyweds were given one full year to adjust to married life, and the husband had no military duty or business responsibilities during that period. Why was this time to be set apart? So the husband could *"bring happiness to his wife."*

Early Mosaic law made it clear that the emotional well-being of a wife was the specific responsibility of her husband. It was his job to "cheer" her. It still is!

Verse 6 protects the weak by not allowing another person to take a millstone for a pledge. Millstones were used daily in homes to grind grain in preparing meals. To take a millstone as collateral for a debt would deprive a person of his daily bread (*"living"*).

Verse 7 deals with the issue of kidnapping, a common practice in the ancient Near East. This act was punishable by death.

The Hebrew word translated *"leprosy"* (v. 8) refers to a broad range of skin diseases, not exclusively to leprosy. Instead of repeating the legislation concerning these diseases, Moses referred the people to God's original instructions for the priests concerning leprosy (Lev. 13–14). He provided motivation to obey this ceremonial legislation by reminding them of Miriam, who was afflicted with leprosy because of her opposition to Moses (Num. 12).

This section deals with society's treatment of the poor. This issue is still relevant three thousand years later. Recently I read an interview given by Jim Wallis concerning the subject of poverty. He read the Bible specifically to find everything it said about the poor. His findings? The Bible was literally filled with references to the poor. In fact, the subject of poverty ranked second only to idolatry.

He took out his scissors and cut out of a Bible every reference to poor people, love for enemies, and reconciliation. After finally accomplishing his mission, he took that Bible with him when he went out to preach. He would hold it up in the air and say, "Brothers and sisters, this is the American Bible, full of holes from all we have cut out, all we have ignored. Our Bible is full of holes."

Moses made certain that Israel's care for the needy was not "full of holes." Verses 10–13 deal with the collection of a pledge. The individual lending the money was not allowed to enter the home of the borrower to collect something as collateral (vv. 10–11). This ensured the borrower's rights of personal property and kept the lender from taking advantage of the man. A very poor person would only have a garment to offer as a pledge. That garment was used as a cloak by day and bed covering by night. The creditor was not to keep that garment overnight (vv. 12–13). Even in a covenant community, one that received God's direct blessing, there would be the disadvantaged. Their hardship was to be alleviated by the spirit of generosity of their brothers and sisters.

"A hired servant who is poor and needy" (v. 14) should receive his wages at the end of each day. The phrase, *"for he is poor and has his heart set on it"* (v. 15) indicates that he needed to be paid daily in order to provide food for his family.

Verse 16, which addresses the issue of capital punishment, stands out in this section dealing with poverty. Many crimes in the Old Testament were punishable by the death penalty. The principle here is that a man is responsible for his own crime and, therefore, he alone must pay the penalty. If a father was condemned to death, the son was not to be executed with him or in his place, and vice versa. This short piece of legislation makes clear a principle underlying all the law in Deuteronomy: namely, that the presence of law and the requirement that it be obeyed placed upon every man the responsibility for his own actions, both within the covenant community and before God.

The rest of this chapter deals with the proper treatment of *"the stranger, the fatherless, and the widow"* (v. 19). Verse 17 commands justice toward the disadvantaged and generosity toward the widow (see also 10:18–19). Verses 19–21 offer one method of providing for these people. The fields, olive trees, and vineyards are not to be picked clean. The landowners were to leave a portion of food so that those who were unfortunate could glean from them. This kept the needy from being humiliated by having to beg or accept welfare; they could still work for their food. We see an example of this in Ruth's providing for herself and her mother-in-law by gleaning the rich man's fields (Ruth 2).

The legislation throughout this chapter not only protects the poor—it also protects the rich! Failure by the wealthy to help the weak brought judgment upon them. Notice the times where God comes into the picture when the wealthy are commanded to give to the poor. When the relationship is positive, *"it shall be righteousness to you before the Lord your God"* (v. 13). If the rich take advantage of the poor, then the poor will *"cry out against you to the Lord, and it be sin to you"* (v. 15). Israel's own past captivity and oppression under the Egyptians (vv. 18, 22) serves as a continual reminder to them to be generous to the less fortunate.

ADMINISTRATION OF BEATINGS

25:1 "If there is a dispute between men, and they come to court, that *the judges* may judge them, and they justify the righteous and condemn the wicked,

2 "then it shall be, if the wicked man deserves to be beaten, that the judge will cause him to lie down and be beaten in his presence, according to his guilt, with a certain number of blows.

3 "Forty blows he may give him *and* no more, lest he should exceed this and beat him with many blows above these, and your brother be humiliated in your sight.

4 "You shall not muzzle an ox while it treads out *the grain."*

Deut. 25:1-4

The purpose of the law in Deuteronomy 25:1-3 is not primarily to prescribe corporal punishment, but to limit it. The maximum number of blows to the guilty party is not to exceed forty.[2] Since the law protected the guilty from receiving more than forty stripes, the Jews often stopped short, at thirty-nine lashes. Paul was beaten by the Jews five times after this manner (2 Cor. 11:24).

CONTINUING A DEAD MAN'S NAME

25:5 "If brothers dwell together, and one of them
dies and has no son, the widow of the dead man
shall not be *married* to a stranger outside *the family;*
her husband's brother shall go in to her, take her
as his wife, and perform the duty of a husband's
brother to her.

6 "And it shall be *that* the firstborn son which she
bears will succeed to the name of his dead brother,
that his name may not be blotted out of Israel.

7 "But if the man does not want to take his
brother's wife, then let his brother's wife go up to
the gate to the elders, and say, 'My husband's
brother refuses to raise up a name to his brother in
Israel; he will not perform the duty of my husband's
brother.'

8 "Then the elders of his city shall call him and
speak to him. But *if* he stands firm and says, 'I do not
want to take her,'

9 "then his brother's wife shall come to him in the
presence of the elders, remove his sandal from his
foot, spit in his face, and answer and say, 'So shall it
be done to the man who will not build up his brother's
house.'

10 "And his name shall be called in Israel, 'The
house of him who had his sandal removed.'"

Deut. 25:5–10

In only one kind of circumstance was marriage permitted to a
close relative. Marriage to a divorced or widowed sister-in-law was
forbidden (Lev. 18:16) except under the following conditions. The
brothers must have been living together (i.e., they inherited their
father's property jointly), and the deceased brother must have died
without a son. If both of these conditions existed, then this type of
marriage was to take place.

The first son born from this brother-in-law marriage was given
*"the name of his dead brother, that his name may not be blotted out of
Israel"* (v. 6). Therefore, if a man died before the Lord fulfilled His
covenant promises made to Abraham and his descendants, he could

still participate, in a sense, in the glorious future of Israel through his legal descendants.

If a widow's brother-in-law refused to fulfill his duty either through greed (not wanting to share the family inheritance with his sister-in-law) or through dislike of his sister-in-law, she could tell the elders of the city about it. If he still refused, she could then *"remove his sandal from his foot, spit in his face,"* and curse him (*"so shall it be done to . . ."*) (v. 9). These actions show her strong disapproval of his refusal. This embarrassment to him, along with the stigma of being known for his refusal to honor his dead brother's right name, illustrates how God used social pressure to motivate His people to obedience.[3]

RESPONSIBILITIES CONCERNING THE WRONG

25:11 "If *two* men fight together, and the wife of one draws near to rescue her husband from the hand of the one attacking him, and puts out her hand and seizes him by the genitals,
12 "then you shall cut off her hand; your eye shall not pity *her.*"

Deut. 25:11–12

This is the only place in the Old Testament where mutilation served as a punishment for an offense. Israel's neighbors often used mutilation as a way to punish the offender (i.e., in Assyrian law a man on the street who kissed a woman who was not his wife had his lip cut off by the sword). In this situation, two men are fighting and the wife of one of the men tries to rescue her husband by grasping the genitals of the other man. As a result, her hand was to be *"cut off."* The law illustrates, in general terms, that the end does not justify the means.

Perhaps the reason for the severe punishment for this crime centers around the issue of procreation. The woman's action could cause permanent injury to the male resulting in his inability to father children.[4] This interpretation is essentially the same as the reasoning behind the previous legislation (vv. 5–10) relating to a man who died before fathering a son to carry on his name.

HONEST WEIGHTS AND MEASURES

25:13 "You shall not have in your bag differing weights, a heavy and a light.

14 "You shall not have in your house differing measures, a large and a small.

15 "You shall have a perfect and just weight, a perfect and just measure, that your days may be lengthened in the land which the LORD your God is giving you.

16 "For all who do such things, all who behave unrighteously, *are* an abomination to the LORD your God."

Deut. 25:13–16

The theme of weights (measures, scales) is common in the Old Testament. Leviticus 19:35–37 gives similar legislation about this subject (see also Prov. 11:1; 16:11; 20:10, 23; Amos 8:5; Mic. 6:11; Hos. 12:7). The customer was at the mercy of the vendor who could easily use heavy weights for buying and small ones for selling. Royal standards for these weights were fixed during the reign of David (2 Sam. 14:26). The Israelites were to be totally honest in their business dealings. They could not afford to be otherwise, since it was ultimately the Lord who would withhold or give prosperity.

Dwight D. Eisenhower saw leadership in the same light as Moses. He said,

> In order to be a leader, a man must have followers. And to have followers, a man must have their confidence. Hence the supreme quality for a leader is unquestionably integrity. Without it, no real success is possible, no matter whether it is on a section gang, a football field, in an army, or in an office. If a man's associates find him guilty of phoniness, if they find he lacks forthright integrity, he will fail. His teachings and actions must square with each other. The first great need, therefore, is integrity and high purpose.

RESPONSIBILITIES CONCERNING THE AMALEKITES

25:17 "Remember what Amalek did to you on the way as you were coming out of Egypt,

18 "how he met you on the way and attacked your rear ranks, all the stragglers at your rear, when you *were* tired and weary; and he did not fear God.
19 "Therefore it shall be, when the LORD your God has given you rest from your enemies all around, in the land which the LORD your God is giving you to possess *as* an inheritance, *that* you will blot out the remembrance of Amalek from under heaven. You shall not forget."

Deut. 25:17–19

The Amalekites were a nomadic desert tribe that traced its genealogy back to Amalek, the grandson of Esau. Two specific battles with the Amalekites are mentioned in the Pentateuch (Exod. 17:8–16; Num. 14:39–45). However, this passage indicates a series of hostilities that are not mentioned elsewhere. Their cowardly attacks on the tired and weary, coupled with their lack of fear of Israel's God, were not to be forgotten! Since the Amalekites had shown no mercy, they were to receive none. Four hundred years later David defeated the Amalekites (2 Sam. 1:1), but they were not completely wiped out until Hezekiah's day, another three hundred years later (1 Chron. 4:41–43). The strong command, *"You shall not forget,"* is the last of nine such commands in Deuteronomy.

There seems to be a clear message that stands out in all the various regulations and responsibilities dealt with in Deuteronomy 24 and 25. The message is this: The Israelites were not to be merely holy individuals; they were to be a holy nation. Therefore, Israel's holiness of heart and mind must be authenticated by her holiness of action. In the celebrated words of John Wesley, "Christianity is essentially a social religion, and to make it into a solitary one is to destroy it. . . . The gospel of Christ knows no religion but social religion; no holiness but social holiness."[5]

NOTES

1. Eduard Dobson, "Divorce in the Old Testament," *Fundamentalist Journal* (October 1985): 39–41.

2. Victor P. Hamilton, *Handbook on the Pentateuch* (Grand Rapids: Baker Book House, 1982), p. 447.

3. John F. Walvoord and Roy B. Zuck, *The Bible Knowledge Commentary, O. T.* (Wheaton, IL: Victor Books, 1978), pp. 306–7.

4. Anthony Phillips, *Ancient Israel's Criminal Law* (New York: Schocken Books, Inc., 1971), p. 94.

5. A. R. G. Deasley and Jack Ford, *Beacon Bible Commentary* (Kansas City, MO: Beacon Hill Press, 1969), p. 586.

CHAPTER TWENTY-THREE

Acknowledgment of God as Benefactor

Deuteronomy 26:1-19

ACKNOWLEDGMENT BY OFFERINGS

26:1 "And it shall be, when you come into the land which the LORD your God is giving you *as* an inheritance, and you possess it and dwell in it,

2 "that you shall take some of the first of all the produce of the ground, which you shall bring from your land that the LORD your God is giving you, and put *it* in a basket and go to the place where the LORD your God chooses to make His name abide.

3 "And you shall go to the one who is priest in those days, and say to him, 'I declare today to the LORD your God that I have come to the country which the LORD swore to our fathers to give us.'

4 "Then the priest shall take the basket out of your hand and set it down before the altar of the LORD your God.

5 "And you shall answer and say before the LORD your God: 'My father *was* a Syrian, about to perish, and he went down to Egypt and dwelt there, few in number; and there he became a nation, great, mighty, and populous.

6 'But the Egyptians mistreated us, afflicted us, and laid hard bondage on us.

7 'Then we cried out to the LORD God of our fathers, and the LORD heard our voice and looked on our affliction and our labor and our oppression.

8 'So the LORD brought us out of Egypt with a

mighty hand and with an outstretched arm, with great terror and with signs and wonders.

9 'He has brought us to this place and has given us this land, "a land flowing with milk and honey";

10 'and now, behold, I have brought the firstfruits of the land which you, O LORD, have given me.' Then you shall set it before the LORD your God, and worship before the LORD your God.

11 "So you shall rejoice in every good *thing* which the LORD your God has given to you and your house, you and the Levite and the stranger who *is* among you.

12 "When you have finished laying aside all the tithe of your increase in the third year—the year of tithing—and have given *it* to the Levite, the stranger, the fatherless, and the widow, so that they may eat within your gates and be filled,

13 "then you shall say before the LORD your God: 'I have removed the holy *tithe* from *my* house, and also have given them to the Levite, the stranger, the fatherless, and the widow, according to all Your commandments which You have commanded me; I have not transgressed Your commandments, nor have I forgotten *them.*

14 'I have not eaten any of it when in mourning, nor have I removed *any* of it for an unclean *use,* nor given *any* of it for the dead. I have obeyed the voice of the LORD my God, and have done according to all that You have commanded me.

15 'Look down from Your holy habitation, from heaven, and bless Your people Israel and the land which You have given us, just as You swore to our fathers, "a land flowing with milk and honey."'"

Deut. 26:1–15

The teacher was lecturing her class on American history. Confident that she had covered her material well, she began the review by asking, "A distinguished foreigner was a big help to the American colonists during the Revolutionary War. Can you give me his name?" Tammy's hand immediately shot up. Unhesitantly she answered: "God."

Moses begins this chapter by again reminding the children of Israel that God will be their supreme Helper. It is He who will provide the land that they are to possess. Notice the phrases that repeatedly point to God as the source of Israel's blessings. *"God is giving you . . . an inheritance"* (v. 1); *"I have come to the country which the Lord swore to our fathers to give us"* (v. 3); *"the Lord heard our voice"* (v. 7); *"the Lord brought us out of Egypt"* (v. 8); *"He . . . brought us to this place"* (v. 9); *"So you shall rejoice in every good thing which the Lord your God has given to you"* (v. 11); *"bless Your people Israel and the land which You have given us"* (v. 15).

Israel must respond with gratitude toward God because of His continual blessing upon them as a people. What can they do to express their appreciation to Yahweh?

Ways to Express Gratitude to God for His Blessings

Use God's gift to His fullest expectations. Israel was expected to *"come into the land . . . possess it and dwell in it"* (v. 1). God's promise to Abraham was a land for his descendants. Up to this time the land had not been taken. It had been promised, but not possessed. It had been spied out, but not seized. The people stood between the promise of God and its fulfillment. Notice the progression of the phrases. They were to arrive at the land, strive for it, and live in it. Until that happened, they would be living below their potential.

God's gift to each of us is our potential. Our gift to Him is what we do with that potential. The chief way that you and I can be disloyal to God is to make small what He intended to make large. The purpose of our lives is to fulfill the expectations of the God who created us. To do so is to concretely express our gratitude to God for His blessing.

Return to God the first of everything He has given you (vv. 2–4). This act was an acknowledgment that God was the source and owner of everything that the people possessed. It was God who promised them the land; it was God who heard their cry in Egypt and delivered them; it was God who protected and provided for the people in the wilderness. Now God was going to give them possession of the land and cause them to prosper!

They were to place some of the firstfruits into a basket and bring it

285

to the priest in the sanctuary. This personal yet public act allowed the Israelite to visibly acknowledge that God was faithful to bring His people into the land *"flowing with milk and honey."*

I can remember learning some "law of firsts" before I entered school as a child. I was taught to give others the first choice of a dessert before I picked mine. Ladies walked through doors first and older people spoke first before children. Prayer was first before the food was eaten and permission must first be given before I left the property. Obeying the "law of firsts" demonstrated my respect for others and was an acknowledgment of my place in society. But the greatest lessons of "firsts" came in my relationship to God. I was taught to give God the first part of every day, the first day of every week, the first priority in my life, and the first tenth of my money. Those firsts have become the greatest joys of my life. My parents, like Moses, knew that teaching me the "law of firsts" would return many blessings from God.

Share the story of God's goodness with others (vv. 5–9). Israel's testimony begins with Jacob, the grandson of Abraham, the father of the sons whose names were given to the twelve tribes. The nation Israel derived its name from him. Jacob, however, is called a Syrian (v. 5) because of his long stay there (Gen. 29–31) and because his two wives and most of his children were born there.

Jacob was 130 years old when he went down to Egypt taking only seventy people with him (Gen. 46:27). Israel's bragging rights could not be traced to their own strength and character. Their testimony was great because it focused upon God's greatness, not theirs.

Sadly, too many Christians share their testimony in a self-centered and boring fashion. I grew up in a church that stressed Wednesday night testimony meetings. Many in the congregation spoke of their "Egypt experiences" and their "wilderness wanderings" without ever getting into the promised land. The result was that people left discouraged instead of uplifted. In professional basketball, the team with the ball must shoot before twenty-four seconds are up or the buzzer goes off and they forfeit the ball to the other team. Perhaps churches should apply the twenty-four-second principle to personal sharing times. If the Christian does not glorify God or provide encouragement for others in twenty-four seconds, he must sit down.

Worship and rejoice before the Lord your God (vv. 10–11). The Israelite would take the basket of firstfruits and *"set it before the Lord your*

God" (v. 10) in a spirit of worship and rejoicing. The phrase *"the Lord your God"* is used 299 times in Deuteronomy. It expresses a personal and exclusive relationship between Yahweh and Israel, and it suggests that there is a fundamental difference between Israel's God and those of other nations.[1] No wonder Israel would worship and rejoice before the Lord. There was no other God beside Him! Their baskets full of firstfruits were another illustration that the God of Abraham, Isaac, and Jacob was faithful.

When God blesses us we should not forget to praise Him. The enemy will continually steal through the door of an ungrateful heart. Our attitude toward God should find exuberant expression. We should all have the spirit that my father had when, while conducting a church dedication, he became emotionally overwhelmed with praise and worship of God. The congregation began singing the Doxology:

> Praise God, from whom all blessings flow;
> Praise Him, all creatures here below;
> Praise Him above, ye heavenly host;
> Praise Father, Son, and Holy Ghost. Amen.

Dad looked out at the worshiping congregation and said, "My heart is overwhelmed with praise to God. Let's sing another verse!"

Make yourself personally accountable to God for your giving (vv. 12–15). There is a relationship between the phrase, *"when you have finished laying aside all the tithe"* (v. 12) and *"then you shall say before the Lord . . ."* (v. 13). After the Israelites obeyed God's instructions concerning giving, then they would come before the Lord and give a report of personal accountability. Notice the first person pronouns in verses 13 and 14. *"I have removed the holy tithe from my house . . . I have not transgressed Your commandments, nor have I forgotten them. I have not eaten any of it when in mourning, nor have I removed any of it. . . . I have obeyed."*

Verse 15 is classic Deuteronomy. The Israelite is saying, "Now that we have listened and obeyed Your commands—bless us." A Christian friend who has always practiced biblical stewardship in his life was telling me about his involvement in a recent car accident. I asked him, "What were you thinking when you realized that you were going to be hit by the other car?" He laughed and said, "My tithe is all paid up!"

Trust and obey, for there's no other way
To be happy in Jesus, but to trust and obey.

John H. Sammis

ACKNOWLEDGMENT BY OBEDIENCE

26:16 "This day the LORD your God commands you to observe these statutes and judgments; therefore you shall be careful to observe them with all your heart and with all your soul.

17 "Today you have proclaimed the LORD to be your God, and that you will walk in His ways and keep His statutes, His commandments, and His judgments, and that you will obey His voice.

18 "Also today the LORD has proclaimed you to be His special people, just as He promised you, that *you* should keep all His commandments,

19 "and that He will set you high above all nations which He has made, in praise, in name, and in honor, and that you may be a holy people to the LORD your God, just as He has spoken."

Deut. 26:16–19

These four verses conclude Moses' explanation of the laws given in Deuteronomy 4:41–26:19. This passage calls for a total commitment to God and to His commands. It also affirms God's commitment to Israel. This section may be viewed as a formal ratification of the covenant between the Lord and Israel, even though the word "covenant" does not appear in these verses. Israel accepted and affirmed her covenantal responsibilities, and the Lord affirmed His promise to exalt an obedient Israel over all the nations of the earth.

I am intrigued by the repetition of the word *"today"* (or *"this day"*). *"This day the Lord your God commands you"* (v. 16); *"Today you have proclaimed the Lord to be your God"* (v. 17); *"Also today the Lord proclaimed you to be His special people"* (v. 18). This word is a crucial one throughout all Deuteronomy. The word *"today,"* or one very close to it, appears fifty-nine times in Deuteronomy.

Simon DeVries has made an interesting study of this word. His conclusion regarding its urgency is worthy of note: "His revelation is now. He is very alive and present. Israel must respond one way or another, because the voice of God is near. The word they must obey is not far off in the heavens or belonging to remote antiquity. Therefore do not defer your choice to still another 'today'!"[2]

NOTES

1. G. T. Manley, *The Book of the Law: Studies in the Date of Deuteronomy* (London: Tyndale Press, 1957), p. 41.
2. Simon J. DeVries, "The Development of the Deuteronomic Promulgation Formula," *Bib* 55 (1974): 316.

CHAPTER TWENTY-FOUR

Emphasizing the Covenant

Deuteronomy 27:1–28:68

The next four chapters to be studied (27–30) contain the third message of Moses to his people. A review of the messages of Moses in Deuteronomy is as follows:

A. Moses' first message: "Learning from the Past" 1:6–4:40

B. Moses' second message: "Laws to Live By" 4:41–26:19

C. Moses' third message: "Keep the Covenant" 27:1–30:20

Moses has finished placing before Israel the law of the Lord. Now is the time for decision and renewal. Throughout Israel's history it will be necessary to call the nation to renewal of the covenant commitment of obedience. These renewals will take place at significant points in Israel's history, such as when they are preparing to enter the promised land (Deut.), at the dedication of Solomon's temple (1 Kings 8), and during a transition of leadership (Josh. 24; 1 Sam. 12).

The success or failure of God's people depended upon their response to God's law. They could choose either to live by it or to disobey it. Neutrality was not an option. In this section of Scripture, Moses concentrates on consequences: what his people choose to sow, that shall they also reap.

If the choice is obedience, the consequence is blessing. If that choice is disobedience, the consequence is a curse. Particularly in this address, the curse includes a future exile from the land, a theme first sounded in 4:23–28. Robert Polzin has captured the shift in emphasis from Moses' second to third address: "The emphasis of the second address was on the immediate future and what Israel had to do to remain in the land God was giving them. Here in the third address, emphasis is on the far-distant future of exile and on what Israel had to do to regain the land."[1]

To aid the people in remembering the covenant, it was . . .

WRITTEN FOR THE PEOPLE TO SEE

27:1 Now Moses, with the elders of Israel, commanded the people, saying: "Keep all the commandments which I command you today.

2 "And it shall be, on the day when you cross over the Jordan to the land which the LORD your God is giving you, that you shall set up for yourselves large stones, and whitewash them with lime.

3 "You shall write on them all the words of this law, when you have crossed over, that you may enter the land which the LORD your God is giving you, 'a land flowing with milk and honey,' just as the LORD God of your fathers promised you.

4 "Therefore it shall be, when you have crossed over the Jordan, *that* on Mount Ebal you shall set up these stones, which I command you today, and you shall whitewash them with lime.

5 "And there you shall build an altar to the LORD your God, an altar of stones; you shall not use an iron *tool* on them.

6 "You shall build with whole stones the altar of the LORD your God, and offer burnt offerings on it to the LORD your God.

7 "You shall offer peace offerings, and shall eat there, and rejoice before the LORD your God.

8 "And you shall write very plainly on the stones all the words of this law."

Deut. 27:1-8

The fact that *"Moses, with the elders"* (v. 1) spoke to the people is significant. Usually Moses addressed the people himself. This joint address is significant. Moses would not be present at the commanded renewal of the covenant; his death would not allow him to enter into Canaan. Therefore, the elders would have to be responsible for seeing that these commands were carried out. This joint address was to place added responsibility upon the elders' shoulders; it would be a visible reminder to the people that they were to follow the elders who stood with Moses.

We are reminded of the importance of great leaders' surrounding themselves with good men. The elders surrounded and supported

Moses at the close of his days of leading the children of Israel. They had also accompanied him to face Pharaoh and ask for the release of the captive Israelites (Exod. 3:16–18). On many occasions between the beginning and close of Moses' career as a leader, others came around him to enhance his leadership and to help carry the heavy responsibilities that had been given him. Is it not true that few people are successful unless a lot of other people want them to be? Great works of God are built by the relay race principle, not by a single runner. Here Moses, the leader, is passing the baton of leadership on to the elders before the entire congregation of Israel. The leaders will change, but not the covenant.

Upon Israel's entrance into the land of promise, they were to do two things. First, they were to prepare stones and write the law upon them. Preparation of the stones consisted of coating them with white plaster (a common practice in Egypt), setting them up on Mount Ebal for the people to see, and writing the book of Deuteronomy upon them.

The stones were to be set up at Mount Ebal, at the base of which lay the city of Shechem. It was at Shechem that the Lord first appeared to Abraham, and there Abraham built his first altar to the Lord (Gen. 12:6–7). There is significance in the choice of this location for the law-engraved stones. It emphasized God's faithfulness in giving Israel the land *just as the Lord God of your fathers promised you* (v. 3). It also hinted that the time for the complete fulfillment of His promises might be near, if only Israel would obey.

The second thing Israel was to do upon entering Canaan was to build an altar and offer sacrifices to the Lord (vv. 5–7). Following the instructions given in Exodus 20:25, they were not to use iron tools in building the altar. Questions have often arisen concerning the prohibition of iron tools in this command. Perhaps God did not want His children, who did not possess iron, to develop a dependence upon any surrounding people for iron; this might risk their being influenced by others in harmful ways. Or perhaps the uncut stones were meant to suggest that neither the law nor the sacrificial system was to suffer any human adornment.

The *burnt offerings* (v. 6) were to be totally consumed on the altar. This expressed the people's total dependence on the Lord. The *peace offerings* (v. 7), which were eaten communally, expressed their thankfulness to God and their joy in His provision.

Spoken for the People to Hear

27:9 Then Moses and the priests, the Levites, spoke
to all Israel, saying, "Take heed and listen, O Israel:
This day you have become the people of the LORD
your God.
10 "Therefore you shall obey the voice of the LORD
your God, and observe His commandments and His
statutes which I command you today."

Deut. 27:9-10

The phrase *"this day you have become the people of the Lord your God"*
(v. 9) does not imply that Israel was not the people of God before that
time. It means that Israel was at a significant turning point in her
history; she had freshly committed herself again to the Lord.

These verses beautifully show the relationship between the covenant and obedience. The covenant was established first; obedience
followed. The covenant was Yahweh's free gift; it was not determined by any prior obedience or good works on Israel's part. Obedience was not a condition for the covenant but the outcome of it.
Obedience was to be motivated by gratitude to God for all He had
done for His people and for His acceptance of them as His people.
Obedience is indeed required, but it is the consequence rather than
the cause of the covenant.

Curses on Disobedience

27:11 And Moses commanded the people on the same
day, saying,
12 "These shall stand on Mount Gerizim to bless
the people, when you have crossed over the Jordan:
Simeon, Levi, Judah, Issachar, Joseph, and Benjamin;
13 "and these shall stand on Mount Ebal to curse:
Reuben, Gad, Asher, Zebulun, Dan, and Naphtali.
14 "And the Levites shall speak with a loud voice
and say to all the men of Israel:
15 'Cursed *is* the one who makes a carved or
molded image, an abomination to the LORD, the work
of the hands of the craftsman, and sets *it* up in secret.'
And all the people shall answer and say, 'Amen!'

16 'Cursed *is* the one who treats his father or his mother with contempt.'
And all the people shall say, 'Amen!'
17 'Cursed *is* the one who moves his neighbor's landmark.'
And all the people shall say, 'Amen!'
18 'Cursed *is* the one who makes the blind to wander off the road.'
And all the people shall say, 'Amen!'
19 'Cursed *is* the one who perverts the justice due the stranger, the fatherless, and widow.'
And all the people shall say, 'Amen!'
20 'Cursed *is* the one who lies with his father's wife, because he has uncovered his father's bed.'
And all the people shall say, 'Amen!'
21 'Cursed *is* the one who lies with any kind of animal.'
And all the people shall say, 'Amen!'
22 'Cursed *is* the one who lies with his sister, the daughter of his father or the daughter of his mother.'
And all the people shall say, 'Amen!'
23 'Cursed *is* the one who lies with his mother-in-law.'
And all the people shall say, 'Amen!'
24 'Cursed *is* the one who attacks his neighbor secretly.'
And all the people shall say, 'Amen!'
25 'Cursed *is* the one who takes a bribe to slay an innocent person.'
And all the people shall say, 'Amen!'
26 'Cursed *is* the one who does not confirm *all* the words of this law.'
And all the people shall say, 'Amen!'"

Deut. 27:11–26

This ceremony was commanded earlier by Moses (11:26–32). After the altar was set up on Mount Ebal, six tribes were to assemble *"on Mount Gerizim to bless the people"* (v. 12) and six were to assemble *"on Mount Ebal to curse"* (v. 13). The six tribes on Mount Gerizim descended from Jacob's wives, Leah and Rachel. Four of the six tribes stationed on Mount Ebal for the curses descended from Jacob's concubines, Bilhah and Zilpah. The other two were Reuben, Jacob's firstborn, who forfeited his birthright through incest (Gen. 35:22; 49:3–4), and Zebulun, Leah's youngest son.

The Levites stood between the two mountains to recite the blessings and curses. Actually, only the priests attending the ark stood in the middle (Josh. 8:33); all other Levites were near Mount Gerizim (Deut. 27:12). Only twelve curses on people who transgressed certain laws are included in this section.

The first curse involves the making of an idol (v. 15). This could be a breach of either the first commandment (if it were an idol of a god other than the Lord) or the second commandment (if it were an attempt to represent God Himself in some visual and physical form). Even though an offender might manage to keep his idol a secret, the idolater would be cursed. The response *"all the people shall answer and say, 'Amen!'"* (v. 15) is an acknowledgment that everyone understood and agreed to the curse.

The second curse relates to one who dishonors his father or mother (v. 16). (See discussion on Deut. 5:16.)

The third curse deals with the removal of a neighbor's landmark (v. 17). (See comments on Deut. 19:14.)

The fourth curse speaks to those who mistreat the weak and oppressed members of the community. Moses used the misleading of a blind person as an illustration (v. 18).

The fifth curse is an elaboration of the fourth (v. 19).

The sixth through ninth curses (vv. 20–23) are directed against anyone who engages in any of four forbidden sexual relationships. The nature of these acts demands secrecy and privacy. Therefore, they would probably not be witnessed by others or brought before a court of law. Yet again we realize that the deed will be exposed before God and will bring a curse upon those who commit such wrongful acts.

The tenth and eleventh curses (vv. 24–25) deal with attempts to secretly attack or murder an innocent victim. (See comments on 5:17.)

The last curse demonstrates that the preceding list was representative (v. 26). Perhaps the eleven examples were chosen because most of them could be done in secret; the offender might not be easily detected. The summary nature of the twelfth curse, however, indicates that God desires wholehearted obedience to His law both in public and in private.

OPTIONS FOR THE PEOPLE TO DECIDE

28:1 "Now it shall come to pass, if you diligently obey the voice of the LORD your God, to observe carefully all His commandments which I command you today, that the LORD your God will set you high above all nations of the earth.

2 "And all these blessings shall come upon you and overtake you, because you obey the voice of the LORD your God:

3 "Blessed *shall* you *be* in the city, and blessed *shall* you *be* in the country.

4 "Blessed *shall be* the fruit of your body, the produce of your ground and the increase of your herds, the increase of your cattle and the offspring of your flocks.

5 "Blessed *shall be* your basket and your kneading bowl.

6 "Blessed *shall* you *be* when you come in, and blessed *shall* you *be* when you go out.

7 "The LORD will cause your enemies who rise against you to be defeated before your face; they shall come out against you one way and flee before you seven ways.

8 "The LORD will command the blessing on you in your storehouses and in all to which you set your hand, and He will bless you in the land which the LORD your God is giving you.

9 "The LORD will establish you as a holy people to Himself, just as He has sworn to you, if you keep the commandments of the LORD your God and walk in His ways.

10 "Then all peoples of the earth shall see that you are called by the name of the LORD, and they shall be afraid of you.

11 "And the LORD will grant you plenty of goods, in the fruit of your body, in the increase of your livestock, and in the produce of your ground, in the land of which the LORD swore to your fathers to give you.

12 "The LORD will open to you His good treasure, the heavens, to give the rain to your land in its season, and to bless all the work of your hand. You

shall lend to many nations, but you shall not borrow.

13 "And the LORD will make you the head and not the tail; you shall be above only, and not be beneath, if you heed the commandments of the LORD your God, which I command you today, and are careful to observe *them.*

14 "So you shall not turn aside from any of the words which I command you this day, *to* the right or the left, to go after other gods to serve them.

15 "But it shall come to pass, if you do not obey the voice of the LORD your God, to observe carefully all His commandments and His statutes which I command you today, that all these curses will come upon you and overtake you:

16 "Cursed *shall* you *be* in the city, and cursed *shall* you *be* in the country.

17 "Cursed *shall be* your basket and your kneading bowl.

18 "Cursed *shall be* the fruit of your body and the produce of your land, the increase of your cattle and the offspring of your flocks.

19 "Cursed *shall* you *be* when you come in, and cursed *shall* you *be* when you go out.

20 "The LORD will send on you cursing, confusion, and rebuke in all that you set your hand to do, until you are destroyed and until you perish quickly, because of the wickedness of your doings in which you have forsaken Me.

21 "The LORD will make the plague cling to you until He has consumed you from the land which you are going to possess.

22 "The LORD will strike you with consumption, with fever, with inflammation, with severe burning fever, with the sword, with scorching, and with mildew; they shall pursue you until you perish.

23 "And your heavens which *are* over your head shall be bronze, and the earth which is under you *shall be* iron.

24 "The LORD will change the rain of your land to powder and dust; from the heaven it shall come down on you until you are destroyed.

25 "The LORD will cause you to be defeated before your enemies; you shall go out one way against them and flee seven ways before them; and you shall become troublesome to all the kingdoms of the earth.

26 "Your carcasses shall be food for all the birds of the air and the beasts of the earth, and no one shall frighten *them* away.

27 "The LORD will strike you with the boils of Egypt, with tumors, with the scab, and with the itch, from which you cannot be healed.

28 "The LORD will strike you with madness and blindness and confusion of heart.

29 "And you shall grope at noonday, as a blind man gropes in darkness; you shall not prosper in your ways; you shall be only oppressed and plundered continually, and no one shall save *you*.

30 "You shall betroth a wife, but another man shall lie with her; you shall build a house, but you shall not dwell in it; you shall plant a vineyard, but shall not gather its grapes.

31 "Your ox *shall be* slaughtered before your eyes, but you shall not eat of it; your donkey *shall be* violently taken away from before you, and shall not be restored to you; your sheep *shall be* given to your enemies, and you shall have no one to rescue *them*.

32 "Your sons and your daughters *shall be* given to another people, and your eyes shall look and fail *with longing* for them all day long; and *there shall be* no strength in your hand.

33 "A nation whom you have not known shall eat the fruit of your land and the produce of your labor, and you shall be only oppressed and crushed continually.

34 "So you shall be driven mad because of the sight which your eyes see.

35 "The LORD will strike you in the knees and on the legs with severe boils which cannot be healed, and from the sole of your foot to the top of your head.

36 "The LORD will bring you and the king whom you set over you to a nation which neither you nor your fathers have known, and there you shall serve other gods—wood and stone.

37 "And you shall become an astonishment, a proverb, and a byword among all nations where the LORD will drive you.

38 "You shall carry much seed out to the field but gather little in, for the locust shall consume it.

39 "You shall plant vineyards and tend *them*, but you shall neither drink *of* the wine nor gather the *grapes*; for the worms shall eat them.

40 "You shall have olive trees throughout all your territory, but you shall not anoint *yourself* with the oil; for your olives shall drop off.

41 "You shall beget sons and daughters, but they shall not be yours; for they shall go into captivity.

42 "Locusts shall consume all your trees and the produce of your land.

43 "The alien who *is* among you shall rise higher and higher above you, and you shall come down lower and lower.

44 "He shall lend to you, but you shall not lend to him; he shall be the head, and you shall be the tail.

45 "Moreover all these curses shall come upon you and pursue and overtake you, until you are destroyed, because you did not obey the voice of the LORD your God, to keep His commandments and His statutes which He commanded you.

46 "And they shall be upon you for a sign and a wonder, and on your descendants forever.

47 "Because you did not serve the LORD your God with joy and gladness of heart, for the abundance of everything,

48 "therefore you shall serve your enemies, whom the LORD will send against you, in hunger, in thirst, in nakedness, and in need of everything; and He will put a yoke of iron on your neck until He has destroyed you.

49 "The LORD will bring a nation against you from afar, from the end of the earth, *as swift* as the eagle flies, a nation whose language you will not understand,

50 "a nation of fierce countenance, which does not respect the elderly nor show favor to the young.

51 "And they shall eat the increase of your livestock and the produce of your land, until you are destroyed; they shall not leave you grain or new wine or oil, or the increase of your cattle or the offspring of your flocks, until they have destroyed you.

52 "They shall besiege you at all your gates until your high and fortified walls, in which you trust, come down throughout all your land; and they shall besiege you at all your gates throughout all your land which the LORD your God has given you.

53 "You shall eat the fruit of your own body, the flesh of your sons and your daughters whom the LORD your God has given you, in the siege and desperate straits in which your enemy shall distress you.

54 "The sensitive and very refined man among you will be hostile toward his brother, toward the wife of his bosom, and toward the rest of his children whom he leaves behind,

55 "so that he will not give any of them the flesh of his children whom he will eat, because he has nothing left in the siege and desperate straits in which your enemy shall distress you at all your gates.

56 "The tender and delicate woman among you, who would not venture to set the sole of her foot on the ground because of her delicateness and sensitivity, will refuse to the husband of her bosom, and to her son and her daughter,

57 "her placenta which comes out from between her feet and her children whom she bears; for she will eat them secretly for lack of everything in the siege and desperate straits in which your enemy shall distress you at all your gates.

58 "If you do not carefully observe all the words of this law that are written in this book, that you may fear this glorious and awesome name, THE LORD YOUR GOD,

59 "then the LORD will bring upon you and your descendants extraordinary plagues—great and prolonged plagues—and serious and prolonged sicknesses.

60 "Moreover He will bring back on you all the

diseases of Egypt, of which you were afraid, and they shall cling to you.

61 "Also every sickness and every plague, which is not written in this Book of the Law, will the LORD bring upon you until you are destroyed.

62 "You shall be left few in number, whereas you were as the stars of heaven in multitude, because you would not obey the voice of the LORD your God.

63 "And it shall be, that just as the LORD rejoiced over you to do you good and multiply you, so the LORD will rejoice over you to destroy you and bring you to nothing; and you shall be plucked from off the land which you go to possess.

64 "Then the LORD will scatter you among all peoples, from one end of the earth to the other, and there you shall serve other gods, which neither you nor your fathers have known—wood and stone.

65 "And among those nations you shall find no rest, nor shall the sole of your foot have a resting place; but there the LORD will give you a trembling heart, failing eyes, and anguish of soul.

66 "Your life shall hang in doubt before you; you shall fear day and night, and have no assurance of life.

67 "In the morning you shall say, 'Oh, that it were evening!' And at evening you shall say, 'Oh, that it were morning!' because of the fear which terrifies your heart, and because of the sight which your eyes see.

68 "And the LORD will take you back to Egypt in ships, by the way of which I said to you, 'You shall never see it again.' And there you shall be offered for sale to your enemies as male and female slaves, but no one will buy you."

Deut. 28:1–68

Moses sets before the congregation of Israel the blessings and the curses of the covenant that they are renewing. Two things about the blessing and cursing sections of this chapter deserve comment: (1) Israel's God comes first to bless His people. The usual order of other ancient covenants is curses, then blessings; here the order is reversed. (2) The blessings (vv. 1–14) are heavily outnumbered by the curses (vv. 15–68). The reason for this probably lies in Israel's tendency to go astray. This trait displayed itself in the journey through the wilderness. Several other ancient Near Eastern law codes and treaties also contained more curses than blessings.

The blessing section (vv. 1–14) follows the condition, *"if you diligently obey . . ."* (v. 1). The cursing section (vv. 15–68) begins with *"if you do not obey . . ."* (v. 15). The blessings of verses 3–6 and the curses of verses 16–19 are concerned with the same issues but reflect opposite results, depending upon Israel's obedience or disobedience. The various blessings and curses may seem insignificant, but they provide a capsulized picture of the basic Deuteronomic theology: "Those who follow the Lord may anticipate blessing in every area of their lives. Those who disobey the Lord may anticipate troubles in every area of their lives."

This issue has divided the Christian community in the past and continues to do so today. Is the system of rewards and punishment really this simple and straightforward? Is it as black and white as it appears? Are one's circumstances always a result of one's character? Are there no exceptions? Or is the Deuteronomic theology misunderstood, and therefore misinterpreted? G. K. Chesterton speaks to this. "When once people have begun to believe that prosperity is the reward of virtue, their next calamity is obvious. If prosperity is regarded as the reward of virtue, it will be regarded as the symptom of virtue. Men will leave off the heavy task of making good men successful. They will adopt the easier task of making out successful men good."[2]

Deuteronomy greatly influences many of the other Old Testament books. Joshua and Kings function primarily as a historical witness to the truthfulness of Deuteronomy's theology vis-à-vis obedience, disobedience, and consequences.[3]

Some of the preaching of Amos in the eighth century B.C. has its basis in Deuteronomy 28 or something very close to it. Such a backdrop makes even more understandable Amos' rhetorical questions such as: "If there is calamity in a city, will not the Lord have done it?" (Amos 3:6). In the very next chapter (4:6–11) this prophet lists the following illustrations of God's trying to bring Israel to an awakening: a shortage of food, no rains for the harvest, a lack of adequate drinking water, disease that wiped out produce of gardens and vineyards, and war and pestilence. God's wrath produces every conceivable misfortune.

A number of the psalms also support this emphasis. One has only to think of passages such as Psalm 1, a contrast between the righteous man who prospers in all that he does and the wicked man who is perishing. David testifies, "I have been young, and now am old; / Yet I have not seen the righteous forsaken, / Nor his descendant begging bread" (Ps. 37:25); and "Many sorrows shall be to the wicked; / But he who trusts in the Lord, mercy shall surround him" (Ps. 32:10).

The first nine chapters of Proverbs provide a number of illustrations that those who fear the Lord will be delivered but the wicked will be cut off and rooted out (2:12, 21–22). To honor the Lord is a guarantee that "Your barns will be filled with plenty, / And your vats will overflow with new wine" (Prov. 3:10). Continually the principle arises that each act has a consequence.

So deeply entrenched was this idea that it was still prevalent among Jesus' disciples. Viewing a man with congenital blindness, they asked, "Rabbi, who sinned, this man or his parents, that he was born blind?" (John 9:2). After His conversation with the rich young ruler, Jesus added the following for the benefit of His disciples: "Assuredly, I say to you that it is hard for a rich man to enter the kingdom of heaven. And again I say to you, it is easier for a camel to go through the eye of a needle than for a rich man to enter the kingdom of God" (Matt. 19:23–24). The disciples' response? "They were greatly astonished, saying, 'Who then can be saved?'" (Matt. 19:25). For had not wealth been considered one of the prime evidences of God's blessing? This theology also explains why they could not accept the Lord's forthcoming crucifixion.

Yet we need to observe that, for all the truthfulness of the curses and blessings of Deuteronomy, they present only a part of the picture. Any conclusions we draw need to be tempered by a study of all Scripture. It is important to observe several things.

First, the historical books themselves present something of a mixed picture. In war "the sword devours one as well as another" (2 Sam. 11:25), so that the innocent suffer along with the guilty. Witness the untimely deaths of the priests of Nob (1 Sam. 22:18–19) and the brothers of Abimelech (Judg. 9:1–6). These are instances in which death had nothing at all to do with retributive justice. On the other side of the ledger one has only to think of the many kings, both Judean and Israelite, who basked in luxury and opulence, and all this in spite of a God-defying lifestyle.

Second, the prophets do not baptize the Deuteronomic theology uncritically. In an emphasis reminiscent of parts of Deuteronomy, Hosea reminds Israel that in spite of her infidelity, God has given her "grain, new wine, and oil, / And multiplied her silver and gold" (Hos. 2:8). Here are gifts of divine blessing, although by all accounts such gifts should have been withheld. Perhaps the primary example of undeserved curse in prophetic literature is the "suffering servant" of Isaiah 53. The servant of the Lord is rejected, afflicted, and treated with contempt. He does not prosper. And this is simply an extension, but in much greater intensity, of the suffering experienced by most of the prophets. Few, if any, escaped persecution and harassment. But at no point is the suggestion made that these trials are a divine rebuke leveled at His spokesmen.[4]

Third, indeed some psalms do support a traditional understanding of reward and punishment. But as many, if not more, challenge the traditional view. Limiting himself to the wisdom psalms, J. K. Kuntz divides these psalms into three categories according to what they espouse in regard to the doctrine of reward and punishment. These categories are the traditional, the realistic, and the futuristic (which hopes in the prospects of immortality).[5] Add to this the large number of psalms of lament (almost one-third of the Psalter), only a few of which move into imprecation, and we are forced to take a more critical look at our possibly shallow understanding of the act-and-consequence relationship.

Fourth, some entire books in the Old Testament canon protest against a frozen interpretation of Deuteronomy. The best examples are Ecclesiastes and Job. As the writer of Ecclesiastes observed, one fate comes to both the wise and the foolish (2:14; 9:2). Both are forgotten quickly (2:16). Man has no advantage over the beast (3:19). God gives wealth and honor, but others who do not deserve these blessings partake of them like scavengers (6:2). The experience of Job is well known. Job's friends were reflecting the theology of Deuteronomy accurately, but their application of it to Job was inaccurate and, thus, irrelevant.

Fifth, the witness of the New Testament is interesting. Jesus certainly taught the eventual relationship of character to destiny. What

He repudiated was the immediate relationship of character to circumstance. Thus, the case of the lad being born blind had nothing at all to do with sin. The eighteen who were crushed to death by the falling tower in Siloam were not quintessential sinners (Luke 13:1–5). Jesus taught that God sends rain and sunshine on unbeliever and believer alike (Matt. 5:45), a point especially interesting in light of Deuteronomy 28:12, which pinpoints rain as one of God's blessings on the obedient.

Two experiences from Paul's life buttress instances taken from the Gospels. Paul's experience on the Mediterranean during a storm may be compared with Jonah's experience much earlier on the same sea and in the same kind of weather. In Jonah's case, God sent the storm to force him to rethink his disobedience and reluctance to go to Nineveh. For Paul the storm was simply a phenomenon of the weather.

The second illustration revolves around Romans 8:31–39. Paul lists certain experiences that Deuteronomy 28 precisely classifies as treaty curses—tribulation, distress, persecution, famine, nakedness, peril, and sword. In the midst of his argument, Paul quotes Psalm 44:22—"For Your sake we are killed all day long"—but does not need to quote 44:23, "Awake! Why do You sleep, O Lord?"

Paul can say, "In all these things we are more than conquerors." The basis for Paul's assurance is not his experiences, but the death and resurrection of Christ (Rom. 8:32–34).

A final point that can be made is that Deuteronomy itself gives us something of a double picture. Moses reminds Israel that God humbled her in the wilderness, not because of any specific sin, but to teach her and to test her (Deut. 8:2–3). It was a way of disciplining Israel (Deut. 8:5). Moses also reminds Israel that she has been given wealth, but it is all a gift of God, not something earned (Deut. 8:18). God is not giving the blessing of the land to Israel because she is more righteous than the other nations (Deut. 9:4–6). And finally, Israel avoided the wrath of God in the episode of the golden calf only because Moses interceded and prayed at length on Israel's behalf (Deut. 9:25–29). She is spared by virtue of Moses' dependence on God.[6] So, even the Book of Deuteronomy cautions us against oversimplifying a very complex area of walking with God.

However, some conclusions may be drawn from the vital question of whether all good and all evil things that happen are caused by God in response to man's actions. (1) Every good gift comes from God. (2) Many blessings and curses are a result of man's response to God. (3) Some blessings and curses are a result of God's plan for man. (4) Blessings can become curses if we fail to glorify God. (5) The teaching ". . . whatever a man sows, that he will also reap" (Gal. 6:7) is a general principle that will be true in the long run, but there will be times when it seems to be a fallacy.

Deuteronomy 28 contains several blessings and curses dealing with various issues. The following outline with brief explanations will help bring some order to this section.

I. The Blessings 28:1-14
   A. Contingent on obedience (vv. 1-2)
   B. The blessings (vv. 3-6)
   C. Elaboration of the blessings (vv. 7-14)
      Verses 3-6 were probably read aloud in covenant renewal ceremonies in order to state the blessing of covenant obedience. Verses 7-14 are Moses' sermonic elaboration of these blessings. Israel will experience blessings in the areas of military might, finance, agriculture, and reputation, but only if she *"shall not turn aside from any of the words"* of God or *"go after other gods to serve them"* (v. 14).
II. The curses 28:15-68
   A. A result of disobedience (v. 15)
   B. The curses (vv. 16-19)
   C. Ultimate result of curses is destruction (v. 20)
      The *"confusion"* or panic that God sent upon Israel's enemies, thus rendering them helpless in battle, would be sent upon Israel if they were disobedient.
   D. By disease (vv. 21-22)
      The plagues were given to Egypt so that the Israelites could possess the land of Canaan. If Israel was disobedient, plagues would in turn drive them out.
   E. By drought (vv. 23-24)
   F. By defeat in battle (vv. 25-26)
      Israel would be defeated so soundly that no one would remain to bury the dead or to frighten away the birds that would eat the bodies.

G. By diseases and the consequences of defeat (vv. 27–35)

The physical and mental afflictions would be so great that the Israelites would not have the strength or presence of mind to complete any task.

H. By exile (vv. 36–37)

Disobedience would result in exile. Instead of other nations honoring Israel and glorifying God, their conversation about Israel would be degrading. How could such a nation with so much potential fall to such depths?

I. By crop failure and economic ruin (vv. 38–42)

No matter how hard the Israelites worked to produce crops, their goal would always be frustrated. They would do the right things and reap the wrong results.

J. By decline in status (vv. 43–44)

The Canaanites, who had been driven out of the land, would again enjoy its benefits because of Israel's disobedience. Contrast these verses with verses 12 and 13.

K. Reason for the curses (vv. 45–48)

1. Disobedience (v. 45)

At this point in the sermon Moses seemed to assume that Israel would receive all the curses. It was no longer a matter of "if you disobey," but rather *you did not obey the voice of the Lord your God"* (v. 45).

2. As a continuing sign of Israel's disobedience (v. 46)

3. Because Israel has lost the joy of serving God (v. 47)

L. The horrors of a besieged city (vv. 49–57)

The two worst possible curses were saved until the conclusion of the sermon; they specifically illustrated the siege (vv. 49–57) and the exile (vv. 58–68). The nation brought from afar would be *"as swift as the eagle"* (v. 49). The Babylonians are compared to a sweeping vulture in Habakkuk 1:6, 8. They would be brutal, *"a nation of fierce countenance, which does not respect . . . ,"* destructive, destroying all the crops and killing the livestock; and thorough, besieging *"all your gates . . . throughout all your land"* (v. 52). The horrors of that siege would come to a climactic manifestation in cannibalism (vv. 53–57; cf. Jer. 19:9). The enemies would eat Israel's livestock and crops, but Israel would devour their own children!

This verse was literally fulfilled when the Arameans besieged Samaria (2 Kings 6:24–29) and when the Babylonians besieged Jerusalem (Lam. 2:20; 4:10).

M. Summary of the curses (vv. 58–68)

Whereas God had multiplied her *"as the stars of heaven,"* Israel would be reduced to *"few in number"* (v. 62). Whereas Israel had dwelt securely in the land, she would be *"plucked from off the land"* (v. 63). Having once served the Lord, she now would *"serve other gods"* (v. 64). Having once lived in security, she would now live in *"anguish of soul"* (v. 65). To escape her daily misery she will long for the night to come, but when it is night she will long for the daytime. The Israelites' condition would be so humiliating that no Egyptian would even purchase them as slaves. All because of disobedience!

NOTES

1. Robert Polzin, *Moses and the Deuteronomist: A Literary Study of Deuteronomic History* (New York: Seabury Press, 1980), p. 70.

2. G. K. Chesterton, "Man Is Most Comforted by Paradoxes," in *The Dimensions of Job: A Study and Selected Readings*, ed. N. Glatzer (New York: Schocken Books, Inc., 1969), pp. 236–37.

3. Victor P. Hamilton, *Handbook on the Pentateuch* (Grand Rapids: Baker Book House, 1982), p. 458.

4. Ibid., p. 460.

5. J. Kenneth Kuntz, "The Retribution Motiv in Psalmist Wisdom," *ZAW* 89 (1977): 232.

6. John G. Gammie, "The Theology of Retribution in the Book of Deuteronomy," *The Catholic Bible Quarterly* 32 (1970): 10–12.

CHAPTER TWENTY-FIVE

Entering into the Covenant

Deuteronomy 29:1–30:20

ENTER ON THE BASIS OF HISTORY

29:1 These *are* the words of the covenant which the LORD commanded Moses to make with the children of Israel in the land of Moab, besides the covenant which He made with them in Horeb.

2 Now Moses called all Israel and said to them: "You have seen all that the LORD did before your eyes in the land of Egypt, to Pharaoh and to all his servants and to all his land—

3 "the great trials which your eyes have seen, the signs, and those great wonders.

4 "Yet the LORD has not given you a heart to perceive and eyes to see and ears to hear, to this *very* day.

5 "And I have led you forty years in the wilderness. Your clothes have not worn out on you, and your sandals have not worn out on your feet.

6 "You have not eaten bread, nor have you drunk wine or *similar* drink, that you may know that I *am* the LORD your God.

7 "And when you came to this place, Sihon king of Heshbon and Og king of Bashan came out against us to battle, and we conquered them.

8 "We took their land and gave it as an inheritance to the Reubenites, to the Gadites, and to half the tribe of Manasseh.

9 "Therefore keep the words of this covenant, and do them, that you may prosper in all that you do."

Deut. 29:1–9

The contents of the covenant clearly show the benefits of obedience and the penalties of disobedience. Now the covenant must be sealed by the taking of an oath. Deuteronomy 29 and 30 call for action on the part of the people. Moses, wanting the people to take a positive step, uses various appeals to encourage them to enter into this covenant. In this section he points to their history to encourage their commitment, reminding Israel of three past blessings received from the Lord: the deliverance from Egypt (vv. 2–3); the miraculous provisions in the wilderness (vv. 5–6); and the victories over Sihon and Og, whose lands they now occupy (vv. 7–8).

Yet, in spite of these displays of supernatural power, the purpose of which was to increase Israel's faith in God, the people are still untrusting. Notice two contrasting sentences in this section. *"You have seen all that the Lord did before your eyes"* (v. 2) and *"Yet the Lord has not given you a heart to perceive and eyes to see and ears to hear, to this very day"* (v. 4). The children of Israel had physically witnessed the direct blessings of God; yet they had not fully understood the implications of God's saving acts. Their natural eyes were not enough! In Romans 10:21, Paul quotes Isaiah, "All day long I have stretched out My hands / To a disobedient and contrary people," and gives Israel's disobedience as the reason for their spiritual blindness (Rom. 11:1–10).

Some years ago a friend of mine was taking his daughter on a cruise around Manhattan Island. It was one of those beautifully clear days. Suddenly the little girl exclaimed, "Daddy, I can look farther than my eyes can see!"

This is what Moses hoped his people would do. Unfortunately, they were more like the two birds who saw a loaf of bread bounce out of a cart and hit the pavement. A small piece broke off and both sparrows instantly swooped for the crumb. They fought for the small piece until one successfully seized the meager breakfast and ate it, while the other went hungry. The large loaf sitting nearby was untouched and unnoticed. With just a little wider range of vision, both birds would have been satisfied. How often Israel fought over crumbs and did not see God's total plan for His people.

We do not need to see greater miracles to trust and obey God; we need to trust and obey God to see greater miracles. A person with a disobedient heart draws the curtains of his soul until he sees no light; an obedient-hearted person opens up the windows of his soul and is awed by the greatness of God. Light is appropriated as we obey and apply God's truth in our lives.

ENTER THAT GOD MAY ESTABLISH YOU

29:10 "All of you stand today before the LORD your God: your leaders and your tribes and your elders and your officers, all the men of Israel,
11 "your little ones and your wives—also the stranger who *is* in your camp, from the one who cuts your wood to the one who draws your water—
12 "that you may enter into covenant with the LORD your God, and into His oath, which the LORD your God makes with you today,
13 "that He may establish you today as a people for Himself, and *that* He may be God to you, just as He has spoken to you, and just as He has sworn to your fathers, to Abraham, Isaac, and Jacob."

Deut. 29:10–13

All of the people of Israel are standing before God. The various groups of people are listed in descending order for a reason. Obedience is taught by example. As the leaders entered into the covenant, the people would follow. It has been facetiously reported that as Moses faced the Red Sea, he exclaimed, "Why must I always go first?" This formal ceremony places the leaders in the forefront so the people could witness their commitment. Notice the urgency with which Moses appeals to them. Three times the word *"today"* is used to encourage them to make an immediate response (vv. 10, 12, 13), *"that He may establish you today as a people for Himself"* (v. 13).

ENTER FOR THE SAKE OF OTHERS

29:14 "I make this covenant and this oath, not with you alone,
15 "but with *him* who stands here with us today before the LORD our God, as well as with *him* who *is* not here with us today

311

16 (for you know that we dwelt in the land of Egypt and that we came through the nations which you passed by,

17 and you saw their abominations and their idols which *were* among them—wood and stone and silver and gold);

18 "so that there may not be among you man or woman or family or tribe, whose heart turns away today from the LORD our God, to go *and* serve the gods of these nations, and that there may not be among you a root bearing bitterness or wormwood;

19 "and so it may not happen, when he hears the words of this curse, that he blesses himself in his heart, saying, 'I shall have peace, even though I follow the dictates of my heart'—as though the drunkard could be included with the sober.

20 "The LORD would not spare him; for then the anger of the LORD and His jealousy would burn against that man, and every curse that is written in this book would settle on him, and the LORD would blot out his name from under heaven.

21 "And the LORD would separate him from all the tribes of Israel for adversity, according to all the curses of the covenant that are written in this Book of the Law,

22 "so that the coming generation of your children who rise up after you, and the foreigner who comes from a far land, would say, when they see the plagues of that land and the sickness which the LORD has laid on it:

23 'The whole land *is* brimstone, salt, and burning; it is not sown, nor does it bear, nor does any grass grow there, like the overthrow of Sodom and Gomorrah, Admah, and Zeboiim, which the LORD overthrew in His anger and His wrath.'

24 "All nations would say, 'Why has the LORD done so to this land? What does the heat of this great anger mean?'

25 "Then *people* would say: 'Because they have forsaken the covenant of the LORD God of their fathers, which He made with them when He brought them out of the land of Egypt;

26 'for they went and served other gods and worshiped them, gods that they did not know and that He had not given to them.

27 'Then the anger of the LORD was aroused against this land, to bring on it every curse that is written in this book.

28 'And the LORD uprooted them from their land in anger, in wrath, and in great indignation, and cast them into another land, as *it is* this day.'

29 "The secret *things belong* to the LORD our God, but those *things which are* revealed *belong* to us and to our children forever, that *we* may do all the words of this law."

Deut. 29:14–29

1. The Responsibility of Leadership (vv. 14–15)

This covenant is for future generations as well as for those who are now being challenged to make this commitment to God. The decision today will affect Israel's destiny for generations to come. At crucial times throughout history, nations have made decisions that have either enhanced or destroyed their futures.

An example of this occurred during World War II. Following the fall of France in 1940, the German Third Reich claimed victory in Europe. Hitler appealed to Great Britain: "I am the victor; I can see no reason why this war need go on." Lord Halifax officially responded that no peace which gave Germany control of non-German territory would be acceptable to Britain.

However, the decision leading to this reply had been made a few weeks earlier, as the fall of France was anticipated. Addressing the nation, Churchill noted, "The battle of France is over; I expect that the battle of Britain is about to begin. Upon this battle depends the survival of Christian civilization. . . . Let us therefore brace ourselves to our duties and so bear ourselves that if the British Empire and its commonwealth last for a thousand years, men will say 'This was their finest hour.'"

As he appeals to his people to enter into this covenant, Moses has this same sense of the importance of the hour of decision for Israel (vv. 14–15).

2. The Power of Experience (vv. 16–18)

Moses reminds Israel that they are not naive concerning idolatry. *"For you know . . . and you saw . . ."* (vv. 16, 17) indicate their firsthand witness to the terribleness of the sin of idolatry. Again Moses appeals to their past to influence their future. The present generation should certainly abstain from idols because of their present experiences (vv. 16–18).

3. The Deceptiveness of Sin (v. 19)

It is possible for sin to deceive man until *"he blesses himself in his heart, saying, 'I shall have peace, even though I follow the dictates of my heart'"* (v. 19). This transgressor imagines that although all others may be detected, he will escape. Because human magistrates and witnesses may not discover his crime, he concludes that God will not either. In fact, he leaves God out of his calculation; he lays his plans and carries them out as if there were no God. He expects to receive blessings in spite of his wicked course.

4. The Judgment of God (vv. 20–23)

But God will intervene. Not only will He punish the one who introduced idolatry, but He will chastise the whole nation because they allowed themselves to be swept away by false worship. This judgment will be so severe that it is compared to the judgment that befell Sodom and Gomorrah (vv. 20–23).

5. The Questions of Nations (v. 24)

Israel's sin has caused the judgment of God to fall upon her. Other nations will wonder why Israel's God would allow this to happen (v. 24). This is certainly not what God desired. No, He wanted to bless Israel until the questions arising from the lips of other nations would ask positive things about His goodness.

6. The Response of the Outsiders (vv. 25–28)

God delights in the earth's fertility. He finds pleasure in fruits and flowers. But His delight in the fruit of the soul is much greater.

Therefore, He blasts all the beauty and fertility of the promised land in order to produce fruits of holiness within His people. People will see this land that once flowed with milk and honey and ask, "What happened?" And the response will be *they have forsaken the covenant of the Lord* (v. 25).

7. The Certainty of God's Word (v. 29)

It may be difficult for some to understand how God could punish His children so severely. Moses explains that *the secret things belong to the Lord* (v. 29). This refers to the hidden causes which motivate God to discipline His people. The purpose of God's revelation is not to gratify our curiosity but to secure our obedience. It is not speculative, but practical. Moses expects obedience to God from the people and reminds them that the law was given not only that the Israelites might *know* what is right, but that they might also *do* what is right.

Today this truth must be followed by the Christian community. The Bible is able to establish us because it is inspired of God (2 Tim. 3:16–17). It is not simply a book of religious ideas or good moral advice; it is the very word of God. It "is profitable for doctrine, for reproof, for correction, for instruction in righteousness, that the man of God may be complete, thoroughly equipped for every good work." "Doctrine" tells us what is right; "reproof" tells us what is not right; "correction" tells us how to get right; and "instruction" tells us how to stay right. Why? So we can be equipped to minister effectively to others. An excellent formula for Bible study is this one: Study it through. Pray it in. Live it out. Pass it on.

A few years ago a man approached me after my first message at a Bible conference and asked, "Will you be speaking on prophecy while you are here?" I responded, "No, but I will be sharing from God's word how we can grow spiritually in our daily walk and in our ministry to others." A look of dejection crossed his face as he replied, "I won't be back; I'm into the end times." How are we going to be ready for the "end times" unless we obey God's word in the "meantime"?

ENTER FOR THE SAKE OF THE NATION

30:1 "Now it shall come to pass, when all these things come upon you, the blessing and the curse which I have set before you, and you call *them* to mind among all the nations where the LORD your God drives you,

2 "and you return to the LORD your God and obey His voice, according to all that I command you today, you and your children, with all your heart and with all your soul,

3 "that the LORD your God will bring you back from captivity, and have compassion on you, and gather you again from all the nations where the LORD your God has scattered you.

4 "If *any* of you are driven out to the farthest *parts* under heaven, from there the LORD your God will gather you, and from there He will bring you.

5 "Then the LORD your God will bring you to the land which your fathers possessed, and you shall possess it. He will prosper you and multiply you more than your fathers.

6 "And the LORD your God will circumcise your heart and the heart of your descendants, to love the LORD your God with all your heart and with all your soul, that you may live.

7 "Also the LORD your God will put all these curses on your enemies and on those who hate you, who persecuted you.

8 "And you will again obey the voice of the LORD and do all His commandments which I command you today.

9 "The LORD your God will make you abound in all the work of your hand, in the fruit of your body, in the increase of your livestock, and in the produce of your land for good. For the LORD will again rejoice over you for good as He rejoiced over your fathers,

10 "if you obey the voice of the LORD your God, to keep His commandments and His statutes which are written in this Book of the Law, *and* if you turn to the LORD your God with all your heart and with all your soul."

Deut. 30:1–10

Moses predicts a positive turning point in the life of Israel. But it will only be after *"all these things come upon you, the blessing and the curse"* (v. 1). One of my greatest joys in pastoral work is to listen as people tell me about their conversion experiences—what caused them to leave sinful lives and begin following Christ. Here, Moses gives the steps to be taken to restore a right relationship between God and His people.

1. A Return to Right Thinking (v. 1)

There is a relationship between the curses and the decision to change. The prodigal son "came to himself" after spending time in a pig pen. The woman with an incurable disease reached out to Jesus after "she had spent all she had." Here Moses predicts that after the curses, captivity, and heartbreak, *Israel will begin to think right.*

Recently, while flying from Chicago to San Diego, I engaged in an interesting conversation with a man named Dave. He was going through some difficult times in his life and began hinting that a change was needed. Yet at the same time, he reveled in some of the sins in his life. He was double-minded. He wanted to be forgiven of his sins; yet he was thoroughly enjoying some of them. He was shocked when I said, "Dave, you're not ready. You are still enjoying the pleasure of sin for a season." At the close of our conversation I prayed that God would make Dave miserable until he would desire above everything to know God.

2. A Return to the Lord (v. 2)

A right thought-life will cause a quick return to God. Repentance means turning around and coming to God. Many of us are like the old mountaineer who was on trial for stealing a horse. He hired a good lawyer and won his case. "You've been acquitted," said the attorney. The mountaineer scratched his head and asked, "Does this mean I get to keep the horse?" Are we not too often like that? We want God's mercy, forgiveness, and grace; yet we want to keep the "horse."

3. Obedience to the Voice of God (v. 2)

The repentance that God expects of Israel is more than merely turning away from an evil past. It involves a wholehearted commitment to obeying God's voice. Present forgiveness and future blessing is contingent upon Israel's obedience to God.

317

Our return to God must be marked not only by acknowledgment of our sin but by a commitment to do it no more. There was a cartoon several years ago in the *Saturday Review of Literature* in which little George Washington is standing with an ax in his hand. Lying on the ground before him is the famous cherry tree. He has already made his smug admission that he did it—after all, he "cannot tell a lie." But his father is standing there, exasperated, saying, "All right, so you admit it! You *always* admit it. The question is, when are you going to stop *doing* it!"

4. Restoration of Previous Position (v. 3)

Israel, after remembering, repenting, and obeying, could now expect God to reestablish her former position. Only her sincere humility could open the gates of God's compassion, which He promises to demonstrate by the following acts: (1) He will gather the people back from all scattered directions (v. 4); (2) He will prosper and multiply the people even more than He did their ancestors (v. 5); (3) He will give them a heart that leans toward obedience to God (v. 6); (4) He will put a curse on Israel's enemies (v. 7); and (5) He will rejoice over His people in their prosperity (v. 9).

Moses declares in verse 6 that *"the Lord your God will circumcise your heart and the heart of your descendants, to love the Lord."* God now is promising Israel that He will replace her former spiritual insensitivity and stubbornness with a new will to obey Him. Moses realizes that in their present state, the people can never love God enough to remain obedient to the law; there must be a change of heart. The key to will power is "want power." People who want something badly enough can usually find the will power to achieve it.

ENTER ON THE BASIS OF UNDERSTANDING

30:11 "For this commandment which I command you today *is* not *too* mysterious for you, nor *is* it far off.

12 "It *is* not in heaven, that you should say, 'Who will ascend into heaven for us and bring it to us, that we may hear it and do it?'

13 "Nor *is* it beyond the sea, that you should say,
'Who will go over the sea for us and bring it to us,
that we may hear it and do it?'
14 "But the word *is* very near you, in your mouth
and in your heart, that you may do it."

Deut. 30:11-14

Recently I saw a plaque inscribed with these words: "I know you believe you understand what you think I said, but I am not sure you realize what I really meant." Successful communicators are able to make their message easily understood. They are careful that their choice of words does not have a hidden double meaning. Mark Twain said, "The difference between the right word and the almost right word is the difference between lightning and lightning bug." Communicators delight in taking a complex thought and reducing it to a simple statement. In a world of technology and complexity, real communicators are a rare breed. Someone has said, "If the safety pin were invented today, it would have two transistors, a regulator, an off and on switch, and require a service check every six months."

Successful leaders realize that followers must understand the order before they can obey it. General Ulysses S. Grant kept a particularly feeble-minded soldier just outside his office. Before issuing an order, he would read it to this soldier. If the young man understood it, the order stood. If not, Grant returned to his desk to simplify or clarify it. Peter Drucker, often called "the father of American management," claims that 60 percent of all management problems are a result of faulty communications.

Moses, a great leader and communicator, does not want his followers to misunderstand God's law. As he faces them, knowing that their crucial decision concerning the covenant is pending, he reminds Israel that the law is not incomprehensible or inaccessible—"*not too mysterious for you, nor is it far off*" (v. 11). Although the law had a heavenly origin, God revealed it clearly to Israel; there was no need for anyone to "*ascend into heaven . . . and bring it to us*" (v. 12). The law was already written down and the Israelites had been familiar with its demands while in the wilderness. Therefore Moses could say that "*the word is very near you*" (v. 14). Israel could speak it ("*in your mouth*") and they knew it ("*in your heart*"). Now Moses says, "*Do it.*"

319

ENTER TODAY WHILE THE OPTION IS CLEAR

30:15 "See, I have set before you today life and good, death and evil,

16 "in that I command you today to love the LORD your God, to walk in His ways, and to keep His commandments, His statutes, and His judgments, that you may live and multiply; and the LORD your God will bless you in the land which you go to possess.

17 "But if your heart turns away so that you do not hear, and are drawn away, and worship other gods and serve them,

18 "I announce to you today that you shall surely perish; you shall not prolong *your* days in the land which you cross over the Jordan to go in and possess.

19 "I call heaven and earth as witnesses today against you, *that* I have set before you life and death, blessing and cursing; therefore choose life, that both you and your descendants may live;

20 "that you may love the LORD your God, that you may obey His voice, and that you may cling to Him, for He *is* your life and the length of your days; and that you may dwell in the land which the LORD swore to your fathers, to Abraham, Isaac, and Jacob, to give them."

Deut. 30:15–20

The greatest power we possess is the power to choose. Our most important choice, whether on the plains of Moab or in today's fast-paced world, is between *"life and good, death and evil"* (v. 15). The appeal to choose between life and death is common in the Old Testament (Josh. 24:14–24; Jer. 8:3; 21:8). In the Book of Proverbs this appeal has a strong individual sense (8:35–36; 11:19; 12:28; 13:14), whereas in Deuteronomy the appeal is to the whole nation. Even so, the individual was not swallowed up in the community so that he could avoid responsibility. Indeed, these final verses (15–20) are expressed in the second person singular. From the early times on, God dealt with individuals, challenging them to respond to His call.

Moses never taught Israel that they were justified by obeying the law. In his first book he stated that Abraham was justified by faith in the Lord (Gen. 15:6). Here Moses is speaking to a believing people

320

about fellowship, not justification. His point is simply that Israel's full enjoyment of life is based on their obedience to God's word. Although the people could not be justified by the law, they could be blessed because of their obedience to it.

But if they persisted in drawing away from God, they would perish. Their response would not only affect their lives, but the lives of their descendants. Again we see Deuteronomy taking into account not only the present community but also its future generations.

Jonathan Edwards said, "Resolved: That all men should live for the glory of God. Resolved: That whether others do or not, I will." This great Puritan preacher made a decision that positively influenced the lives of his descendants. Hundreds of members of his family over the next two hundred years entered the ministry and other areas of public service. The power of choice was emphasized by Moses, but is still realized today.

CHAPTER TWENTY-SIX

Preparation for the Land Which Lies Ahead

Deuteronomy 31:1–33:29

A LEADER TO BE SELECTED

31:1 Then Moses went and spoke these words to all Israel.

2 And he said to them: "I *am* one hundred and twenty years old today. I can no longer go out and come in. Also the LORD has said to me, 'You shall not cross over this Jordan.'

3 "The LORD your God Himself crosses over before you; He will destroy these nations from before you, and you shall dispossess them. Joshua himself crosses over before you, just as the LORD has said.

4 "And the LORD will do to them as He did to Sihon and Og, the kings of the Amorites and their land, when He destroyed them.

5 "The LORD will give them over to you, that you may do to them according to every commandment which I have commanded you.

6 "Be strong and of good courage, do not fear nor be afraid of them; for the LORD your God, He *is* the One who goes with you. He will not leave you nor forsake you."

7 Then Moses called Joshua and said to him in the sight of all Israel, "Be strong and of good courage, for you must go with this people to the land which the LORD has sworn to their fathers to give them, and you shall cause them to inherit it.

8 "And the LORD, He *is* the One who goes before

you, He will be with you, He will not leave you nor
forsake you; do not fear nor be dismayed."

Deut. 31:1-8

Dr. Warren Bennis, professor of management at the School of Business Administration at the University of Southern California, has recently completed a four-year study of outstanding leaders. After examining the source of their strength, Dr. Bennis discovered what he believes are five strengths common to all "superleaders."

1. *Vision*—the capacity to create a compelling vision of a desired state of affairs.

2. *Communication*—the capacity to communicate that vision in a way that gains the support of others.

3. *Persistence*—the capacity to maintain the organization's direction, especially when the going gets rough.

4. *Empowerment*—the capacity to create a social structure that harnesses the energies and abilities of others to get the best results.

5. *Organizational learning*—the capacity to monitor an organization's performance, learn from past actions, and use the resulting knowledge to forge a course for the future.[1]

Moses, the greatest leader in the Old Testament, was competent in all five categories. There is something wonderfully pathetic in this scene (v. 2). Moses, the great leader whose eye is yet undimmed, is laying down his mantle of leadership before Israel crosses the Jordan. The congregation of Israel could have become discouraged, but Moses here exhibits one of those competencies common to all superleaders—empowerment. Notice how Moses first focuses his attention on the congregation, encouraging them as they face this leadership transition (vv. 3–6). Then he turns to Joshua and also encourages him (vv. 7–8). Good leaders inspire others by showing confidence in them; great leaders inspire others with confidence in themselves!

God has prepared another effective leader to follow Moses. A tremendous task lay ahead of him, but he was ready. Verses 3–8 give us insight into the reasons for Israel to be encouraged during this transition.

1. The Encouragement of Joshua

Moses boldly declares to all the people that God will overthrow the enemy and assist them in their entrance into Canaan. Then he specifically addresses Joshua and says, *"You must go with this people to the land which the Lord has sworn to their fathers to give them, and you shall cause them to inherit it"* (v. 7). These instructions certainly will encourage Joshua as the reins of leadership are placed in his hands.

2. The Experience of Joshua

Joshua had already received important preparation for this time in his life. He first associated closely with Moses at Mount Sinai, when the law was given. Therefore, he has not only a reverence for God and His power but an appreciation for the law. He has proved himself skillful in the exercise of field battle. He has also had experience acquired as a spy, when he became thoroughly acquainted with Canaan and when his ability to judge a situation was reinforced by Caleb's encouraging spirit. He had shown himself to be a man who obeyed God even if it meant facing ridicule. When Moses tells the people that Joshua will cross over before them, they understand why.

3. The Example of Joshua

The commissioning of Joshua by Moses is not done in a private ceremony. It is important for the congregation to also experience this process. Therefore, *"Moses called Joshua and said to him in the sight of all Israel . . ."* (v. 7). Thomas Carlyle said, "Show me the man you honor and I will know what kind of man you are, for it shows me what your ideal of manhood is and what kind of a man you long to be." Albert Schweitzer said, "Example is not the main thing in influencing others; it is the only thing." Moses stands before the people he has led for forty years and puts his hand upon their next leader—a man they can trust, a man like himself.

4. The Empowerment of Joshua

Joshua is divinely appointed: *". . . just as the Lord has said"* (v. 3). He is divinely led: Moses said to Joshua concerning God's guidance, *"He is the One who goes before you"* (v. 8). Joshua is divinely empowered: *"He will be with you, He will not leave you nor forsake you; do not fear nor be dismayed"* (v. 8).

LAW TO BE READ REGULARLY

31:9 So Moses wrote this law and delivered it to the priests, the sons of Levi, who bore the ark of the covenant of the LORD, and to all the elders of Israel.

10 And Moses commanded them, saying: "At the end of *every* seven years, at the appointed time in the year of release, at the Feast of Tabernacles,

11 "when all Israel comes to appear before the LORD your God in the place which He chooses, you shall read this law before all Israel in their hearing.

12 "Gather the people together, men and women and little ones, and the stranger who *is* within your gates, that they may hear and that they may learn to fear the LORD your God and carefully observe all the words of this law,

13 "and *that* their children, who have not known it, may hear and learn to fear the LORD your God as long as you live in the land which you cross the Jordan to possess."

Deut. 31:9-13

Moses prepares the people for Canaan by emphasizing the important place that God's word must hold in the community's life. His turning the leadership over to Joshua illustrates the importance of divine guidance. It is interesting that one of the few times the word "success" is mentioned in the Bible is when Joshua has just been appointed and the law is being emphasized. "This Book of the Law shall not depart from your mouth, but you shall meditate in it day and night, that you may observe to do according to all that is written in it. For then you will make your way prosperous, and then you will have good success" (Josh. 1:8).

Moses gives the priests the responsibility of teaching the law to the congregation of Israel. He instructs them to read the law to the people every seven years at the Feast of Tabernacles. This section deals with the value of God's word to the entire Israelite assembly.

Everyone was to receive this teaching. Only the men were required to make the pilgrimage to the central sanctuary for the major feasts (16:16). But every seven years the *"men and women and little ones, and the stranger"* (v. 12) were to gather at the place of God's choice to

hear His word. This experience was important for the following reasons: (1) It was rare for an individual to possess a copy of the Scriptures. Knowledge was gained only through the public reading of
God's word or the teaching of the parents. (2) The experience of the
pilgrimage to the central sanctuary, trusting God for their homes left
behind and for the journey ahead, symbolically reenacted something
of the original exodus from Egypt.

*The object of the reading and teaching of the law was reverence for it
and obedience to it.* The *"children, who have not known it, may hear and
learn to fear the Lord"* (v. 13). Those who know it will be reminded,
so they can *"carefully observe all the words of this law"* (v. 12). Admonitions to carefully observe God's word appear frequently in the
later chapters of Deuteronomy (16:12; 17:19; 26:16; 28:1, 13, 15, 58;
31:12). This repetition shows Moses' concern for strict obedience.

Recently when my father was reading the Bible, I asked him,
"Dad, are you learning anything new in the Bible?" This godly man
who has been in the ministry for forty-four years closed the Bible
and said, "Son, I always read the Bible through twice a year. But
every day God's word teaches me something new."

George Mueller, that man of great faith, said, "The vigor of our
spiritual life will be in exact proportion to the place held by the
Word in our life and thoughts. I solemnly state this from experience
of fifty-four years. I have read the Bible through a hundred times
and always with increasing delight. Each time it seems like a new
book to me. Great has been the blessing from consecutive, diligent,
daily study." Moses would totally agree!

A WARNING MESSAGE

31:14 Then the LORD said to Moses, "Behold, the days
approach when you must die; call Joshua, and present
yourselves in the tabernacle of meeting, that I may in-
augurate him." So Moses and Joshua went and presented themselves in the tabernacle of meeting.

15 Now the LORD appeared at the tabernacle in a
pillar of cloud, and the pillar of cloud stood above
the door of the tabernacle.

16 And the LORD said to Moses: "Behold, you will
rest with your fathers; and this people will rise and

326

play the harlot with the gods of the foreigners of the land, where they go *to be* among them, and they will forsake Me and break My covenant which I have made with them.

17 "Then My anger shall be aroused against them in that day, and I will forsake them, and I will hide My face from them, and they shall be devoured. And many evils and troubles shall befall them, so that they will say in that day, 'Have not these evils come upon us because our God *is* not among us?'

18 "And I will surely hide My face in that day because of all the evil which they have done, in that they have turned to other gods.

19 "Now therefore, write down this song for yourselves, and teach it to the children of Israel; put it in their mouths, that this song may be a witness for Me against the children of Israel.

20 "When I have brought them to the land flowing with milk and honey, of which I swore to their fathers, and they have eaten and filled themselves and grown fat, then they will turn to other gods and serve them; and they will provoke Me and break My covenant.

21 "Then it shall be, when many evils and troubles have come upon them, that this song will testify against them as a witness; for it will not be forgotten in the mouths of their descendants, for I know the inclination of their behavior today, even before I have brought them to the land of which I swore *to give them.*"

Deut. 31:14-21

Two significant things happen in these verses: (1) Joshua is commissioned by the Lord to lead Israel (vv. 14-15). (2) A prophecy of Israel's rebellion is given (vv. 16-21).

Moses, Joshua, and God held a private meeting in the tabernacle. In this touching scene God breaks some bad news to these past and future leaders of Israel. Moses, after a life of service to God and Israel, hears the Lord say, *"This people will rise and play the harlot with the gods of the foreigners of the land, where they go to be among them, and they will forsake Me and break My covenant which I have made with them"* (v. 16).

Verses 16–21 make several statements about God. (1) The future is known by God (v. 16). (2) God judges and punishes disobedience (vv. 17–18). (3) God is faithful to faithless man (vv. 19–21). (4) God knows our inclinations (v. 21).

They also make several statements about Israel. (1) God's provision for the well-being of His people is not always accepted. He has given them leadership (Moses and now Joshua), the law to guide them, and has performed countless miracles. Yet, they *play the harlot* and are unfaithful to Him (v. 16). Unfaithfulness is not always caused by unmet needs. (2) In adversity Israel will remember God (v. 17). (3) In prosperity Israel will forget God (v. 20).

The point of this speech is that Israel, once a land of promise, will follow other gods and will forget the God who is responsible for her very existence. God is saying to Joshua: "Be prepared for difficult days ahead. Your leadership will not deter Israel from disobedience." It is significant that throughout these events Joshua never speaks. He only listens. It would be a heavy experience to be informed beforehand that your mission as a leader would meet with mixed results. Even the reading of the law every seven years would not be a deterrent. Notice that the Lord does not speak of the coming apostasy as a possibility, but as an inevitability. I am impressed with Joshua's faithfulness to his task regardless of the bleak picture of the future. A mature leader looks beyond the circumstances and receives strength from his calling.

A MESSAGE TO BE DELIVERED

31:22 Therefore Moses wrote this song the same day, and taught it to the children of Israel.

23 Then He inaugurated Joshua the son of Nun, and said, "Be strong and of good courage; for you shall bring the children of Israel into the land of which I swore to them, and I will be with you."

24 So it was, when Moses had completed writing the words of this law in a book, when they were finished,

25 that Moses commanded the Levites, who bore the ark of the covenant of the LORD, saying:

26 "Take this Book of the Law, and put it beside

the ark of the covenant of the LORD your God, that it
may be there as a witness against you;

27 "for I know your rebellion and your stiff neck. *If*
today, while I am yet alive with you, you have been
rebellious against the LORD, then how much more after my death?

28 "Gather to me all the elders of your tribes, and
your officers, that I may speak these words in their
hearing and call heaven and earth to witness against
them.

29 "For I know that after my death you will become utterly corrupt, and turn aside from the way
which I have commanded you. And evil will befall
you in the latter days, because you will do evil in the
sight of the LORD, to provoke Him to anger through
the work of your hands."

Deut. 31:22–29

Perhaps the most sobering fact of leadership is that it is a lonely
position. A leader has no one with whom he shares the responsibility of final decisions. It is human to stand with the crowd; it is divine
to stand alone. It is manlike to follow the people, to drift with
the tide; it is Godlike to follow a principle and stem the tide. Noah
built and voyaged alone; his neighbors laughed at his strangeness
and perished. Abraham wandered and worshiped alone; Sodomites
smiled at the simple shepherd, followed the fashion, and fed the
flames. Daniel dined and prayed alone. Elijah sacrificed and witnessed alone. Jeremiah prophesied and wept alone. Jesus loved and
died alone. "No man stood with me, but all forsook me" wrote the
battle-scarred apostle in describing his appearance before the emperor. Joshua, too, must stand alone. Yet in that vacant spot he will
find God: *"I will be with you"* (v. 23).

Moses completes the book that is to be read every seven years and
hands it to the Levites, the overseers of the ark of the covenant. The
law was to be placed beside the ark, not in it (v. 26). Only the Ten
Commandments were placed inside the ark. Moses' angry words to
the congregation reflect both his righteous indignation and his disappointment in the people after he has heard God foretell their
apostasy. Moses knew from experience that they were rebellious and

stiff-necked, and he had no trouble believing they would transgress after his death. This knowledge was a heavy load for a dying leader to carry.

A SONG TO BE SUNG

31:30 Then Moses spoke in the hearing of all the assembly of Israel the words of this song until they
were ended:
32:1 "Give ear, O heavens, and I will speak;
   And hear, O earth, the words of my mouth.
  2 Let my teaching drop as the rain,
   My speech distill as the dew,
   As raindrops on the tender herb,
   And as showers on the grass.
  3 For I proclaim the name of the LORD: Ascribe
   greatness to our God.
  4 *He is* the Rock, His work *is* perfect;
   For all His ways *are* justice,
   A God of truth and without injustice;
   Righteous and upright *is* He.
  5 "They have corrupted themselves;
   They are not His children,
   Because of their blemish:
   A perverse and crooked generation.
  6 Do you thus deal with the LORD,
   O foolish and unwise people?
   Is He not your Father, *who* bought you?
   Has He not made you and established you?
  7 "Remember the days of old,
   Consider the years of many generations.
   Ask your father, and he will show you;
   Your elders, and they will tell you:
  8 When the Most High divided their inheritance
    to the nations,
   When He separated the sons of Adam,
   He set the boundaries of the peoples
   According to the number of the children of
    Israel.
  9 For the LORD's portion *is* His people;
   Jacob *is* the place of His inheritance.

330

10 "He found him in a desert land
   And in the wasteland, a howling wilderness;
   He encircled him, He instructed him,
   He kept him as the apple of His eye.

11 As an eagle stirs up its nest,
   Hovers over its young,
   Spreading out its wings, taking them up,
   Carrying them on its wings,

12 So the Lord alone led him,
   And *there was* no foreign god with him.

13 "He made him ride in the heights of the earth,
   That he might eat the produce of the fields;
   He made him draw honey from the rock,
   And oil from the flinty rock;

14 Curds from the cattle, and milk of the flock,
   With fat of lambs;
   And rams of the breed of Bashan, and goats,
   With the choicest wheat;
   And you drank wine, the blood of the grapes.

15 "But Jeshurun grew fat and kicked;
   You grew fat, you grew thick,
   You are obese!
   Then he forsook God *who* made him,
   And scornfully esteemed the Rock of his
     salvation.

16 They provoked Him to jealousy with foreign
     gods;
   With abominations they provoked Him to
     anger.

17 They sacrificed to demons, not to God,
   To gods they did not know,
   To new *gods,* new arrivals
   That your fathers did not fear.

18 Of the Rock *who* begot you, you are
     unmindful,
   And have forgotten the God who fathered
     you.

19 "And when the Lord saw *it,* He spurned *them,*
   Because of the provocation of His sons and His
     daughters.

20 And He said: 'I will hide My face from them,
   I will see what their end *will be,*

331

> For they *are* a perverse generation,
> Children in whom *is* no faith.
> 21 They have provoked Me to jealousy by *what* is
>   not God;
> They have moved Me to anger by their foolish idols.
> But I will provoke them to jealousy by *those*
>   *who are* not a nation;
> I will move them to anger by a foolish nation.
> 22 For a fire is kindled in My anger,
> And shall burn to the lowest hell;
> It shall consume the earth with her increase,
> And set on fire the foundations of the
>   mountains.
> 23 'I will heap disasters on them;
> I will spend My arrows on them.
> 24 *They shall be* wasted with hunger,
> Devoured by pestilence and bitter destruction;
> I will also send against them the teeth of
>   beasts,
> With the poison of serpents of the dust.
> 25 The sword shall destroy outside;
> *There shall be* terror within
> For the young man and virgin,
> The nursing child with the man of gray hairs.
> 26 I would have said, "I will dash them in pieces,
> I will make the memory of them to cease from
>   among men,"
> 27 Had I not feared the wrath of the enemy,
> Lest their adversaries should misunderstand,
> Lest they should say, "Our hand *is* high;
> And it is not the LORD who has done all this."'
> 28 "For they *are* a nation void of counsel,
> Nor *is there any* understanding in them.
> 29 Oh, that they were wise, *that* they understood
>   this,
> *That* they would consider their latter end!
> 30 How could one chase a thousand,
> And two put ten thousand to flight,
> Unless their Rock had sold them,
> And the LORD had surrendered them?
> 31 For their rock *is* not like our Rock,
> Even our enemies themselves *being* judges.

32 For their vine *is* of the vine of Sodom
   And of the fields of Gomorrah;
   Their grapes *are* grapes of gall,
   Their clusters *are* bitter.

33 Their wine *is* the poison of serpents,
   And the cruel venom of cobras.

34 'Is this not laid up in store with Me,
   Sealed up among My treasures?

35 Vengeance is Mine, and recompense;
   Their foot shall slip in *due* time;
   For the day of their calamity *is* at hand,
   And the things to come hasten upon them.'

36 "For the LORD will judge His people
   And have compassion on His servants,
   When He sees that *their* power is gone,
   And *there is* no one *remaining*, bond or free.

37 He will say: 'Where *are* their gods,
   The rock in which they sought refuge?

38 Who ate the fat of their sacrifices,
   And drank the wine of their drink offering?
   Let them rise and help you,
   And be your refuge.

39 'Now see that I, *even* I, *am* He,
   And *there is* no God beside Me;
   I kill and I make alive;
   I wound and I heal;
   Nor *is there any* who can deliver from My hand.

40 For I raise My hand to heaven,
   And say, "As I live forever,

41 If I whet My glittering sword,
   And My hand takes hold on judgment,
   I will render vengeance to My enemies,
   And repay those who hate Me.

42 I will make My arrows drunk with blood,
   And My sword shall devour flesh,
   With the blood of the slain and the captives,
   From the heads of the leaders of the enemy."'

43 "Rejoice, O Gentiles, *with* His people;
   For He will avenge the blood of His servants,
   And render vengeance to His adversaries;
   He will provide atonement for His land *and*
      His people."

44 So Moses came up with Joshua the son of Nun and spoke all the words of this song in the hearing of the people.

45 Moses finished speaking all these words to all Israel,

46 and he said to them: "Set your hearts on all the words which I testify among you today, which you shall command your children to be careful to observe—all the words of this law.

47 "For it *is* not a futile thing for you, because it *is* your life, and by this word you shall prolong *your* days in the land which you cross over the Jordan to possess."

Deut. 31:30–32:47

One of the best ways to memorize something is to put it to music. My daughter Elizabeth was having some difficulty remembering the multiplication tables until her teacher taught her to sing them. Immediately there was a positive change in Elizabeth's grasp of numbers.

God instructs Moses to write a song and teach it to all Israel (Deut. 31:19–22). The song will be a witness to the faithfulness of God and will help Israel *"remember the days of old"* (32:7) after they fall into apostasy. This song has the following characteristics: (1) It has an abundance of pictures, metaphors, and poetic expressions that show the feelings of God; (2) it is a witness against a disobedient nation that has been blessed far above all other nations on earth; and (3) the song is a prophetic anticipation of future judgment. This poetic composition offers a graphic contrast between the nature of God and the nature of His people. He is *"the Rock"* (vv. 4, 18, 30, 31). They are on the rocks (v. 37).

Many see this chapter as having the literary form of a covenant lawsuit, thereby linking it closely with the rest of Deuteronomy. The fact that the chapter is not completely parallel to the standard covenant lawsuit can be explained. This poem is described in verse 2 as *"my teaching."* Moses' intent could be to write a didactic poem based on a covenant lawsuit document.[2]

This analysis is most generally accepted. G. D. Mendenhall suggests another alternative. He feels the poem is not a covenant lawsuit but rather a prophetic oracle. He states, "Here Yahweh is not suing anyone for breach of covenant; instead the breach had taken place, the consequence had been suffered and the issue is whether or not Yahweh would be a reliable refuge for the future."³

This interpretation shifts the major portion of the poem from a prolonged and bitter discourse against the people to a doxology to God. In the past God may have hid His face (v. 20), but now Moses will try to let Israel see that face again. Whether they will see it is uncertain; Moses himself is unsure. For that reason, in the introduction of the poem he can only speak wishfully, *"Let my teaching drop as the rain, / My speech distill as the dew, / As raindrops on the tender herb, / And as showers on the grass"* (v. 2).⁴ This interpretation will help divide this lengthy chapter of Deuteronomy.

1. *God's faithfulness is compared to Israel's foolishness (vv. 3–9).* The declared intention of this poem is to *"proclaim the name of the Lord"* and *"ascribe greatness to our God"* (v. 3). God is prominently pictured as *"a Rock"* in this poem (vv. 4, 18, 30, 31). This metaphor is often used by the psalmist, and it appears at other places in the Bible. It represents the divine unchangeability and security to which men come for refuge in a world filled with physical and spiritual foes. This imagery has found its way into the music of the Christian church in such songs as "Rock of Ages" and "The Solid Rock." For Moses, the characterization of God as a Rock was born out of personal experience: the law was proclaimed on the rock of Sinai; Moses hid himself in the cleft of a rock; out of a smitten rock the waters gushed forth. How natural it was for Moses to apply this image to the eternal God!

Yet Israel was corrupt and doubly foolish. First, they flouted the grace of God, and second, they forgot about His power. Moses once again calls upon the people to *"remember the days of old"* (v. 7). This repeated challenge is given sixteen times in Deuteronomy, beginning in 4:10 and concluding here.

2. *God chooses Israel but Israel forgets God (vv. 10–18).* Verses 10–14 emphasize the goodness of God. He led Israel (vv. 10, 12); He developed Israel (vv. 10, 11); He provided for Israel (vv. 13–14); He loved Israel. The metaphor of the eagle speaks of God's loving parental care. Moses uses a pregnant phrase when describing Israel as *"the apple of His eye"* (v. 10). The Hebrew reads literally, "He kept them as the 'little men' of His eye." How close do you have to get to another person before you see yourself reflected in that person's eye? God has gotten that close to Israel. He knows His people face to

face.[5] God blessed Israel (vv. 13–14). The phrase *"He made him draw honey from the rock"* (v. 13) suggests that even the most barren places became fertile for Israel. Their blessing was supernatural.

Israel's response was unnatural. She became like an animal kicking its feeder (v. 15). The depths of Israel's perversity can be seen in verse 18 where Moses compares the Lord to a mother *"who begot you"* and as a father *"who fathered you."* Yet Israel forgets His parental love. Martin Luther said, "A full stomach does not promote piety, for it stands secure and neglects God."

3. *Israel's apostasy provokes God to great anger and judgment (vv. 19–25).* In His righteous indignation, God will withdraw His beneficial presence (v. 20). The metaphor of fire (v. 22) points to the awful consequences and comprehensive nature of God's judgment. He will also use hunger, pestilence, wild beasts, poisonous serpents, and war to carry out His destruction (vv. 23–25).

4. *God deliberates with Himself (vv. 26–33).* God is about to unleash the ultimate punishment on His people—annihilation—but then He stops after further reflection. Here we have an instance of God deliberating with Himself. Gerhard von Rad, commenting on these verses, said, "This section is therefore an interlude which takes us out of the turmoil of historical processes and allows us to overhear a soliloquy within the depths of the divine heart."[6] God's decision is to exercise restraint, not because Israel deserves it, but because His honor is at stake. Israel's lack of understanding keeps her from considering her coming calamity.

5. *God displays both vengeance and compassion (vv. 34–43).* Even if God exercises restraint on Israel's behalf, her enemies cannot expect the same treatment. Though the Lord would allow Israel's enemies to execute judgment upon Israel, He would still hold them accountable for their wickedness and repay them (vv. 41–43). The children of Israel will not experience Yahweh's compassion until they relinquish all their trust in their own efforts, *"When He sees that their power is gone"* (v. 36). God's goal in judging Israel is not to annihilate her; it is to bring her to the point where she understands that *"there is no God beside Me"* (v. 39).

After sharing with the congregation all the words of the song, Moses tells them to *"set your hearts on all the words"* (v. 46), to know them and take them seriously. If they will meditate on the certainty and severity of the judgment that God will send them for apostasy, the Song of Moses can serve as a powerful deterrent to future rebellion. A healthy fear of judgment will also help their descendants to obey God's word. Once again, Moses concludes with a reminder that Israel's existence and longevity depended on the people's obedience to God (v. 47).

A LAND TO BE DENIED

32:48 Then the LORD spoke to Moses that very same day, saying:
49 "Go up this mountain of the Abarim, Mount Nebo, which *is* in the land of Moab, across from Jericho; view the land of Canaan, which I give to the children of Israel as a possession;
50 "and die on the mountain which you ascend, and be gathered to your people, just as Aaron your brother died on Mount Hor and was gathered to his people;
51 "because you trespassed against Me among the children of Israel at the waters of Meribah Kadesh, in the Wilderness of Zin, because you did not hallow Me in the midst of the children of Israel.
52 "Yet you shall see the land before *you*, though you shall not go there, into the land which I am giving to the children of Israel."

Deut. 32:48-52

Mount Nebo is one of the most prominent peaks in Moab. It overlooks the north end of the Dead Sea. It is here that Moses will die. God will allow Moses the privilege of seeing the promised land but only from a distance. God's reason for not allowing Moses the privilege of leading Israel into Canaan is recorded in Numbers 20:1-13. God had commanded Moses to speak to a rock in order to bring forth water for the people who were grumbling against him and Aaron. Moses disobeyed the Lord by hitting the rock twice instead of speaking to it (Num. 20:11). He also arrogantly suggested that he and Aaron, not the Lord, had brought forth the water (20:10). For this act of unbelief and haughtiness, Moses forfeited his right to lead the people into the land which flowed with milk and honey.

I vividly remember the thoughts that rushed through my mind a few years ago when I stood on top of Mount Nebo and reflected on this incident. As a communicator and spiritual leader, I tried to place myself in the shoes of Moses. No doubt he was both glad and sad. What a joy to see the land that he had worked so hard to reach. What a sorrow to know the effects of a few brief self-indulgent moments of sin. Many times previously Moses had wrestled with God, asking permission to enter the land. Now he rested, knowing that God had another leader and the mission would be accomplished. Moses would be an example to all of Israel that God will not allow His people to get away with disobedience.

A BLESSING TO BE GIVEN

33:1 Now this *is* the blessing with which Moses the man of God blessed the children of Israel before his death.
 2 And he said:
 "The LORD came from Sinai,
 And dawned on them from Seir;
 He shone forth from Mount Paran,
 And He came with ten thousands of saints;
 From His right hand
 Came a fiery law for them.
 3 Yes, He loves the people;
 All His saints *are* in Your hand;
 They sit down at Your feet;
 Everyone receives Your words.
 4 Moses commanded a law for us,
 A heritage of the congregation of Jacob.
 5 And He was King in Jeshurun,
 When the leaders of the people were gathered.
 All the tribes of Israel together.
 6 "Let Reuben live, and not die,
 Nor let his men be few."
 7 And this he said of Judah:
 "Hear, LORD, the voice of Judah,
 And bring him to his people;
 Let his hands be sufficient for him,
 And may You be a help against his enemies."

8 And of Levi he said:
"*Let* Your Thummim and Your Urim *be* with
   Your holy one.
Whom You tested at Massah,
And with whom You contended at the waters
   of Meribah,
9 Who says of his father and mother,
  'I have not seen them';
Nor did he acknowledge his brothers,
Or know his own children;
For they have observed Your word
And kept Your covenant.
10 They shall teach Jacob Your judgments,
And Israel Your law.
They shall put incense before You,
And a whole burnt sacrifice on Your altar.
11 Bless his substance, LORD,
And accept the work of his hands;
Strike the loins of those who rise against him,
And of those who hate him, that they rise not
   again."
12 Of Benjamin he said:
"The beloved of the LORD shall dwell in safety
   by Him,
Who shelters him all the day long;   '
And he shall dwell between His shoulders."
13 And of Joseph he said:
"Blessed of the LORD *is* his land,
With the precious things of heaven, with the
   dew,
And the deep lying beneath,
14 With the precious fruits of the sun,
With the precious produce of the months,
15 With the best things of the ancient mountains,
With the precious things of the everlasting
   hills,
16 With the precious things of the earth and its
   fullness,
And the favor of Him who dwelt in the bush.
Let *the blessing* come 'on the head of Joseph,
And on the crown of the head of him *who was*
   separate from his brothers.'

17 His glory *is like* a firstborn bull,
 And his horns *like* the horns of the wild ox;
 Together with them
 He shall push the peoples
 To the ends of the earth;
 They *are* the ten thousands of Ephraim,
 And they *are* the thousands of Manasseh."
18 And of Zebulun he said:
 "Rejoice, Zebulun, in your going out,
 And Issachar in your tents!
19 They shall call the peoples *to* the mountain;
 There they shall offer sacrifices of
  righteousness;
 For they shall partake *of* the abundance of the
  seas
 And *of* treasures hidden in the sand."
20 And of Gad he said:
 "Blessed *is* he who enlarges Gad;
 He dwells as a lion,
 And tears the arm and the crown of his head.
21 He provided the first *part* for himself,
 Because a lawgiver's portion was reserved
  there.
 He came *with* the heads of the people;
 He administered the justice of the LORD,
 And His judgments with Israel."
22 And of Dan he said:
 "Dan *is* a lion's whelp;
 He shall leap from Bashan."
23 And of Naphtali he said:
 "O Naphtali, satisfied with favor,
 And full of the blessing of the LORD,
 Possess the west and the south."
24 And of Asher he said:
 "Asher *is* most blessed of sons;
 Let him be favored by his brothers,
 And let him dip his foot in oil.
25 Your sandals *shall be* iron and bronze;
 As your days, *so shall* your strength *be.*
26 "*There is* no one like the God of Jeshurun,
 Who rides the heavens to help you,
 And in His excellency on the clouds.

27 The eternal God *is your* refuge,
   And underneath *are* the everlasting arms;
   He will thrust out the enemy from before you,
   And will say, 'Destroy!'
28 Then Israel shall dwell in safety,
   The fountain of Jacob alone,
   In a land of grain and new wine;
   His heavens shall also drop dew.
29 Happy *are* you, O Israel!
   Who *is* like you, a people saved by the LORD,
   The shield of your help
   And the sword of your majesty!
   Your enemies shall submit to you,
   And you shall tread down their high places."

Deut. 33:1-29

Moses is described in verse 1 as *"the man of God."* This title is used elsewhere in the Old Testament to characterize a prophet (1 Sam. 9:6; 1 Kings 13:1–3; 2 Kings 4:7, 16). Deuteronomy declares Moses to be a prophet par excellence (18:15; 34:10). Here Moses gives a blessing to the individual tribes before his death, as did the patriarchs (Gen. 27:7; 49:1–28). Such blessings were more than empty wishes; once uttered, they carried the promise of fulfillment.

The blessings that Moses pronounces on the tribes differ in content from those that Jacob gave. The oracles in Genesis 49 are sometimes judgmental. By contrast, these oracles are consistently redeeming and promissory. They promised continued existence (v. 6), priestly prerogatives (v. 10), safety (v. 11), choice gifts (vv. 13–16), affluence (vv. 18–19), reward of land (vv. 20–21), possession (v. 23), prosperity and strength (vv. 24–25).

An excellent example of the difference between the words of Jacob and Moses can be seen in their words to Reuben. Jacob says, "Reuben . . . unstable as water, you shall not excel, / Because you went up to your father's bed; / Then you defiled it" (Gen. 49:3–4). But Moses says to the Reubenites, "Let Reuben live, and not die, / Nor let his men be few" (33:6).

Observing that this chapter contains no exhortation, but rather invocations of future blessings, Brevard Childs remarks, "The canonical function of chapter 33 serves to place the law fully within the perspective of divine sovereignty, shifting the focus from Israel's behavior to God's ultimate purpose. The Mosaic legislation is thus subordinated to the overriding purpose of God for his people, and the final eschatological realization of his will is attested to in spite of the nation's failure."[7]

This closing blessing of Israel's great leader must have been the highlight of the people's lives. I remember reading about the late Dr. George Truett who pastored forty years at First Baptist Church in Dallas, Texas. At the close of his great ministry, the church board approached this man of God and asked what they could give him—a home, a car—what would he like? He replied, "Give me the privilege of praying for my people." Then, on his last Sunday for a solid hour while the congregation was standing, this great pastor-leader poured out his soul in prayer for the people he loved so dearly. Those who were there never forgot that hour. No doubt the same could be said about those who listened as Moses bestowed blessings upon his people.

Moses begins once more by describing the Lord's appearance at Sinai when He gave the law to the people. This was a major event in Israel's history. To become a nation it was necessary to have a common people (v. 5), a common constitution (v. 4), and a common land. Soon Israel would be a complete nation. Now Moses would give a blessing to the tribes.

Reuben (*v. 6*). The resolution for Reuben to live may suggest that this tribe would face some special adversity or defect in character that might bring disaster. In Jacob's blessing (Gen. 49:4), the instability of the tribe had been indicated; in a later military affair the Reubenites are criticized for their lack of participation (Judg. 5:15, 16). After an incident in the eleventh century B.C. (1 Chron. 5:18–22), very little is heard of this tribe, though they continued to exist and are mentioned as late as the time of Ezekiel (48:7).

Judah (*v. 7*). Jacob had promised that the scepter would not depart from Judah (Gen. 49:10), which meant that the Messiah would come through this tribe. Since Judah marched at the head of the tribes (Num. 2:2–9), they were first in battle. This blessing in verse 7 is essentially a prayer for Judah's military success, a petition for Yahweh's presence.

Levi (*vv. 8–11*). Levi had proven faithful to God when other tribes were faithless. The *"Thummim"* and *"Urim"* were probably

342

two precious stones used in the casting of lots to receive divine answers in difficult matters (Exod. 28:30). The blessing indicates three principal duties assigned to Levi on the basis of past actions and dedication to divine service: (1) They were to be the medium of God's revelation (v. 8); (2) they were to have an educational role in teaching the Israelites the law of God (v. 10a); and (3) they were to be responsible for Israel's formal system of worship (v. 10b). The blessing in verse 11 is a prayer for the Levites' success in using their skills in God's work.

Benjamin (v. 12). In Genesis 49:27 a very warlike and fierce character is ascribed to Benjamin. Yet here Benjamin is promised security in the midst of battle. The prediction that Benjamin would *"dwell between His shoulders"* brings to mind the figure of a father carrying his son on his back. This verse reflects Benjamin's special status as Jacob's youngest and particularly loved son (Gen. 44:20).

Joseph (vv. 13-17). Jacob had great ambitions for Joseph. Moses also has great ambitions for this tribe. Moses prays first for Joseph's material prosperity. Notice the repetition of the word *"precious"* in reference to this tribe. The land given to this tribe included Carmel, where there was an abundance of timber, down to Joppa and the central province of Samaria; they were rich in land. Moses also prays for their military strength. They are pictured as a bull or an ox goring the nations. This tribe, the largest of the northern tribes, was divided. The two divisions were named after Manasseh, Joseph's firstborn, and Ephraim, Joseph's second son. Though Manasseh was the older son, Jacob gave Ephraim the blessing of the firstborn (Gen. 48:17-20). Therefore, Ephraim is mentioned first and credited with *"ten thousands,"* while Manasseh is only credited with *"thousands."*

Zebulun and Issachar (vv. 18-19). These two tribes are called upon to *"Rejoice, Zebulun, in your going out, / And Issachar in your tents!"* (v. 18). In other words, they are to rejoice in every aspect of their daily lives because of God's blessing. These two tribes were blessed with riches from the sand and seas. The most important information given about them is their responsibility in sharing the blessings of God with others (v. 19).

Gad (vv. 20-21). This tribe had already been allocated its territory east of the Jordan before the covenant renewal in Moab. Although

Gad already had its land, it fought valiantly (*"as a lion"*) along with the rest of Israel until the Lord gave them rest (Josh. 22:1–6).

Dan (*v. 22*). When Jacob blessed Dan, he compared him to a serpent that bites a horse's heels and causes the rider to fall backward (Gen. 49:17). Now Moses compares the tribe to a young lion which suddenly springs from ambush to make an attack. He could be referring to the impetuous nature of the Danites, who were quick to follow their own inclinations.

Naphtali (*v. 23*). This tribe settled in a fertile area around the Sea of Galilee and found favor with the Lord.

Asher (*vv. 24–25*). The name Asher means "blessed, happy." This tribe would be the happiest and most blessed among the tribes of Israel. To *"dip his foot in oil"* is an extravagant act. Secure from their enemies, Asher could expect a long, happy life.

Moses concludes with praise to the Lord (v. 26–29). The reference to Jeshurun (v. 26) links these concluding verses of praise to the introductory portion of the blessing where Jeshurun is also mentioned (v. 5). God, who is Israel's King, is a leader who is beyond comparison. His kingship is celebrated in these concluding verses by the reference to His own power and the power He gives to His people, who would win great victories in the coming conflict. After a victory in the past, the Israelites had sung, "Who is like You, O Lord, among the gods?" (Exod. 15:11). Now, before the battle, the old rhetorical question is turned into an affirmative note of praise, *"There is no one like the God of Jeshurun!"* (v. 26).

NOTES

1. Warren G. Bennis, *More Power to You* (New York: Doubleday & Co., Inc.).

2. J. A. Thompson, *Deuteronomy*, Tyndale Old Testament Commentary Series, ed. D. J. Wiseman (Downers Grove, IL: Inter Varsity Press, 1975), p. 297.

3. George E. Mendenhall, "Samuel's Broken Rib: Deuteronomy 32." In *No Famine in the Land: Studies in Honor of J. L. McKinzie*, ed. J. W. Flanigan and A. W. Robinson (Chico, CA: Scholars Press, 1975), pp. 63–74.

4. Victor Hamilton, *Handbook on the Pentateuch* (Grand Rapids; Baker Book House, 1982), p. 469.

5. Ibid., p. 470.

6. Gerhard von Rad, *Deuteronomy: A Commentary*, Old Testament Library (Philadelphia: Westminster Press, 1966), p. 198.

7. Brevard S. Childs, *Introduction to the Old Testament as Scripture* (Philadelphia: Fortress Press, 1979), pp. 219–21.

CHAPTER TWENTY-SEVEN

A Change of Leaders

Deuteronomy 34:1-12

THE DEATH OF MOSES

34:1 Then Moses went up from the plains of Moab to Mount Nebo, to the top of Pisgah, which is across from Jericho. And the LORD showed him all the land of Gilead as far as Dan,

2 all Naphtali and the land of Ephraim and Manasseh, all the land of Judah as far as the Western Sea,

3 the South, and the plain of the Valley of Jericho, the city of palm trees, as far as Zoar.

4 Then the LORD said to him, "This *is* the land of which I swore to give Abraham, Isaac, and Jacob, saying, 'I will give it to your descendants.' I have caused you to see *it* with your eyes, but you shall not cross over there."

5 So Moses the servant of the LORD died there in the land of Moab, according to the word of the LORD.

6 And He buried him in a valley in the land of Moab, opposite Beth Peor; but no one knows his grave to this day.

7 Moses *was* one hundred and twenty years old when he died. His eyes were not dim nor his natural vigor diminished.

8 And the children of Israel wept for Moses in the plains of Moab thirty days. So the days of weeping *and* mourning for Moses ended.

Deut. 34:1-8

Moses is dying and he knows it. His blessings and exhortations to the people he has led for forty years are over and must be remem-

346

bered. His last words hold a special significance for Israel. The deathbed statements of any great person are always of interest to his or her followers. As people age, they gain a sense of what really matters, what is really significant. Moses, the great communicator, has endeavored in his last speech to get Israel to live right after he's gone.

Now he climbs the mountain range alone. His ministry ends as it began—in the very presence of God. He gazes at the land which he cannot enter. As he views it, there must be joy deep within, for he is looking at his lifetime goal. Moses then *"died . . . according to the word of the Lord"* (v. 5). This phrase has been interpreted by the rabbis to mean that "he died by the kiss of the Lord." This interpretation comes from the literal meaning of this phrase, which is "he died at the mouth of the Lord."

God arranged for the private burial of Moses; *"no one knows his grave to this day"* (v. 6). Attempts to discover the place of his burial to satisfy our curiosity will never be realized. The beauty of Moses' death lies not in the physical details of his death but in the fact that he was with God in that hour of transition. The God who called him to lead the people of Israel was with him even in his dying hour. After his death, the people spent thirty days *"weeping and mourning for Moses"* (v. 8).

Recently I read the story of a father who was always greeted by his son, Mark, when he came home from work. But on one particular day, it was different. Mark was nowhere to be seen as Dad drove up to the house. Expecting to find Mark just inside the front door, Dad hurried up the sidewalk. Once inside the house, he began calling Mark, but each call was answered by silence.

Then Dad noticed that Mom was in the backyard, chatting with one of the neighbors. In his anxiety, he rudely interrupted, asking "Where's Mark?" She casually replied, "I don't know where he is." "What-do-you-mean-you-don't-know-where-he-is?" he fired back. But before he could begin to question her fitness as a mother, she interrupted: "Honey, I don't know where he is, but I know who he's with. Your parents have taken him out for the afternoon."

Dad began to calm down immediately when he knew with whom Mark was spending the afternoon. Many people grieve like the bereaved congregation of Israel, and in their sadness ask, "Where has my loved one gone?" Our comfort comes from knowing what God's word teaches us about the death of one of His children. We do not know where they have gone, but we do know with whom they are.

Frances Havergal, the songwriter, lived and moved in the word of God. His word was her constant companion. On the last day of her life, she asked a friend to read Isaiah 42 to her. When the friend read the sixth verse, "I, the Lord, have *called* You in righteousness, / And will *hold* Your hand; / I will *keep* You . . . ," Miss Havergal stopped her. She whispered, "'Called . . . held . . . kept.' I can go home on that." So could Moses.

MOSES REMEMBERED

34:9 Now Joshua the son of Nun was full of the spirit of wisdom, for Moses had laid his hands on him; so the children of Israel heeded him, and did as the LORD had commanded Moses.

10 But since then there has not arisen in Israel a prophet like Moses, whom the LORD knew face to face,

11 in all the signs and wonders which the LORD sent him to do in the land of Egypt, before Pharaoh, before all his servants, and in all his land,

12 and by all that mighty power and all the great terror which Moses performed in the sight of all Israel.

Deut. 34:9–12

Verses 10–12 of Deuteronomy 34 constitute Moses' epitaph. They form a fitting conclusion to the Pentateuch, of which the last four books contain an account of the life and works of Moses in Israel. The words *"there has not arisen in Israel a prophet like Moses"* encourage the reader to reflect on this leader's greatness. Moses holds a unique position among prophets; he was a spiritual pioneer. Moses was the first to proclaim the attributes of God. He was the first to give love as the impetus for obedience (5:9; 6:5). Moses was the first to give us God's law. And he was the first to give a plan of education in the family.

Upon final evaluation, the character of Moses also points to his greatness. He enjoyed a uniquely intimate fellowship with God

(v. 10). It is not Moses' knowledge of God that is stressed, but rather God's knowledge of Moses! God had sought him out and appointed him to a particular task; over the years the relationship became intimate. Israel knew that Moses communicated personally with God. Moses was unequaled in the performance of signs and wonders (v. 11). Moses displayed awesome power among the people of Israel (v. 12).

Sometimes at funerals we paint too beautiful a picture of the deceased; we make him or her out to be a far better person than he or she really was. All of the deceased's good works are magnified and, of course, all shortcomings are passed over. I am often reminded of Lincoln's remark at the burial of one of his generals: "If he had known he would get a funeral like this, he'd have died sooner."

But the greatness of Moses stood the test of time. The earthly kingdom of God, which Moses played an important part in founding, came to an end as represented by the independent state of Israel early in the sixth century B.C. The prophets who followed Moses began to point forward to a new covenant. It was in the formation of the new covenant that at last *a prophet like Moses* appeared again, but He was more than a prophet. Whereas Moses was a servant in the household of God, the coming Prophet was a Son, Jesus Christ (Heb. 3:1–6).[1]

NOTE

1. P. C. Craigie, *Commentary on the Book of Deuteronomy*, New International Commentary on the Old Testament (Grand Rapids: Wm. B. Eerdmans Publishing Co., 1976), p. 406.

Bibliography

Bennis, Warren G. *More Power to You*. New York: Doubleday & Co., Inc.

Carmichael, Calum M. "A Time for War and a Time of Peace: The Influence of the Distinction upon Some Legal and Literary Material." In *Studies in Jewish Legal History: Essays in Honor of David Daub*, edited by B. S. Jackson, 50–63. London: Jewish Chron. Pub., 1974.

Chesterton, G. K. "Man Is Most Comforted by Paradoxes." In *The Dimensions of Job: A Study and Selected Readings*, edited by N. Glatzer, 228–37. New York: Schocken Books, Inc., 1969.

Childs, Brevard S. *Introduction to the Old Testament as Scripture*. Philadelphia: Fortress Press, 1979.

Clarke, Adam. *The Holy Bible with a Commentary and Critical Notes*. Vol. 1. London: William Tegg & Co., 1854.

Craigie, P. C. *Commentary on the Book of Deuteronomy*. New International Commentary on the Old Testament. Grand Rapids: Wm. B. Eerdmans Publishing Co., 1976.

Daube, David. "One from Among Your Brethren Shall You Set King over You." *JBL* 90 (1971): 480–81.

Deasley, A. R. G. and Jack Ford. *Beacon Bible Commentary*. Kansas City, MO: Beacon Hill Press, 1969.

DeVries, Simon J. "The Development of the Deuteronomic Promulgation Formula." *Bib* 55 (1974): 301–16.

Dobson, Eduard. "Divorce in the Old Testament." *Fundamentalist Journal* (October 1985).

Driver, Samuel R. *Deuteronomy*. 3rd ed. Geneva, AL: Allenson, 1902.

———. *An Introduction to the Literature of the Old Testament*. Utica, NY: Meridian Pub., 1957.

Fuller, R. C., ed. "Deuteronomy." *A New Catholic Commentary on Holy Scripture*. Camden, NJ: Thomas Nelson, Publishers, 1969.

Gammie, John G. "The Theology of Retribution in the Book of Deuteronomy." *The Catholic Bible Quarterly* 32 (1970): 1–12.

Hamilton, Victor P. *Handbook on the Pentateuch*. Grand Rapids: Baker Book House, 1982.

Henry, Matthew. *An Exposition of the Old and New Testaments*. London: James Nisbet and Company, 1857.

Jones, E. Stanley. *Abundant Living*. Nashville: Abingdon Press, Festival Books, 1976.

Kaufmann, Stephen. "Structure of the Deuteronomic Law." *Maaraz* 1 (1979): 105–58.

Kuntz, J. Kenneth. "The Retribution Motiv in Psalmist Wisdom." *ZAW* 89 (1977): 223–33.

Macht, D. I. "An Experimental Pharmacological Appreciation of Leviticus 11 and Deuteronomy 14." *Bulletin of the History of Medicine* 27 (1953).

Manley, G. T. *The Book of the Law: Studies in the Date of Deuteronomy.* London: Tyndale Press, 1957.

Maxwell, John C. *Your Attitude: Key to Success.* San Bernardino, CA: Here's Life Publication, 1984.

Mendenhall, George E. "Samuel's Broken Rib: Deuteronomy 32." In *No Famine in the Land: Studies in Honor of J. L. McKinzie,* edited by J. W. Flanigan and A. W. Robinson, 63–74. Chico, CA: Scholars Press, 1975.

Morgan, Brian. *Discovery Papers Catalogue* no. 3817 (November 7, 1982).

Nicholson, E. W. *Deuteronomy and Tradition.* Oxford: Basil Blackwell, 1967.

Patrick, Dale. *Old Testament Law.* Atlanta: John Knox Press, 1985.

Patterson, J. Randall. *The Bible Newsletter.* Evangelical Ministries, Inc., 1984.

Peckham, B. "The Composition of Deuteronomy 9:1–10:11." In *Word and Spirit,* 3–59. Willowdale, Ontario: Regis College Press, 1975.

Phillips, Anthony. *Ancient Israel's Criminal Law.* New York: Schocken Books, Inc., 1971.

Polzin, Robert. *Moses and the Deuteronomist: A Literary Study of Deuteronomic History.* New York: Seabury Press, Inc., 1980.

Smith, William R. *The Prophets of Israel.* 2nd ed. London: Adam and Charles Black, 1897.

Thompson, J. A. *Deuteronomy: An Introduction and Commentary,* edited by D. J. Wiseman. Tyndale Old Testament Commentary Series. Downers Grove, IL: Inter Varsity Press, 1975.

von Rad, Gerhard. *Deuteronomy: A Commentary.* Old Testament Library. Philadelphia: Westminster Press, 1966.

———. *Studies in Deuteronomy.* Translated by D. Stalker. London: SCM Press, Ltd., 1953.

Walvoord, John F. and Roy B. Zuck. *The Bible Knowledge Commentary, O.T.* Wheaton, IL: Victor Books, 1978.

Weinfeld, C. M. *Deuteronomy and the Deuteronomic School.* Oxford: Clarendon Press, 1972.

Wenham, Gordon J. "Deuteronomy and the Central Sanctuary." *TB* 22 (1971).

Wright, G. Ernest. *God Who Acts.* London: SCM Press, Ltd., 1952.

———. *The Old Testament against Its Environment.* London: SCM Press, Ltd., 1950.